PAPAL INFALLIBILITY

Papal Infallibility

A Protestant Evaluation of an Ecumenical Issue

Mark E. Powell

WILLIAM B. EERDMANS PUBLISHING COMPANY
GRAND RAPIDS, MICHIGAN / CAMBRIDGE, U.K.

© 2009 Mark E. Powell
All rights reserved

Published 2009 by
Wm. B. Eerdmans Publishing Co.
2140 Oak Industrial Drive N.E., Grand Rapids, Michigan 49505 /
P.O. Box 163, Cambridge CB3 9PU U.K.

Printed in the United States of America

15 14 13 12 11 10 09   7 6 5 4 3 2 1

Library of Congress Cataloging-in-Publication Data

Powell, Mark E.
Papal infallibility: a Protestant evaluation of an ecumenical issue / Mark E. Powell.
p.   cm.
Includes bibliographical references.
ISBN 978-0-8028-6284-6 (pbk.: alk. paper)
1. Popes — Infallibility.   2. Catholic Church — Doctrines.
3. Catholic Church — Teaching office.   4. Catholic Church — Infallibility.
5. Church — Infallibility.   I. Title.

BX1806.P69   2009
262′.131 — dc22

2008039495

www.eerdmans.com

To Debbie

Contents

Preface   ix

1. Introduction   1

2. The Origin and Exercise of Papal Infallibility   20

3. Maximal Infallibility: Henry Edward Cardinal Manning   49

4. Moderate Infallibility: John Henry Cardinal Newman   84

5. Moderate Infallibility: Avery Cardinal Dulles   123

6. Minimal Infallibility: Hans Küng   163

7. Conclusion: Orthodoxy Without Infallibility   202

   Bibliography   214

   Index   221

Preface

This book needs some explanation. After all, why does a Protestant, and a free-church Protestant at that, take up a critical study of a Roman Catholic doctrine like papal infallibility? It should be stated up front that this project was never an attempt to attack and denounce the Catholic Church, although I do find papal infallibility untenable for the epistemological reasons laid out in this work, as well as biblical and historical reasons. Instead, and perhaps surprisingly, this project began with the uneasy realization that Protestantism's appeal to *sola scriptura* faced limitations when dealing with the major christological heresies faced by the patristic church. The basic problem is that scripture, taken alone, can be interpreted in any number of ways that depart from the historic Christian faith, a problem that is verified by either studying church history or browsing the internet. One can affirm this observation and, as I do, still have the highest regard for scripture, both as a source for knowledge of God and a guide for spiritual formation. The patristic church, which held the biblical writings in the highest regard and fervently appealed to scripture in theological argumentation, never limited its response to heresy by simply handing the Bible to its opponents, even after the canon of the New Testament was finalized.[1] Likewise, conservative Protestants, even those that are non-

---

1. Tertullian wanted to take scripture away from the Gnostic heretics! Athanasius reluctantly accepted the use of the unbiblical term *homoousios* in the Creed of Nicea once it became clear that such a term was necessary to exclude Arianism.

creedal, have always insisted that scripture be interpreted within certain bounds.

Catholics have in hand a response to the limitations of *sola scriptura*. However, from the beginning I felt that the Catholic position, epitomized by papal infallibility, was fraught with problems as well. Unlike John Henry Newman, I never seriously considered accepting belief in the Marian dogmas and papal infallibility in order to secure the doctrine of the Trinity and Chalcedonian christology. Still, I sensed and hoped that a careful investigation of papal infallibility, to which I am not committed, would bring insights into similar proposals in conservative Protestantism that are much closer to home. This has been the case, and the publication of this work has encouraged me to begin "part two" of this project, that is, applying what I have learned to epistemic proposals in conservative Protestantism.

This work was originally a doctoral dissertation at Southern Methodist University titled "Papal Infallibility as Religious Epistemology: Manning, Newman, Dulles, and Küng." As this earlier title makes clear, the focus of this work is on papal infallibility as a proposal in religious epistemology. This focus explains why I do not emphasize biblical and historical problems with the doctrine of papal infallibility, although these issues are discussed in this work and are considered important. Biblical and historical issues regarding papal infallibility have been adequately treated before, and a familiar response from Catholic theologians has emerged, namely, an appeal to doctrinal development. The traditional discussion has led me to believe that one cannot prove or disprove papal infallibility, at least to the committed apologist; but one can offer for consideration a more compelling paradigm for conceiving religious epistemology and ecclesial authority. Focusing on epistemological issues allows the discussion to move forward and new ways of thinking about religious epistemology and ecclesial authority to emerge. The focus on epistemological issues also explains why I do not take up other aspects of the papacy, such as the Catholic structure of church government. My recommendations to Catholic theologians in the final chapter are limited to constructive ways of dealing with the pope as the final piece of a complex epistemology.

I do agree with a growing number of conservative Protestants that the age of Reformation polemics is over, and the way forward on the traditional disagreements between Catholics and Protestants is constructive and forthright dialogue.[2] In my own intellectual journey I have found that both Catholic and Protestant responses to the Reformation create problems that transcend one side being right and the other being wrong. Further, I fully expect both Catholicism and the various forms of Protestantism to continue to flourish in the future. We will need to work together to untangle the knots we have tied and tightened over the years, and this book is offered as one constructive proposal for wider consideration.

This book was conceived and nurtured in two academic communities. First, the Graduate Program in Religious Studies at Southern Methodist University provided an academic environment that is truly remarkable for its balance of high standards and personal interaction. As should be clear throughout this work, I am deeply indebted to my doctoral advisor, William Abraham, and feel particularly fortunate to have participated in the Canonical Theism research group which he led. Other participants include Frederick Aquino, Pavel Gavrilyuk, Chuck Gutenson, Douglas Koskela, Natalie Van Kirk, Jason Vickers, and David Watson. This work was greatly improved by the feedback I received at our meetings, and I hope my contribution illuminates the fruitfulness and implications of this larger project, the results of which are now available in *Canonical Theism: A Proposal for Theology and the Church*.[3] William Babcock and Bruce Marshall, as well as Brian Daley of the University of Notre Dame, served as readers of the dissertation. This work is much stronger because of their keen insights and recommendations.

Second, I wrote the majority of this work while teaching at Harding University Graduate School of Religion, an institution that combines academic excellence with a clear mission of training ministers and scholars for the church. Interaction with colleagues and students, particularly after numerous attempts to present parts of this work in the classroom setting, have helped me state my concerns more precisely. My dean, Evertt Huffard, was especially encouraging and supportive as I balanced new class preparations and completing my dissertation. My

---

2. See, for instance, D. H. Williams, *Evangelicals and Tradition: The Formative Influence of the Early Church* (Grand Rapids: Baker Academic, 2005), 179-80.

3. William J. Abraham, Jason E. Vickers, and Natalie B. Van Kirk, eds., *Canonical Theism: A Proposal for Theology and the Church* (Grand Rapids: Eerdmans, 2008).

graduate assistant, Jordan Guy, prepared the index and engaged me in helpful dialogue over lunch.

Two church communities have nurtured my family and me during my graduate studies and the writing of this book: the Preston Road Church of Christ in Dallas, Texas, and the Sycamore View Church of Christ in Memphis, Tennessee. Both are wonderful communities of worship and spiritual formation, and they represent the best of my own religious heritage.

It has been an honor to work with the staff at Eerdmans Publishing, including William B. Eerdmans Jr., Reinder Van Til, Amy Kent, Linda Bieze, Jennifer Hoffman, and Victoria Fanning. Eerdmans has earned a reputation of quality academic publishing in theological studies, and I am grateful to have my work included in their catalog.

Finally, my family deserves special thanks. I am blessed to have two wonderful parents, Eddie and JoAnn Powell, who have always encouraged and supported my education and ministry. Of course, my wife Debbie has sacrificed, suffered, triumphed, and put up with me throughout this entire project. This work is dedicated to her with much love and appreciation. And my three young children have made all of my work more enjoyable. My third-grade daughter is especially excited to see the appearance of this book, though I have tried to warn her that it will be some time before she actually understands it.

CHAPTER 1

Introduction

Doctrines of inerrancy and infallibility have secured a prominent place in Western discussions of theological prolegomena. It is increasingly becoming apparent, though, that these doctrines are substantial problems. Pope Paul VI himself observed that the papacy is the greatest stumbling block in the ecumenical arena, and his successors continue to be painfully aware of the problem.[1] While the issue of the papacy extends beyond the doctrine of papal infallibility, the doctrine is widely considered to be the primary obstacle in ecumenical dialogue. Further, there are countless searching believers who are distressed when they find an error or contradiction in a biblical text or papal teaching. Motivated by intellectual virtue, they adopt another epistemic method, along with the supposed conclusions, advocated by proponents of revisionist versions of the faith or unbelief altogether. For these reasons and more, there is a need to revisit the assumptions underlying doctrines of inerrancy and infallibility. Must there be agreement on religious epistemology before further ecumenical progress can be made? And is it true that the Christian faith stands or falls with an inerrant scripture or an infallible teacher?

The justification of religious belief became a pressing issue in the

1. In 1967 Pope Paul VI stated, "We are aware that the pope is undoubtedly the greatest obstacle in the path of the *Oecumene*." In 1995 Pope John Paul II again brought attention to the issue in *Ut unum sint*. See the discussion in Carl E. Braaten and Robert W. Jenson, eds., *Church Unity and the Papal Office* (Grand Rapids: Eerdmans, 2001), pp. 1-2.

1

West during the Protestant Reformation.[2] Because of the rampant abuse of papal authority in the sixteenth century, Protestants sought a new authority to trump that of the pope and ecumenical councils. For Protestants, religious truth was secured by the plain sense of scripture as interpreted by the individual under the guidance of the Holy Spirit.[3] However, this appeal to scripture as an epistemic criterion was not without problems. Individuals, churches, and nations disagreed on the proper interpretation of scripture, leading to further divisions in the Western church. Some, like the Socinians, rejected foundational Christian beliefs such as the Trinity and the incarnation because they held that scripture, when properly interpreted, opposes these surviving remnants of ecclesial tradition.[4] The application of historical criticism to scripture and the rise of Liberal Protestantism led conservative Protestants to buttress the epistemic status of scripture with doctrines of biblical inerrancy. These defenders of *sola scriptura* offered ingenious explanations for the purported errors and contradictions in scripture, and warned that rejecting the epistemic doctrine of biblical inerrancy was the first step to denying the Christian faith as a whole.[5]

In response to the Protestant challenge, Catholics rightly argued that scripture alone is inadequate for religious certainty. In addition to an inerrant scripture, an infallible teacher is needed who properly interprets scripture and tradition with the assistance of the Holy Spirit. Many Catholics, conveniently ignoring similar problems in their own

---

2. A good account of this debate is found in Richard H. Popkin's *The History of Scepticism from Erasmus to Descartes* (Assen: Van Gorcum, 1960), chap. 1.

3. For a classic statement of the Protestant position, see John Calvin, *Institutes of the Christian Religion,* vol. 1, ed. John T. McNeill, trans. Ford Lewis Battles (Philadelphia: Westminster Press, 1960), pp. 35-96.

4. A clear presentation of Socinian doctrine is found in Thomas Rees, ed., *The Racovian Catechism* (London: Longman, Hurst, Rees, Orme & Brown, 1818; Lexington, KY: American Theological Library Association, 1962). See especially pp. 25-75, 116-25, and 164-67.

5. For early presentations of biblical inerrancy, see Charles Hodge, *Systematic Theology,* vol. 1 (New York: Scribner, Armstrong & Co., 1874), pp. 151-88, and Benjamin B. Warfield, *The Inspiration and Authority of the Bible,* ed. Samuel G. Craig (Philadelphia: Presbyterian and Reformed Publishing Co., 1948), pp. 71-128. For a contemporary statement, see "Chicago Statement on Biblical Inerrancy," *Journal of the Evangelical Theological Society* 21, no. 4 (December 1978): 289-96.

history, proposed that the schism and heresy pervading Protestantism resulted from the lack of an infallible teacher.[6] The desire for an epistemic method to secure religious certainty led to the definition of papal infallibility at Vatican I. Like the Protestant proponents of biblical inerrancy, the defenders of papal infallibility offered creative explanations for the alleged errors and contradictions in papal and conciliar pronouncements, and warned that rejecting papal infallibility was the first step to unbelief. However, as will be demonstrated throughout this work, the doctrine of papal infallibility did not deliver on its promise to secure epistemic certainty.

In this work, papal infallibility is critiqued as a form of religious epistemology, and a new paradigm for conceiving religious epistemology and ecclesial authority is proposed. While there are similarities between the various doctrines of inerrancy and infallibility, papal infallibility is taken up for two reasons. One, papal infallibility represents the culmination of the desire for religious epistemic certainty that has characterized the West at least since the Reformation. Papal infallibility was proposed to resolve the epistemic issues that are not settled by an appeal to scripture or tradition alone. And two, papal infallibility has been formally canonized in the Catholic tradition, and therefore the doctrine presents a significant challenge to anyone who questions it. While some Protestant churches and parachurch organizations have formally and informally adopted the doctrine of biblical inerrancy, the status of biblical inerrancy for these groups is less clear. Numerous Protestants have distanced themselves from biblical inerrancy more easily, and with fewer consequences, than appears to be the case for Catholics and papal infallibility.

---

6. While the claim is made, it is difficult to see how the Catholic Church escaped the problems faced by Protestants. Obviously orthodox doctrines of the Trinity and the incarnation were challenged in the fourth and fifth centuries by the Arians and various christological proposals, well before the Reformation. The Western church had formally split from the Eastern church, and Protestant churches were offshoots of the Western church. After Vatican I, the "Old Catholics" led by Johann Joseph Ignaz von Döllinger separated from the Catholic Church. Catholic scholar Richard Simon was among the first to apply historical criticism to scripture. In the nineteenth and twentieth centuries, Modernism in Roman Catholicism had similarities to Liberal Protestantism. We can question whether these are good or bad developments, but they occur in the Catholic tradition just as in the Protestant tradition.

Before offering an analysis of papal infallibility, it will be helpful to compare the approach taken here to other contemporary treatments of the doctrine. The oldest critique of papal infallibility submits papal teachings to historical scrutiny and emphasizes errors and contradictions in papal and conciliar proclamations.[7] One example of such historical problems is the condemnation of the monothelite christology of Pope Honorius I by the Sixth Ecumenical Council at Constantinople, a condemnation confirmed by subsequent popes and councils. Another is the conflict between the conciliarism of *Haec Sancta* from the Council of Constance in the early fifteenth century and the definition of papal infallibility at Vatican I. Catholic apologists typically respond by arguing that the problematic papal teaching was not an *ex cathedra* definition, and therefore cannot be infallible. The problem with this defense, of course, is that the qualification *ex cathedra* does not receive extensive comment until Vatican I, so nearly all problematic papal pronouncements can be exonerated in this way. Or, Catholic apologists argue that the supposed error or contradiction, when properly interpreted, is no error or contradiction after all. A similar critique of infallibility is to question the antiquity of certain Catholic doctrines, such as the doctrine of papal infallibility itself.[8] In this case, Catholic apologists usually appeal to the notion of doctrinal development. Doctrines may be implicit in scripture and tradition without being explicit, and in due time the doctrine develops in the Catholic Church under the guidance of the Holy Spirit.

The historical approach will surface from time to time in this work, particularly since Hans Küng stresses historical issues in his critique of infallibility. Further, this work assumes that these historical issues pose a real problem for papal infallibility, a fact that even the Catholic apologist should be willing to acknowledge. But the historical approach

---

7. A classic work in this genre is George Salmon's *The Infallibility of the Church,* 4th ed. (Searcy, AR: James D. Bales, 1914). While this work first appeared in 1888, it received substantial replies from Catholic apologists as late as 1954. See B. C. Butler, *The Church and Infallibility: A Reply to the Abridged "Salmon"* (New York: Sheed & Ward, 1954). Salmon continues to be cited in contemporary polemical works from conservative Protestants. For example, see William Webster, *The Church of Rome at the Bar of History* (Edinburgh: Banner of Truth Trust, 1995).

8. For an important study, see Brian Tierney, *Origins of Papal Infallibility: 1150-1350* (Leiden: E. J. Brill, 1972).

will not be followed here for at least two reasons. One, these debates have grown stale, and the responses from both sides are highly predictable. A fresh approach that is less polemical needs to be considered. And two, most proponents of this approach simply replace papal infallibility with another epistemic method that is equally problematic, typically biblical inerrancy or historical-critical exegesis of scripture combined with a revisionist version of the Christian faith. An example of this problem will be seen in chapter 6 with Hans Küng. On the whole, participants in this debate share assumptions in epistemology that are questioned in this work.

A second contemporary approach is to critique the hierarchical structure of the Catholic Church, as exemplified in the doctrine of papal infallibility, in favor of an egalitarian ecclesiology. Typically, such proposals are combined with an egalitarian understanding of the Trinity that not only rejects the ontological subordination of the persons in the Godhead, but functional or relational subordination as well.[9] This approach is not followed here for several reasons. One, though this is not the place to support this point, the egalitarian doctrine of the Trinity is not convincing. The traditional position is right to reject the ontological subordination of the persons of the Godhead while retaining functional or relational subordination.

Furthermore, this approach tends to favor an optimistic anthropology and ignore the importance of authority for communal living, ironically with the intention of establishing more just communities. Egalitarian proposals leave one wondering exactly what concrete structures should be in place for ordering our lives together. In a philosophical analysis of authority, E. D. Watt states,

> The sphere of authority is public, not private, social, not individual. That is why it is at odds with egalitarian assumptions and notions, which are individualistic: they ask us to imagine mankind as a myriad of monads, with no parents, no infancy, no childhood,

9. Representatives of this approach from a variety of theological perspectives include Jürgen Moltmann, *The Trinity and the Kingdom* (Minneapolis: Fortress Press, 1993); Catherine Mowry LaCugna, *God for Us: The Trinity and Christian Life* (San Francisco: HarperCollins, 1991); Leonardo Boff, *Trinity and Society* (Maryknoll, NY: Orbis Books, 1988); and Miroslav Volf, *After Our Likeness: The Church as the Image of the Trinity* (Grand Rapids: Eerdmans, 1998).

no past, none of whom was ever an apprentice, a student, a recruit, or a member of a team. But human beings as we know them are social and interdependent beings.[10]

Catholic theologian Terence Nichols agrees that any sizeable society needs hierarchical structures to allow the society to function as a whole. A consistent egalitarianism only leads to chaos and the inability to act. He states, "Egalitarians are right in stressing the basic equality of *persons* before God, and with respect to basic rights. They err, however, in extending this to mean that there cannot be hierarchical *roles* within a society."[11] Authority is exercised in all churches, and all churches have ecclesial authorities of various sorts, even if these leaders function informally.

To the extent that egalitarians argue against the abusive exercise of authority and for checks and balances by appealing to, for instance, the doctrine of sin or the historical practice of the early church, such proposals are commended. To the extent that authority itself is challenged, egalitarians are idealistic in the worst sense of the term. In another widely regarded philosophical account of authority, Richard De George suggests that attacks on authority are most successful when they challenge abuses of authority rather than authority itself.[12] This work assumes that Protestant and Orthodox Christians are right to resist excessive papal power because of past and present abuses of papal authority, including the abuse of ecclesiastical power that can result from the exercise of papal infallibility. However, this work does not recommend egalitarianism or present specific proposals for governing ecclesial bodies.

A third approach is to treat Christian doctrine as a religious language system or form of life rather than cognitive or propositional statements. The Lutheran theologian George Lindbeck has popularized one form of this approach under the name postliberal or narrative theology. In addition, he has examined doctrines of inerrancy and infallibility at length.[13]

---

10. E. D. Watt, *Authority* (New York: St. Martin's Press, 1982), p. 105.

11. Terence L. Nichols, *That All May Be One: Hierarchy and Participation in the Church* (Collegeville, MN: Liturgical Press, 1997), pp. 6-7.

12. Richard T. De George, *The Nature and Limits of Authority* (Lawrence, KS: University Press of Kansas, 1985), p. 1.

13. His mature position is found in *The Nature of Doctrine: Religion and Theology in a Postliberal Age* (Philadelphia: Westminster Press, 1984), pp. 98-104. Earlier works in-

According to Lindbeck, doctrines are better viewed as grammatical rules within a religious community rather than ontological truth claims. While he notes that religious believers may go on to make ontological truth claims, the function of doctrines, properly speaking, is to regulate the speech and practice of the religious community.

Within this framework, Lindbeck argues that there must be doctrines that are infallible, or "guaranteed," for religious communities. He proposes that "those affirmations which guarantee, which ground, a religion are for it infallible. These are those central propositions which are essential to its identity and without which it would not be itself."[14] For example, he states, "One can agree that 'Jesus is the Son of God' is an infallible proposition within the Christian language system even if one thinks of this as a piece of baseless mythology."[15] While he affirms the need for infallible propositions, Lindbeck questions the idea of an infallible teaching office. Nevertheless, he does believe ecumenical agreement between Catholics and Protestants is at least theoretically possible given a moderate interpretation of *Pastor Aeternus* and an added condition of reception by the ecumenical church.[16]

Lindbeck's proposal is a subtle one that should not be quickly dismissed.[17] However, his approach is inadequate in that it only allows us to examine the intrasystemic truth, and not the ontological truth, of religious doctrines. Using his own example, we can know that "Jesus is the Son of God" is not only infallible but intrasystemically true if the statement coheres with the rest of the Christian faith. The statement can be intrasystemically true for Christianity even if the man Jesus never lived, or even if there is no referent for the word "God." For Lindbeck, one cannot and should not argue for the ontological truth of this doctrine. It can only be known by faith or "existential commitment."[18] Further, Lindbeck's approach makes it difficult to adjudicate

---

clude George Lindbeck, in *The Infallibility Debate,* ed. John J. Kirvan (New York: Paulist Press, 1971), pp. 107-52, and *Infallibility* (Milwaukee: Marquette University Press, 1972).

14. Lindbeck, in *The Infallibility Debate,* p. 117.

15. Lindbeck, *The Infallibility Debate,* p. 117.

16. Lindbeck, *The Infallibility Debate,* pp. 59-60 and *The Nature of Doctrine,* p. 99.

17. For a more thorough critique of Lindbeck's proposal, see Alister E. McGrath, *The Genesis of Doctrine* (Grand Rapids: Eerdmans, 1990), chaps. 1-3.

18. Lindbeck, *The Nature of Doctrine,* p. 101.

the truth claims of different religious communities. The approach taken in this work offers a more adequate religious epistemology in that it does allow one to pursue the issue of ontological truth and critically evaluate the truth claims of competing belief systems.

A fourth approach is to stress important epistemic principles in an attempt to bypass difficulties with doctrines of inerrancy and infallibility. Examples of such principles include the importance of intellectual and moral virtue for knowers,[19] and the importance of communal discernment in epistemology and hermeneutics.[20] Many moderate proponents of inerrancy and infallibility appeal to these principles when faced with shortcomings in their epistemic doctrines. For instance, problems with inerrancy and infallibility are addressed by stressing the need for the church community when interpreting an inerrant scripture or infallible papal pronouncements. However, this move only covers over, and never really addresses, the problems inherent in doctrines of inerrancy and infallibility. In this work, the importance of virtue and communal discernment are strongly affirmed. However, we must continue to deal with pressing conceptual issues raised by doctrines of inerrancy and infallibility, while not neglecting the importance of healthy epistemic principles.

Further, virtuous persons and religious communities have disagreed with one another and made false knowledge claims. For example, Arian and Socinian communities pursued epistemic and moral virtue, but denied beliefs that, historically, Christians have viewed as foundational. Even more orthodox communities regularly make wrong decisions concerning their beliefs. Sound epistemic principles must be accompanied by the profession and, when appropriate, justification of key particular beliefs.

The approach taken in this work follows and develops further the proposal of William Abraham in *Canon and Criterion in Christian Theology*.[21]

---

19. Two excellent treatments of this position are W. Jay Wood, *Epistemology: Becoming Intellectually Virtuous* (Downers Grove, IL: InterVarsity Press, 1998), and Linda Zagzebski, *Virtues of the Mind* (Cambridge: Cambridge University Press, 1996).

20. A fine treatment here is Luke Timothy Johnson, *Scripture and Discernment: Decision Making in the Church* (Nashville: Abingdon Press, 1996).

21. William J. Abraham, *Canon and Criterion in Christian Theology* (Oxford: Clarendon Press, 1998). See also *Canonical Theism: A Proposal for Theology and the Church*, ed. William J. Abraham, Jason E. Vickers, and Natalie E. Van Kirk (Grand Rapids: Eerdmans, 2008).

Abraham argues that, while it is typically done, it is a conceptual mistake to confuse ecclesial canons with epistemic criteria. The widespread acceptance of this move is evident in the prominent use of the term "norm" in discussions of theological prolegomena. A criterion or norm is a standard of truth, whether of Christian belief or other areas of knowledge such as history and science. The discussion of criteria, though, is a complex one that properly belongs in the field of epistemology, which focuses on issues of rationality, justification, and knowledge.[22] As will be demonstrated throughout this work, proposing an inerrant book or an infallible teacher as a criterion of truth is simply an inadequate epistemology.

Abraham suggests that ecclesial canons properly belong in the field of soteriology, not epistemology. That is, canons are primarily means of grace that lead one to salvation. To say that ecclesial canons are interested in soteriology rather than epistemology is not to suggest that ecclesial canons are disinterested in truth. In fact, it is difficult to see how the Christian faith can be saving if it is not true. However, it is one thing to be concerned with the nature of God and salvation, and another to be concerned with issues of epistemology. Just as historians and scientists make proposals in their respective fields without feeling compelled to offer a comprehensive epistemology, so too does the church in its ecclesial canons. Ecclesial canons present beliefs about God and salvation without giving an epistemology that is intended to secure these beliefs. Abraham proposes that many longstanding problems in Western theology result from this basic conceptual confusion of viewing ecclesial canons as epistemic criteria.[23]

Abraham offers a broad understanding of "ecclesial canons" that extends beyond the canon of scripture. The church has a rich canonical heritage that includes a canon of scripture, but also a canon of doctrine, a canon of saints, a canon of Fathers, a canon of theologians, a canon of liturgy, a canon of bishops, a canon of councils, a canon of ecclesial regulations, and a canon of icons.[24] The canonical heritage of the church presents a particular understanding of God and the Christian faith which Abraham calls "canonical theism."[25] Canonical theism

22. See, for instance, Roderick Chisholm, *The Problem of the Criterion* (Milwaukee: Marquette University Press, 1973).

23. Abraham, *Canon and Criterion in Christian Theology*, pp. 1-3.

24. Abraham, *Canon and Criterion in Christian Theology*, pp. 37-39.

25. See Abraham, Vickers, and Van Kirk, eds., *Canonical Theism*.

is first and foremost Trinitarian, and it presents a rich picture of God, human sin, redemption, and eschatology. Rather than being the recommendation of an individual theologian or ecumenical committee, canonical theism is articulated in the historic, public decisions of the undivided church. The canonical heritage of the church is a gift of divine grace that exists to pass on this vision of God and the Christian life. Through the working of the Holy Spirit, the canonical heritage continues to bring about the salvation and transformation of individuals and communities.

While Abraham locates ecclesial canons outside the realm of epistemology, he continues to take epistemological issues seriously. To begin with, he believes it is a mistake to canonize an epistemology, especially in the ecumenical arena. Primacy should be given to the adherence of a basic Christian ontology, the theism found in the canonical heritage of the church, instead of an epistemic method intended to secure this ontology. As long as this ontology is confessed, there should be flexibility concerning the epistemology one uses to arrive at this theism.[26] Therefore, a Protestant might arrive at this ontology by an appeal to *sola scriptura*, arguing that the plain reading of scripture supports the ontology of the canonical heritage of the church. A Catholic may maintain this ontology because it is based in scripture and tradition as interpreted by the Catholic Church and, ultimately, the pope. The Orthodox may affirm this ontology because it is defined in the ecumenical councils of the undivided church. Postliberals like Lindbeck may affirm this ontology both by a radical faith commitment, and because it coheres with, and is even an infallible foundation for, the Christian form of life. What is important is that none of these epistemologies be canonized in the ecumenical arena.

While Abraham wants to limit the role of epistemology in the ecumenical arena, he does offer a compelling proposal in religious epistemology.[27] Central to his position is a shift from methodism to particularism.[28] According to methodism, one must begin with the proper method for attaining knowledge before one can have particular

---

26. Abraham, *Canon and Criterion in Christian Theology,* pp. 470-80.

27. See also William J. Abraham, *Crossing the Threshold of Divine Revelation* (Grand Rapids: Eerdmans, 2006).

28. Abraham, *Canon and Criterion in Christian Theology,* pp. 17-20. For a concise discussion of methodism and particularism, see Chisholm, *The Problem of the Criterion.*

knowledge claims. Methodism has been dominant in Western philosophy at least since the Enlightenment, as illustrated by René Descartes's rationalism and John Locke's empiricism. It has been equally dominant in theology. As we have already seen, proponents of biblical inerrancy and papal infallibility argue that the Christian faith stands or falls with these epistemic methods. But a strong commitment to methodism is also found in a diverse array of recent theological proposals. For example, Paul Tillich presents the "method of correlation," James Cone argues for a norm that unites the Black experience of oppression with the revelation of God in Jesus Christ, and process theology proceeds by beginning with a persuasive ontology and then revisioning the Christian faith in light of this ontology.[29] The concern to establish and begin with the right theological method has dominated Western theology at least since the Reformation.

The recent fortunes of methodism have not been good, though. In philosophical circles the pursuit of a comprehensive epistemic method has been largely abandoned. The demise of strong foundationalism, the dominant theory of rationality in classic modernity, has led many to believe that only two serious alternatives remain. One is a skepticism that says there is no way to know truth, or at best a nihilism that denies any reality behind linguistic concepts that are said to be socially constructed for the exercise of power.[30] The other alternative is a fideism[31] that refuses to offer justification for belief systems, but instead calls for

29. Paul Tillich, *Systematic Theology*, vol. 1 (Chicago: University of Chicago Press, 1951), pp. 47-66; James H. Cone, *A Black Theology of Liberation*, twentieth anniversary ed. (Maryknoll, NY: Orbis Books, 1990), 35-39; and John B. Cobb and David Ray Griffin, *Process Theology: An Introductory Exposition* (Philadelphia: Westminster Press, 1976), pp. 7-11.

30. See the postmodern philosophy of Jacques Derrida, *A Derrida Reader: Between the Blinds,* ed. Peggy Kamuf (New York: Columbia University Press, 1991), and Michel Foucault, *A Foucault Reader,* ed. Paul Rabinow (New York: Pantheon, 1984). For a theological appropriation, see Mark C. Taylor, *Erring: A Postmodern A/theology* (Chicago: University of Chicago Press, 1987).

31. While the term "fideism" is often used in a derogatory way, I do not intend to use it so here. I take fideism to be a substantial option in religious epistemology that has been vigorously defended by past and present proponents. Broadly speaking, fideists hold that religious belief is rational, but not on the basis of arguments or evidences that are external to a religious belief system. Ultimately, fideists argue that the adoption of any belief system, religious or otherwise, is a matter of faith.

a radical faith commitment. This second alternative has been particularly influential in theological circles, as seen in the influence of Karl Barth, postliberal theology, and recent proposals like radical orthodoxy.[32] It is easy to see how these two alternatives result from the failure of methodism. If we cannot have a comprehensive method to evaluate knowledge claims, it appears that skepticism and fideism are all that remain.

Thankfully, this is not the case. Particularism is another viable alternative that is advocated in contemporary epistemology. Instead of beginning with an epistemic method and then proceeding to particular knowledge claims, particularism begins with particular knowledge claims and defends the rationality of these claims by employing various *ad hoc* arguments. In other words, particularists are more convinced of the truth of particular knowledge claims than they are of epistemic methods used to justify these claims. To take a well-known example, neither Descartes's rationalism nor Locke's empiricism are able to establish the rationality of belief in the external world or other minds, among other beliefs we tend to treat as knowledge. Given this situation, particularists are content to say that there must be a problem with rationalism or empiricism, because we do know that there is an external world and other minds. Particularists would not give up firm knowledge claims simply because they cannot be justified by a proposed epistemic method.

One truth claim that Abraham is especially interested in is canonical theism, which is actually a vast web of interrelated beliefs. However, he does not adopt this web of beliefs simply by means of a faith commitment that excludes rational justification. While canonical theism is found in the public decisions of the undivided church, Abraham believes that good reasons were given for these claims by the early church. And good, though possibly different, reasons can continue to be given for these claims today. Further, the rationality of canonical theism as a whole can be evaluated alongside other specific, competing belief systems. One way this can occur is by presenting cumulative case argu-

32. Karl Barth, *Church Dogmatics: A Selection with Introduction by Helmut Gollwitzer*, trans. and ed. G. W. Bromiley (Louisville: Westminster John Knox Press, 1994), pp. 49-65; John Milbank, Catherine Pickstock, and Graham Ward, eds., *Radical Orthodoxy: A New Theology* (New York: Routledge, 1999), pp. 1-37; and R. R. Reno, "The Radical Orthodoxy Project," in *First Things* 100 (February 2000): 37-44.

ments for each position and making an intuitive judgment in favor of the stronger position.[33] Other proposals in theology can be evaluated in the same manner. *Ad hoc* arguments are employed to justify proposed beliefs without the need for an inerrant scripture, an infallible teacher, or a comprehensive epistemic method.

Abraham's particularism illuminates his understanding of ecclesial canons. While ecclesial canons should not be confused with epistemic criteria, this does not mean they cannot be appealed to in cumulative case arguments for particular beliefs. For example, Abraham believes it is a categorical mistake to view the canon of scripture as an inerrant criterion. Scripture does contain some errors in details. The biblical writers do assume a false cosmology, where the sun revolves around the earth. Scripture must be properly interpreted. For these reasons and more, scripture does not in fact function as an epistemic criterion. However, scripture does give us access to divine revelation, and for this reason it can and should be used in arguments for the rationality of particular beliefs. An appeal to scripture, then, is better viewed as an appeal to divine revelation rather than an appeal to an inerrant criterion.[34] And again, while scripture can be used to justify particular beliefs, its primary function is soteriological. Like other ecclesial canons, scripture is a means of grace that, through the working of the Holy Spirit in the church, brings about salvation and spiritual transformation in the lives of believers.

In summary, it is helpful to distinguish two aspects of Abraham's work, his ecumenical proposal and his epistemological proposal. Abraham's ecumenical vision is grounded in the theism articulated in the canonical heritage of the church. He argues that it is this ontology, and not proposals in epistemology, that should be the basis for ecumenical unity. Proposals in epistemology should not be canonized in the ecumenical arena. However, this does not mean that serious work in epistemology should be abandoned. In his epistemological proposal, Abraham offers a particularist, weak foundational epistemology that allows one to offer arguments for the rationality of particular beliefs and en-

33. For a concise presentation of his weak foundationalist epistemology, see William J. Abraham, *An Introduction to the Philosophy of Religion* (Englewood Cliffs, NJ: Prentice-Hall, 1985), chap. 9.
34. Abraham, *Canon and Criterion in Christian Theology*, pp. 4-6.

tire belief systems. Other serious work in epistemology could be pursued and would be encouraged as well. Still, Abraham believes it is best not to conceive the canons of the church as epistemic criteria, but rather as means of grace that are soteriological in nature.

With the assistance of Abraham's convincing proposal, we can identify at least four conceptual errors in the doctrine of papal infallibility. The first two, and in many instances the third, also characterize doctrines of biblical inerrancy. First, the doctrine of papal infallibility views the canons of the church as epistemic criteria. This point needs careful elaboration, especially in light of how Catholics conceive infallible papal definitions. For Catholics, the infallible decisions of the pope are not viewed as new revelations, and the charism the pope enjoys is not conceived as inspiration, even if papal definitions are not clearly found in scripture and early church tradition. Rather, the charism is conceived as a negative one that keeps the pope, and the church, from error in interpreting and applying scripture and tradition in each new generation. Properly speaking, the pope serves as an infallible belief-producing mechanism[35] who properly interprets scripture and tradition. The phrase "infallible belief-producing mechanism" is used throughout this work to describe the epistemic function of the pope, not as a criterion *per se,* but as an epistemic resource of the church that infallibly interprets the criteria of scripture and tradition. Therefore, an infallible pope is the capstone of an epistemic tower built on scripture and tradition, with scripture and tradition clearly conceived as epistemic criteria.

However, as a proposal to secure religious certainty, papal infallibility has obvious shortcomings. One problem is that of interpreting papal pronouncements. While scripture and tradition are preserved in texts and must be interpreted, papal pronouncements are also preserved in texts that must be interpreted. Instead of solving the problem of interpretation, the doctrine of papal infallibility only pushes the problem one step back. The only way out of this infinite regression is for each individual to possess infallibility so that each person can know that one

---

35. The term "belief-producing mechanism" has become prominent in contemporary epistemology. Memory, sense-perception, and conscience are examples of reliable belief-producing mechanisms. These mechanisms give us reliable beliefs, but they are not infallible since they can be wrong and therefore are defeasible. I use "infallible belief-producing mechanism" as a way to describe the pope's function within the Catholic Church as defined at Vatican I and affirmed at Vatican II.

has properly interpreted infallible papal pronouncements. But if each individual must possess infallibility to attain epistemic certainty, there is hardly a need for the pope to have a special charism of infallibility.

Another problem, which is interrelated to the problem of interpretation, is the issue of identifying infallible doctrines. How do Catholics know which doctrines meet the criteria for infallibility, whether the doctrine in question is infallibly taught by the pope or by the bishops in communion with the pope? As we turn to the four theologians that are examined in this work, it will become evident that the problem of identifying and interpreting infallible doctrines is not a hypothetical one. Such difficulties make the appeal to the pope as an infallible belief-producing mechanism problematic. At least it is difficult to see how Catholic doctrines of infallibility bring more epistemic certainty than what is enjoyed by other Christians.

This work proposes that there is a better way of conceiving ecclesial authority and the canons of the church. Instead of viewing the episcopacy as an item in epistemology, it is better to conceive ecclesial authority as a means of grace whose primary function is soteriological. The role of ecclesial authority, then, is not to secure epistemic certainty, but to teach the faith, shepherd believers, and lead the church, all the while looking to the Holy Spirit for guidance. Ecclesial authority fulfills its soteriological role by building up the church and participating in the salvation and transformation of the body of Christ.

A second conceptual error with papal infallibility is that it is deeply wedded to methodism in epistemology as an attempt to secure certainty. A commitment to methodism is evident when proponents of papal infallibility argue that, without an infallible pope, the church cannot remain in the truth of the gospel. The only options, then, appear to be papal infallibility and skepticism. However, this claim is highly doubtful, especially given the relatively late definition of papal infallibility and the orthodox character of numerous Christian communities that deny the doctrine. Further, as we have already seen, an infallible method for securing religious doctrine is neither available nor necessary. The failure of papal infallibility, or any other method, to secure religious epistemic certainty indicates that particularism is a better way to proceed in the epistemology of theology. We should begin with the theism found in the canonical heritage of the church rather than seek an unattainable method that will secure this theism and all other beliefs.

Third, papal infallibility canonizes an epistemology. The Catholic Church defined the doctrine of papal infallibility at Vatican I, but this has been regrettable for at least two reasons. One, while the content of the gospel does not change, the intellectual currents within which the gospel is articulated and defended do change. For example, the strong foundationalism assumed by the participants at Vatican I has been vigorously criticized and largely abandoned in the last century. The church needs the flexibility to present and defend the gospel in light of contemporary developments in epistemology, although the church should also critically interact with these developments.

More importantly, it should be stressed that the church does not seek to present an epistemology to the world, but the gospel of salvation. While there will and should be Christian epistemologists, epistemology is not the primary work of the church and, for this reason, religious epistemologies should not be defined. Christians may choose to define particular beliefs at times, but the definition of epistemologies only leads to unnecessary division in the church. This work proposes that agreement on religious epistemology is not necessary for ecumenical unity on particular beliefs. At the conclusion, suggestions for Catholic theologians will be proposed in light of the definition of papal infallibility at Vatican I.

Fourth, papal infallibility confuses epistemic certainty with the effective exercise of teaching and organizational authority.[36] According to many Catholic theologians, papal infallibility not only safeguards doctrine but also allows for the effective exercise of authority in the church, which in turn secures church unity. Infallibility, it is maintained, gives the pope the right to decide doctrinal disputes regarding the authentic teaching of the church, to admonish and correct, and to protect the church through discipline. However, epistemic certainty is not logically required for the effective exercise of teaching and organizational authority.

Consider the following analogy. Legal courts make effective and binding interpretations of the law, which the state effectively enforces, without claims of infallibility and irreformability. In fact, laws are periodically revisited and amended in light of extended reflection or chang-

36. A thorough philosophical analysis of authority is found in Richard T. De George, *The Nature and Limits of Authority*.

ing circumstances, in many instances for the good. In this case, authority is effectively exercised without epistemic certainty. The Catholic Church has also exercised effective authority without appealing to epistemic certainty. Catholic officials maintained teaching and organizational authority without definitive claims of papal infallibility until 1870. Further, the current exhortation that papal pronouncements should be obeyed even if they are not infallible supports the notion that infallibility is not logically required for effective teaching and organizational authority.[37] The pope can still function as an important spiritual leader, and even as the final judge of Catholic doctrine, without being conceived as an infallible belief-producing mechanism in a complex epistemology.

This work will examine the doctrine of papal infallibility in light of these proposed conceptual errors. Immediately, though, we are faced with a problem. Various Catholic theologians have interpreted the doctrine of papal infallibility differently, a fact which actually supports the claim that papal infallibility cannot bring religious epistemic certainty. Nonetheless, we will try to overcome this difficulty by examining four interpretations of papal infallibility from four prominent Catholic theologians.

The theologians selected allow us to trace both a chronological and theological spectrum. Chronologically, the first two theologians, William Edward Cardinal Manning and John Henry Cardinal Newman, lived during the definition of papal infallibility at Vatican I and represent early responses to the doctrine. The second two theologians, Avery Cardinal Dulles and Hans Küng, represent mature, contemporary reflections on papal infallibility. Theologically, three typologies are represented which are called maximal, moderate, and minimal infallibility.[38] Manning is a representative of maximal infallibility, Newman and Dulles are representatives of moderate infallibility, and Küng is a representative of minimal infallibility. By combining the use of typologies and the study of specific theologians, we hope to avoid the possibility of

37. This exhortation is found, for instance, in *Lumen Gentium* 25 in Pelikan and Hotchkiss, *Creeds and Confessions of Faith in the Christian Tradition*, vol. 3 (New Haven: Yale University Press, 2003), p. 597.

38. Here we are following a recognized typology. See, for example, J. Robert Dionne, *The Papacy and the Church: A Study of Praxis and Reception in Ecumenical Perspective* (New York: Philosophical Library, 1987), pp. 20, 29-32.

misleading generalizations that can result from the use of typologies alone.[39] Further, it should be noted that representatives of all three types can be found in the period surrounding Vatican I and in the contemporary period.[40]

A few more observations should be made concerning the theologians we will examine. The first three theologians have all been prominent English-speaking figures in the discussion of papal infallibility. All three were elevated to the rank of Cardinal, so their positions represent those of prominent and recognized Catholic figures. And, interestingly enough, all three were converts to Catholicism: the first two from the Church of England, and the third from atheism. As converts, all three were concerned with issues of religious epistemology, and all three turned to Catholic doctrines of infallibility to relieve these concerns.[41] For these reasons, these three figures are excellent representatives for examining papal infallibility as a form of religious epistemology. The last representative, Hans Küng, breaks the mold in nearly every respect. The German-speaking Swiss was born and raised Catholic, and he had his canonical mission to teach Catholic theology revoked because of his opposition to doctrines of infallibility. However, his influence on the discussion of papal infallibility has been immense, and this work would be incomplete without considering his contribution. Further, while Küng rejects doctrines of infallibility, he continues to view ecclesial canons as epistemic criteria and holds methodist commitments in epistemology. Therefore he offers another example of the epistemic assumptions questioned in this work.

Chapter 2 introduces the doctrine of papal infallibility by exploring the historical events surrounding Vatican I and the documents that define and confirm papal infallibility. Chapters 3 through 6 take up the

39. H. Richard Niebuhr discusses this inadequacy of typologies in his classic work *Christ and Culture* (New York: Harper & Row, 1951), pp. 43-44.

40. A prominent example of minimal infallibility during the definition of papal infallibility was Johannes Joseph Ignaz von Döllinger. J. Robert Dionne discusses several contemporary representatives of maximal infallibility, including Joaquín Salaverri de la Torre, Paul Nau, Fidelis Gallati, and Arthur Pfeiffer. See *The Papacy and the Church*, pp. 31-39.

41. Of course, Manning and Newman converted to the Catholic Church before the definition of papal infallibility. Nonetheless, the Catholic teaching of the infallibility of the church was attractive to them both.

four theologians already introduced. Each of these chapters follows a common outline. First, biographical comments are made about the theologians that provide a historical context for their reflections on papal infallibility. Second, other significant theological concerns are presented that illuminate and deepen their understanding of papal infallibility. Third, their position on papal infallibility is given. And fourth, an analysis of each position is offered based on the four conceptual errors already presented. Chapter 7 concludes the work by summarizing the findings and offering Catholic theologians suggestions for dealing with papal infallibility.

This work has several objectives. First, it offers a broad introduction to the doctrine of papal infallibility. Papal infallibility is a remarkable epistemic proposal whose complexity and subtlety is often underestimated. The overview of the doctrine in the second chapter, and the specific interpretations of the doctrine in the following chapters, offer a good introduction to papal infallibility. Second, this work presents a Protestant critique of papal infallibility. However, as already suggested, it recommends a proposal in religious epistemology that critiques much Protestant work in theology as well. And third, this work suggests a way forward. It is hoped that the proposal presented here can help overcome some of the impasses currently found in Christian theology and ecumenical dialogue.

CHAPTER 2

The Origin and Exercise of Papal Infallibility

Before examining specific interpretations of papal infallibility, we will first give a general introduction to the doctrine. This chapter begins with an overview of the pontificate of Pius IX and the historical setting of Vatican I. This overview is important for at least two reasons. One, it provides a historical context for the definition of papal infallibility. And two, it clearly shows that, in addition to the desire for religious epistemic certainty, a number of other factors were involved in the definition. What was in fact defined at Vatican I was a proposal in religious epistemology. However, a basic knowledge of these other factors will be helpful as we suggest how Catholic theologians might deal with *Pastor Aeternus* today.[1] Next we will turn specifically to the doctrine of papal infallibility. Here we will focus primarily on *Pastor Aeternus* from Vatican I and *Lumen Gentium* from Vatican II. Then we will examine specific examples of the exercise of papal infallibility. While Catholic theologians disagree over which doctrines have been infallibly defined, most accept the two Marian dogmas, the immaculate conception of the Blessed Virgin Mary and the assumption of the Blessed Virgin Mary, as clear examples of the exercise of papal infallibility. These two doctrines will be briefly considered in the last part of the chapter.

---

1. This issue is picked up again in chapter 7.

Pius IX and the First Vatican Council

Vatican I, like most church councils, was convened in a time of crisis. Alec Vidler aptly calls this period in the history of the church "an Age of Revolution."[2] The French Revolution of 1789 attacked the *ancien régime* of monarchy and the Gallican church under the principles of "Liberty, Equality, Fraternity." The projects of theological reconstruction and biblical criticism that were popular in Germany were perceived as a threat by the Catholic Church and conservative Protestants.[3] Darwin's theory of evolution offered a viable scientific explanation for the origin of the universe that challenged the traditional Christian view. And various social movements that either rejected religion or separated church and state were perceived by Catholic leaders as marginalizing the authority and influence of church officials in all spheres of life.[4]

During the nineteenth century a loosely defined movement called Liberal Catholicism arose. As Vidler explains,

> Broadly speaking, in the nineteenth century Liberals were those people who were in favour of the new kind of state and society that had issued from the Revolution. They were in favour of constitutional and representative governments, of religious toleration, and of the separation of Church and State ("a free Church in a free State" was the slogan of both Cavour and Montalembert). Liberals were in fact for liberty all round: liberty of the press, of association, of education, etc.[5]

Nineteenth-century liberals were also captivated by ideas that today are closely associated with modernity and the Enlightenment, such as "the

2. Alec R. Vidler, *The Church in an Age of Revolution: 1789 to the Present* (London: Hodder & Stoughton, 1962).

3. Important representatives of theological reconstruction include Friedrich Schleiermacher and G. W. F. Hegel. Biblical critics of this period include David Strauss and F. C. Baur.

4. For a more thorough account of these events, see Vidler and Owen Chadwick, *The Secularization of the European Mind in the Nineteenth Century* (Cambridge: Cambridge University Press, 1975).

5. Vidler, *The Church in an Age of Revolution*, p. 148. C. B. Cavour was an Italian nationalist, and Charles Montalembert was a Liberal Catholic historian.

natural perfectibility of human nature, the inevitability of progress, a vaguely conceived utopia on earth, and romantic notions about nationality."[6] Therefore the Catholic Church had good reason to be suspect of liberalism. Christianity, with its more realistic view of human nature and its belief that governing authorities are under God, had in hand a needed critique of popular liberalism. But in the nineteenth century this critique went too far. Liberalism was viewed by some, both within the Catholic Church and without, as an unequivocal evil that rejected all authority and only led to anarchy. Liberal Catholics, on the other hand, sought to baptize the "Principles of '89" by combining the positive elements of liberalism with the Christian faith.

In the first half of the nineteenth century, Ultramontanism was associated with Liberal Catholicism, though not all Liberal Catholics were Ultramontane. Ultramontanism emphasizes the centralization of authority in the papacy over the independence of the national churches, while Gallicanism emphasizes the independence of the national churches over Roman control. At the time, the French church was thoroughly Gallican and under government control. Nonetheless, the Roman authorities accepted this situation for numerous reasons: it provided some measure of social order during a turbulent political time; the papacy had a strong alliance with the French extending back to the Middle Ages; and the relationship provided several benefits, including the defense of the Papal State by the French army. Some Liberal Catholics saw Ultramontanism as a way to free the church from government control and develop the church's own spiritual resources under the pope. In the 1830s, 1840s, and even 1850s, Ultramontanism was associated with liberalism and the liberty of the church from state control. However, by the 1860s and Vatican I, Ultramontanism was no longer associated with liberalism but with a strong anti-liberal response to the events of the nineteenth century.

In 1846 Mastai Ferretti was elected Pope Pius IX to succeed the conservative Gregory XVI. Pius IX, or Pio Nono as he is affectionately called, would go on to become one of the most significant and controversial figures of the nineteenth century. While he enjoyed unprecedented popularity at the beginning of his pontificate, when he died the Roman masses threw mud at his coffin as it passed through the streets by night

6. Vidler, *The Church in an Age of Revolution*, p. 149.

en route to the Church of *San Lorenzo Fuori le Mure.* The debate over Pius IX continues among contemporary historians and in discussions concerning his canonization. For example, August Hasler portrays Pius IX as an uneducated, abusive megalomaniac, and Vatican I as a council that was not free. Hasler, though, is engaged in heated polemic and obviously exaggerates his picture of Pius IX.[7] Accounts like Hasler's, which paint Pius IX and Vatican I in the most negative terms, are adequately refuted by the testimony of participants at Vatican I, as illustrated in Dom Cuthbert Butler's classic *The Vatican Council: 1869-1870.*[8] As we will see, though, this is not to say that Pius IX and the proceedings of Vatican I were without fault.

A more balanced account would portray Mastai as a pious man who was deeply devoted to the Blessed Virgin and who, as Bishop of Imola and later Bishop of Rome, saw pastoral duties as his foremost concern. He was a charismatic figure who naturally attracted people, though at times he could display his temper. His pontificate lasted over thirty-one years, which is longer than that of any other pope. E. E. Y. Hales rightly calls him "the creator of the Modern Papacy."[9] However, he was not an intellectual, nor was he politically savvy, and this during "an Age of Revolution" when the Catholic Church needed astute leadership.

At the beginning of his pontificate, Pius IX was known as a liberal pope who brought sweeping reforms. He offered amnesty to over 1000 prisoners and return from exile to hundreds more, many of whom were political revolutionaries. He pursued plans to build railways and provide gas lighting in the streets; began the Agricultural Institute and held scientific congresses in the Papal State; and excused the Jews from the weekly obligation of listening to a Christian sermon. Pius IX established

---

7. For example, in one place Hasler states, "At bottom, however, [Pius IX] understood nothing. He could give a rational account of nothing, not even his own words." See August Bernhard Hasler, *How the Pope Became Infallible: Pius IX and the Politics of Persuasion,* trans. Peter Heinegg (Garden City, NY: Doubleday & Co., 1981), p. 123. This is a popularization of Hasler's larger work, *Pius IX (1846-1878), papstliche Unfehlbarkeit und 1. Vatikanisches Konzil. Dogmatisierung einer Ideologie,* 2 vols., in Papste und Papsttum, no. 12 (Stuttgart: Verlag Anton Hiersemann, 1977).

8. Edward Cuthbert Butler, *The Vatican Council: 1869-1870: Based on Bishop Ullathorne's Letters,* ed. Christopher Butler (Westminster, MD: Newman Press, 1962).

9. E. E. Y. Hales, *Pio Nono: A Study in European Politics and Religion in the Nineteenth Century* (Garden City, NY: Image Books, 1954), p. 15.

a press that was subject to the council of five censors, four of whom were laymen; and permitted the establishment of a Civic Guard, a volunteer police force.[10] In 1848 Pius IX even granted a constitution to his people. These reforms made Pius IX extremely popular, and many saw Pius IX as the leader of the Italian Risorgimento, the movement for a unified nation state. Pius IX himself was influenced by the political thought of Gioberti, who pictured Italy as a federation of states where princes would rule their own states and the pope would serve as head of the federation. The reforms of Pius IX, though, ultimately played into the hands of the Italian revolutionaries, who sought power for themselves.

1848 was a year of revolution and political turmoil, and the events of this year ended Pius IX's experiment with liberalism. In February revolution broke out in Paris against the Bourbon government, and in March revolution erupted in Vienna. The Austrian revolution was especially problematic for Pius IX, as Italian revolutionaries and the Piedmontese saw this as the perfect opportunity to drive Austrian forces out of the northern Italian states, a necessary advance if Italy was to be unified. Pius IX, though, could not endorse an offensive war on the Catholic Austrians, his children in the faith and, along with the French, the traditional defenders of the Papal State. Instead of blessing Italian offensives against Austria, Pius IX reproved the revolutionaries and, in effect, parted company with the Risorgimento. Pio Nono's enormous popularity with the Italian masses plummeted immediately.

Revolution reached Rome by the end of 1848. On November 15 the revolutionaries assassinated Rossi, Pius IX's premier in the new constitutional government. The pope's dream of a constitutional government compatible with the papal office died with Rossi. Most government officials fled Rome, and the angry mob attacked the Quirinal, the pope's palace. During the night of November 24, a disguised Pius IX fled to Gaeta. Revolutionaries throughout Italy poured into Rome, including Garibaldi and his army, and a new republic was established under the leadership of the revolutionary Mazzini. Pius IX remained in Gaeta for two years until he returned to Rome with the assistance of French troops.

10. The establishment of the Civic Guard, which put arms in the hands of Roman citizens, was too liberal even for Gizzi, the liberal candidate for the papacy in 1946 and now Secretary of State, and led to his resignation.

Pius IX's return to Rome was characterized by a thorough repudiation of anything liberal. As Hales observes, the uprising in Rome "impressed upon him that liberalism . . . was normally the forerunner of revolution, and was inimical to the Church as well as to the Papal State." While before Pius IX was open to moderate reform, "he had now seen the marks of the beast in his own city; henceforth he would warn the world of those marks, not merely in order to save the Papal State, but in order to save the world."[11]

An important idea that deeply influenced Pius IX, both before and after the events of 1848, was the inseparability of the temporal and spiritual power of the pope. Indeed, his predecessors, as well as a vast majority of Catholics at the time, also held this conviction. The temporal power of the pope was considered necessary for the proper exercise of his spiritual authority since it guaranteed his spiritual independence. Of course, temporal power brought with it many difficulties. For instance, when the pope refused to support an offensive attack against Austria, the pope's role as an Italian ruler could be incompatible with his role as a spiritual leader. But without the temporal power, the pope would be reduced to the status of the Patriarch of Constantinople, who was only allowed "to bless and to pray."

Owen Chadwick summarizes well the position of Pius IX.

> The [Papal] State must be treated as exceptional in Europe because of its history and its vocation as the safeguard of the spiritual independence of the Vicar of Christ. Whether or not other governments were rightly absolute, this government must in the last resort be so because the pope's power as the Vicar of Christ could not be truly exercised unless he had the ultimate authority.[12]

However, this vision of papal power and authority is given a more realistic assessment by Derek Holmes.

> The Pope was frequently regarded as a minor Italian prince rather than a spiritual leader with universal and world-wide responsibili-

---

11. Hales, *Pio Nono*, pp. 142, 143.

12. Owen Chadwick, *A History of the Popes: 1830-1914* (Oxford: Clarendon Press, 1998), p. 92.

ties. But his temporal sovereignty which in theory guaranteed his international independence was often more apparent than real. The Pope had practically no control over the rulers who theoretically recognized his authority; his temporal interests were ignored and he was denied a voice at international meetings. Secular rulers had no intention of allowing the Pope to interfere in their affairs and that included church affairs, whereas most secular governments felt free to intervene in ecclesiastical matters.[13]

Nevertheless, Pius IX fought for his temporal power until his death, even after Victor Emmanuel II, King of Sardinia and first King of Italy, conquered the Papal State during the First Vatican Council.

Two additional events in Pius IX's pontificate are significant for what transpired at Vatican I, the definition of the immaculate conception of the Blessed Virgin and the publication of the Syllabus of Errors. The definition of the immaculate conception was an important step in the development of the Ultramontanism that prevailed at Vatican I. However, as Chadwick observes, it should be emphasized that "the people wanted this doctrine; no one should think it was forced upon the simple people by hierarchs."[14] The popular desire for the definition of the doctrine grew rapidly in the nineteenth century. Though it was well known that Pius IX himself was deeply devoted to the Blessed Virgin — he attributed his speedy return from exile to her — the impetus for the definition came from the laity, and especially from French Catholics. When Pius IX asked bishops for prayer and advice regarding the definition, the vast majority agreed that the doctrine should be defined.

The doctrine itself will be examined more carefully below. What should be emphasized here is the manner in which the doctrine was defined. Pius IX solemnly proclaimed the definition, with an accompanying anathema, on December 8, 1854. As Chadwick notes, "No previous Pope in eighteen centuries had made a definition of doctrine quite like this." He continues,

13. J. Derek Holmes, *The Triumph of the Holy See: A Short History of the Papacy in the Nineteenth Century* (London: Burns & Oates; Shepherdstown, WV: Patmos Press, 1978), p. 5.

14. Chadwick, *A History of the Popes: 1830-1914,* p. 119.

The Pope did not believe that he was an innovator. He was satisfied that this faith was Catholic because it was held for centuries by many. He was declaring what the Church always believed and what the faithful ought to believe. He was sure that in his office as supreme teacher of the Church he was protected by God from error. Therefore he took it for granted that he did not need any consent by the organs of the Church at large to what he proposed to do.[15]

Hales highlights the significance of the occasion as well.

A suggestion that the Bishops should be associated with the Pope in the proclamation was not taken up; the dogma was pronounced upon the sole authority of the Pope, after he had fully consulted both the theologians and the episcopate. A precedent of the greatest importance was thus set, which had its influence upon the form in which the dogma of Papal Infallibility came later to be defined, in 1870.[16]

Of course, the definition established a precedent for future *ex cathedra* papal definitions as well. The definition of the assumption of the Blessed Virgin by Pius XII in 1950 followed the same basic procedure used by Pius IX in 1854.

A second key event leading up to Vatican I was the publication of the Syllabus of Errors at the end of the papal encyclical *Quanta Cura* on December 8, 1864. The appearance of the Syllabus was especially distressful for many Catholics and supporters of the pope, though those who supported strong papal authority approved of the pronouncement. The enemies of the pope found great delight in ridiculing the Syllabus and its condemnations, especially the final proposition. Vidler aptly summarizes the contents of the Syllabus as

an over-all condemnation in the most unqualified terms of rationalism, indifferentism, socialism, communism, naturalism, freemasonry, separation of Church and State, liberty of the press, lib-

---

15. Chadwick, *A History of the Popes: 1830-1914*, p. 121.
16. Hales, *Pio Nono*, p. 154.

PAPAL INFALLIBILITY

erty of religion, culminating in the famous denial that "the Roman pontiff can and ought to reconcile himself and reach agreement with progress, liberalism and modern civilization."[17]

It seemed to many that the pope had taken a stand against modern Western civilization altogether.

It helps to read the Syllabus of Errors in light of its historical setting. The document was a compilation of condemnations Pius IX had already issued, now taken out of their original context. And in several instances, the context is important. In Italy, "progress, liberalism, and modern civilization" were associated with the secularism and anticlericalism of the French Revolution and the Risorgimento, the effects of which Pius IX had experienced firsthand. Nevertheless, the document was still unbearable to many Catholics.

Like the definition of the immaculate conception, the Syllabus of Errors helped create a new Ultramontanism which looked to the papacy as a bedrock in times of instability and a defense against modernity's assault on the Christian faith. With the aid of his charismatic personality, Pius IX promoted this cult of the Holy Father. As Vidler observes,

[Pius IX's] charm and spontaneity won him passionate affection, all the more so on account of his sufferings and political adversities which gave him the halo of a martyr. The mystique about the Holy Father, and what often seems an unwholesome adulation of his person, date from Pius IX. . . . It was Pio Nono who created and encouraged the intense veneration for the Vicar of Christ which is such a striking feature of modern Roman Catholicism.[18]

This cult of the Holy Father was encouraged by Ultramontanes like Louis Veuillot in France, and Cardinal Wiseman and Archbishop Manning in England.[19] For instance, Veuillot's newspaper *L'Univers* answered the question, "Who is the Pope?" with the response "He is Christ on earth."[20] Similar statements abounded, and this growing cult

17. Vidler, *The Church in an Age of Revolution*, p. 151.
18. Vidler, *The Church in an Age of Revolution*, p. 153.
19. Manning, who was elevated to Cardinal in 1875, is the subject of chapter 3.
20. As quoted in Holmes, *The Triumph of the Holy See*, p. 153.

of the Father had a strong influence on the proceedings of Vatican I. It is interesting to note that the cult of the Holy Father developed simultaneously with the growth of centralization and imperialism in secular governments.[21]

Vatican I formally opened on the Feast of the Immaculate Conception, December 8, 1869. When the council began, there were three main positions on the issue of papal infallibility. The Ultramontanes maintained an extreme position on the infallibility of the pope. The "inopportunists" maintained a qualified version of papal infallibility but felt that it was inopportune to define the doctrine because of the harm it would bring to relationships with Protestants and the Orthodox and because of the volatile social climate. A small group opposed the doctrine altogether on historical and theological grounds.[22] At the council, it became clear that the first two positions were the only real options, and of these the inopportunists were in the minority.

Once the council was called, papal infallibility was almost sure to be defined. Many of the political events of the time focused on the nature of the authority of the pope, and a Gallican victory at the council would have been a major blow to the papacy at a time when the pope was under fierce attack from secular enemies. As Chadwick notes,

> The mass of the bishops with not very decided minds on such matters wanted to do all they could for the Pope under the terrible pressure of Italian nationalists and the threats that lay over Rome. The Curia could not bear the idea of a "defeat" of central Roman authority that would happen if the opponents got their way and, after all this world publicity, forced the Council to say nothing about the pope's teaching office.

Chadwick goes on to argue that,

> from the point of view of the historical situation, once the Council was summoned the point of infallibility had to be discussed and, if discussed, then defined. For if it was not defined, the Pope would

---

21. Holmes, *The Triumph of the Holy See*, p. 154.
22. For instance, the famous German historian Johannes Joseph Ignaz von Döllinger.

be shatteringly troubled in ecclesiastical influence at just the time when he was shatteringly troubled in politics.[23]

The inopportune position was weak because, if the infallibility of the pope was indeed true, the times cried out for a strong affirmation and explanation of papal authority. Manning himself argued that the pressure exerted to prevent the definition of infallibility actually strengthened the resolve of the council to proceed with the definition. He states,

> The effect of this deliberate, wide-spread, and elaborate attempt to hinder the definition of the infallibility of the head of the Church, by controlling the Council and obstructing its freedom, was as might be expected. It insured the proposing and passing of the definition. It was seen at once that not only the truth of a doctrine, but the independence of the Church, was at stake. If the Council should hesitate or give way before an opposition of newspapers and of governments, its office as Witness and Teacher of Revelation would be shaken throughout the world. The means taken to prevent the definition made the definition inevitable by proving its necessity.[24]

While Manning spoke of a "deliberate, wide-spread, and elaborate" attempt to impede the freedom of the council, the counter-charge has been made against the Ultramontanes as well. Almost all of the theologians who were invited to Rome to draft the *schemata* for the council were Ultramontane. All of the presidents over the council were Italian, and a disproportionate number of Italian bishops attended the council due to the traditionally small size of Italian bishoprics. The Deputation on the Faith, headed by Manning, did not include a single member of the minority, though one member converted to the minority position after arriving at Rome. Pius IX pledged neutrality at the beginning of the council. However, beginning in the spring of 1870, Pius IX used his influence to push an Ultramontane definition of papal infallibility. In April 1870, the presidents of the council rejected a request to consider

---

23. Chadwick, *A History of the Popes: 1830-1914*, pp. 199, 200.
24. Henry Edward Manning, *The True Story of the Vatican Council* (London: Henry S. King, 1877), pp. 70-71.

the issue of papal infallibility out of its original context in the *schema de Ecclesia*. Manning appealed directly to Pius IX, and the pope agreed that it would be unwise to postpone the decision over papal infallibility because of the heated debates already rising over the issue. In another famous instance in June 1870, Pius IX privately rebuked the Dominican Cardinal Guidi, who, in a rousing speech at the council, insisted that the pope is not infallible on his own independent of the church. Pius IX is reported to have yelled at Guidi, "I, I am tradition, I, I am the Church."[25] These events and others like them were fuel for critics of Vatican I like Lord Acton, as well as contemporary critics like Hasler.

Although the inopportunists did not prevent the definition of papal infallibility, they did attempt to qualify the maximal views the Ultramontanes wanted defined. For instance, the inopportunists worked to ensure that infallibility extends only to solemn definitions addressing matters of faith and morals. While many Catholic theologians and historians see these qualifications as a victory for the inopportunists, these qualifications were still interpreted by the Ultramontanes along maximal lines. The inopportunists also sought a statement in the definition that would require the pope to consult the church before defining doctrines. The Deputation on the Faith, under the recommendation of Pius IX, rejected this request and instead added a strong clause that was intended to settle the Gallican debate once for all. The clause *ex sese non autem ex consensu ecclesia* was added to the final draft of *Pastor Aeternus*. The solemn definitions of the pope are irreformable "of themselves, and not by the consent of the church."

Pastor Aeternus was defined on July 18, 1870. The inopportunists left Rome on the day of the final vote, refusing to vote against the decree. As the decree was ratified in St. Peter's, there was a terrible thunderstorm that some interpreted as a sign of God's displeasure. Manning, though, replied, "They forgot Sinai and the Ten Commandments."[26] The next day, France declared war against Prussia, and by the beginning of August, France had to withdraw the troops that protected Rome. The armies of Victor Emmanuel II easily defeated Rome in September, marking the beginning of a unified Italy and the end of the pope's temporal

25. Regarding this incident, see Chadwick, *A History of the Popes: 1830-1914,* pp. 210-11 and footnote 39.
26. Manning, *The True Story of the Vatican Council,* p. 145.

power. Of course, the council could not continue under these conditions, so it was adjourned. Initially, popes spoke out against the seizure of the Papal State. In 1929, though, Catholic officials accepted the creation of a separate state in Rome, which exists to this day.

Almost all of the bishops, including those in the minority at the council, signed a statement showing their acceptance of the definition of papal infallibility. Several moderate interpretations of the definition appeared, most notably Joseph Fessler's *The True and the False Infallibility of the Popes,* which was favorably received by Pius IX.[27] Most Catholics felt that, since the church defined the decree, it must be true for the church cannot err. A small group, led by Johann Joseph Ignaz von Döllinger, left the Catholic Church to start the Old Catholic Church in Germany.

The Doctrine of Papal Infallibility

The doctrine of papal infallibility has a long history that exceeds the events of Vatican I. Papal infallibility is one of a number of developments of papal claims. Of course, the traditional Catholic position maintains that papal claims are implicit in Christ's promises to Peter in the New Testament. A brief survey of the development of these claims could begin with Irenaeus (c. 130–c. 200) and Tertullian (c. 160–c. 225), who were the first to propose theories of apostolic succession to combat Gnosticism.[28] Tertullian, in his desire to elevate episcopal authority, spoke of the unique position of Peter as the first of the apostles. He did maintain, though, that the powers Christ granted to Peter were attributes of the whole episcopacy and not the Roman bishop alone.

Victor I (189-198), bishop of Rome, emphasized the relationship between Peter and Rome in a dispute over the dating of Easter. This time the appeal to apostolic succession, and the unique relation of Peter and Rome, was not used against heretics but against other churches in Asia

27. Joseph Fessler, *The True and False Infallibility of the Popes* (New York: Catholic Publication Society, 1875).

28. This brief survey is indebted to Geoffrey Barraclough, *The Medieval Papacy* (New York: Harcourt, Brace & World, 1968). For a more recent account, see Eamon Duffy, *Saints and Sinners: A History of the Popes,* 2nd ed. (New Haven: Yale University Press, 2001).

Minor. In the third century Cyprian, Bishop of Carthage (d. 258), stressed the equality of all bishops when his position on the validity of heretical or schismatic baptism was opposed by Stephen, Bishop of Rome (d. 257). While it is not certain, Cyprian likely revised *The Unity of the Catholic Church,* in which he originally stressed the primacy of Peter and Rome, to emphasize the equality of all the bishops.

When the capital of the Roman Empire moved to Constantinople, Roman bishops, beginning with Damasus I (366-384), further stressed their claims of primacy due to the rising threat of the bishop of the "New Rome." Leo I (440-461) was the first to present the Petrine monarchical form of government. Here the Bishop of Rome was understood to exercise authority over the Roman Emperor and ecclesiastical officials of other apostolic sees, namely Alexandria, Antioch, Constantinople, and Jerusalem. Of course, this claim was resisted by other Western bishops, Eastern bishops, and secular rulers. The resistance on the part of the East eventually culminated in the great schism of 1054, a tragedy brought about as much by Rome's claims to primacy as by the theological issues surrounding the addition of *filioque* to the Nicene Creed. Nonetheless by the time of Gregory VII (1073-85), the theory of Leo I became reality in the West as the Roman church did indeed exercise authority over lay rulers, as seen in the Investiture Controversy and the excommunication and deposition of emperor Henry IV. From the middle of the thirteenth century on, "the pope's power as head of the church is essentially unlimited, at least in theory."[29]

According to Brian Tierney, theories of papal infallibility begin to appear at this time. Papal infallibility was first proposed in the thirteenth century by the Franciscan theologian Peter Olivi. The survival of the Franciscans depended heavily on the support of the pope. However, some viewed the Franciscan doctrine of apostolic poverty as an innovation that contradicted the traditional teaching of the church. Olivi's proposal of papal infallibility was an attempt to safeguard the doctrine of apostolic poverty, which was approved by Pope Nicholas III. In the fourteenth century John XXII explicitly rejected Olivi's doctrine of papal infallibility because of the longstanding theory of sovereignty in Roman law, where the ruler is not bound by the laws of his predecessor. John XXII thought such sovereignty was needed for the pope to enact re-

29. Barraclough, *The Medieval Papacy,* p. 122.

newal and reform in the church. Tierney argues, "Since the canonists all believed that the doctrinal pronouncements of a pope might well be in error and so need to be corrected by a later pope they could not have developed such a doctrine [of irreformability] without gross self-contradiction."[30]

Tierney's historical presentation is intended to serve as a critique of the contemporary doctrine. However, he notes that within a half-century of Olivi's proposal, Bishop Guido Terreni presented a doctrine of papal infallibility more like the one adopted at Vatican I. In fact, Francis Sullivan remarks that Terreni "so closely anticipated the doctrine of Vatican I that in the judgment of B. M. Xiberta, the Carmelite scholar who edited [Terreni's] work, 'if he had written it after Vatican I he would have had to add or change hardly a single word.'"[31] Thus we can say that the doctrine of papal infallibility defined at Vatican I had its origins in the fourteenth century and was itself part of a long development of papal claims.

Tierney's presentation of the origins of papal infallibility deserves further comment. The attacks on the doctrine of apostolic poverty led Bonaventure to introduce a significant shift in the understanding of tradition, a shift with similarities to contemporary understandings of doctrinal development. The Franciscans could not deny, and did not want to deny, that St. Francis had introduced a new understanding of the Christian faith. However, Bonaventure "persistently maintained that the current teachings of the church could provide an unerring guide to the truths of faith which Christ had revealed to the first apostles — even when there was no obvious warrant for those teachings in ancient sources."[32] Peter Olivi seized Bonaventure's view of tradition in his arguments for papal infallibility. Olivi argued that the pope, as the supreme judge of the Christian faith, could explicate what had been implicit in the faith and could even verify new revelations. The pope, though, could not reverse truths of faith that were already verified.[33] While most contemporary views of doctrinal development would not

30. Brian Tierney, *Origins of Papal Infallibility: 1150-1350* (Leiden: E. J. Brill, 1972), p. 57. See also pp. 30, 49.

31. Francis Sullivan, *Magisterium: Teaching Authority in the Catholic Church* (New York: Paulist Press, 1983), p. 92.

32. Tierney, *Origins of Papal Infallibility*, p. 73.

33. Tierney, *Origins of Papal Infallibility*, p. 114.

argue for new revelations, the view of Olivi anticipates later understandings of doctrinal development, which appeared and slowly gained popularity in the second part of the nineteenth century.

Here is the definition of papal infallibility from *Pastor Aeternus,* followed by several initial observations:

> Therefore, faithfully adhering to the tradition received from the
> beginning of the Christian faith, to the glory of God our Savior, for
> the exaltation of the Catholic religion and for the salvation of the
> Christian people, with the approval of the sacred council, we teach
> and define as a divinely revealed dogma that when the Roman
> pontiff speaks *ex cathedra,* that is, when, in the exercise of his of-
> fice as shepherd and teacher of all Christians, in virtue of his su-
> preme apostolic authority, he defines a doctrine concerning faith
> or morals to be held by the whole church, he possesses, by the di-
> vine assistance promised to him in blessed Peter, that infallibility
> which the divine Redeemer willed his church to enjoy in defining
> doctrine concerning faith or morals. Therefore, such definitions
> of the Roman pontiff are of themselves, and not by the consent of
> the church, irreformable.
>
> So then, should anyone, which God forbid, have the temerity to
> reject this definition of ours: let him be anathema.[34]

1. The doctrine of papal infallibility is not understood to be an invention or new teaching of the council, but seeks to faithfully adhere to "the
tradition received from the beginning of the Christian faith." As such,
the definition is presented as a "divinely revealed dogma." Also, the infallibility of the pope is viewed as a negative charism. In other words, the
charism involves protection from error, not inspiration or new revelations. The pope, with the aid of the Holy Spirit, is able to faithfully interpret divine revelation, which may require careful reflection and study.
But the pope is not inspired so as to impart new revelation.

2. The pope is infallible when he speaks *"ex cathedra,"* literally,
"from the chair [of Peter]." *Ex cathedra* refers to the solemn definition

---

34. *Pastor Aeternus,* in Jaroslav Pelikan and Valerie Hotchkiss, eds., *Creeds and Confessions of Faith in the Christian Tradition,* vol. 3 (New Haven: Yale University Press, 2003), p. 358.

of doctrines as qualified in the subsequent exegetical phrase presented in points 3-5 below. The phrase *ex cathedra* has led Catholic theologians to distinguish "extraordinary papal magisterium," when the pope exercises his infallible teaching authority to solemnly define a doctrine; and "ordinary papal magisterium," when the pope teaches a doctrine authoritatively but not infallibly.[35] The term "magisterium" can refer either to those who exercise teaching authority in the Catholic Church, that is, the pope and episcopal college; or to the teaching authority that is exercised by these ecclesial authorities.

3. The infallibility of the pope is connected to "the exercise of his office" and not his person *per se.* For the pope to speak *ex cathedra* is to speak officially as "shepherd and teacher of all Christians." Thus we can distinguish official actions of the pope from his actions as a private theologian. If a pope were to resign from office he would no longer possess the charism of infallibility.

4. The realm of the pope's infallible teaching authority is "doctrine concerning faith or morals." The pope's infallibility does not extend to other areas, such as scientific investigation and political decisions. Catholics readily admit that the pope can and has made errors in these areas, as seen in the condemnation of Galileo in the seventeenth century and the support of fascism in the twentieth century. The charism given to the office of the papacy extends only to solemn decisions about doctrines of faith or morals so as to preserve the church in the truth of the gospel.

5. The realm "doctrine concerning faith or morals" is further qualified by the statement "to be held by the whole church." To speak *ex cathedra* is to define a doctrine for the church universal, not simply to decide in a regional dispute or offer private counsel. Further, some would argue that, when defining a doctrine, the pope simply articulates more fully the faith already implicitly held by the whole church. To summarize the last four points, the pope enjoys the charism of infallibility only when speaking *ex cathedra:* that is, when defining doctrine in an official, solemn manner, in the realm of faith or morals, for the church universal.

---

35. See, for example, J. Robert Dionne, *The Papacy and the Church: A Study of Praxis and Reception in Ecumenical Perspective* (New York: Philosophical Library, 1987), pp. 19, 21.

6. The charism the pope enjoys is the "divine assistance promised to him in blessed Peter." Here we see the traditional Catholic claim that the bishops are the successors of the apostles, and the bishop of Rome is the successor of Peter. Since the pope is the successor of Peter, the promises of Christ to Peter are the promises of Christ to the pope. *Pastor Aeternus* cites several New Testament passages to support the doctrine, the most important of which are the three promises of Christ to Peter:

> And I tell you, you are Peter, and on this rock I will build my church, and the gates of Hades will not prevail against it. I will give you the keys of the kingdom of heaven, and whatever you bind on earth will be bound in heaven, and whatever you loose on earth will be loosed in heaven.[36]

> Simon, Simon, listen! Satan has demanded to sift all of you like wheat, but I have prayed for you that your own faith may not fail; and you, when once you have turned back, strengthen your brothers.[37]

> When they had finished breakfast, Jesus said to Simon Peter, "Simon son of John, do you love me more than these?" He said to him, "Yes, Lord; you know that I love you." Jesus said to him, "Feed my lambs." A second time he said to him, "Simon son of John, do you love me?" He said to him, "Yes, Lord; you know that I love you." Jesus said to him, "Tend my sheep." He said to him the third time, "Simon son of John, do you love me?" Peter felt hurt because he said to him the third time, "Do you love me?" And he said to him, "Lord, you know everything; you know that I love you." Jesus said to him, "Feed my sheep."[38]

These three passages continue to be used as the primary scriptural support of the doctrine of papal infallibility. While, for the most part, Protestant and Orthodox Christians agree that these texts give a pri-

---

36. Matthew 16:18-19, NRSV.
37. Luke 22:31-32, NRSV.
38. John 21:15-17, NRSV.

macy to Peter, they disagree that this primacy is to be passed on through history, and that the bishop of Rome is to be identified as the successor of Peter.

7. The infallibility of the pope is placed within the context of the "infallibility which the divine Redeemer willed his church to enjoy." As seen in Matthew 16:18, cited above, "the gates of Hades will not prevail against [the church]." At the close of Matthew's Gospel, Jesus promises his disciples, "And remember, I am with you always, to the end of the age."[39] The infallibility of the pope is connected to the indefectibility of the people of God and Jesus' promise to be with his church for all time. The church is preserved from error because of the charism of infallibility that resides in the papal office.

8. As discussed earlier, the clause *ex sese non autem ex consensu ecclesiae* was added by the Deputation on the Faith in the final draft of *Pastor Aeternus.* The clause opposed elements of the Gallican movement by emphasizing that *ex cathedra* definitions are infallible "of themselves, and not by the consent of the church." In other words, papal definitions are infallible apart from the approval of a council. It should be noted, though, that the pope consulted the bishops and received ardent support before defining the two uncontested *ex cathedra* doctrines, the Marian dogmas. This practice has established a precedent that will most likely be followed in the future.

9. Doctrines defined *ex cathedra* are irreformable. This, of course, is perfectly logical. If a doctrine is true and infallibly defined, it cannot be reformed in the future if the church is to remain in the truth.

When the First Vatican Council was adjourned, many important issues regarding the church, which provided the original context for *Pastor Aeternus,* were never addressed. On October 11, 1962, the Second Vatican Council opened under Pope John XXIII. Here, ecclesiology was taken up again, and *Lumen Gentium,* the dogmatic constitution on the church, was issued on November 21, 1964. *Lumen Gentium,* especially chapter 3, continues the unfinished task of placing the infallibility of the pope within a larger ecclesial framework. The bulk of the chapter explains the role and function of the bishops and confirms that their authority comes directly from Christ, not the pope, provided that the bishops remain in communion with the pope, who is the church's

39. Matthew 28:20, NRSV.

head. Section 25 reaffirms the doctrine of papal infallibility, but also includes several new details.

The faithful are to give religious assent to the teaching of the bishops, but especially to the teaching of the pope.

> The religious assent of will and intellect is to be given in a special way to the authentic teaching authority of the Roman pontiff even when he is not speaking *ex cathedra;* in such a way, that is, that his supreme teaching authority is respectfully acknowledged, and sincere adherence given to decisions he has delivered, in accordance with his manifest mind and will which is communicated chiefly by the nature of the documents, by the frequent repetition of the same doctrine, or by the style of verbal expression.[40]

First, the faithful are to give assent to the teaching of the pope even when his teaching is not *ex cathedra.* This is stated to address one of the perhaps unforeseen consequences of papal infallibility. If the pope is able to infallibly declare doctrine, but does not do so in a particular instance, then his teaching in that instance is tentative and, it would seem, open to dissent. Vatican II addresses this problem by emphasizing that the pope's teaching authority is to be "respectfully acknowledged" and all of his teachings are to be given "sincere adherence."

Second, doctrinal statements can be given various interpretations. Papal teaching could be interpreted in such a way as to disregard the primary concern the pope intends to address. Since this is the case, the faithful must seek to follow the pope's teaching "in accordance with his manifest mind and will." While, undoubtedly, it can be difficult to discern the pope's mind, the quotation from *Lumen Gentium* closes with some practical suggestions on how this can be done.

The following paragraph from *Lumen Gentium* is quoted in full.

> Although individual bishops do not enjoy the prerogative of infallibility, nevertheless, even though dispersed throughout the world, but maintaining the bond of communion among themselves and with the successor of Peter, when in teaching authentically matters concerning faith and morals they agree about a judgment as one

---

40. *Lumen Gentium* 25, in Pelikan and Hotchkiss, p. 597.

that has to be definitively held, they infallibly proclaim the teaching of Christ. This takes place even more clearly when they are gathered together in an ecumenical council and are the teachers and judges of faith and morals for the whole church. Their definitions must be adhered to with the obedience of faith.[41]

The infallible teachings of the church extend beyond the *ex cathedra* definitions of the pope. The bishops of the church can and have spoken infallibly under two circumstances. First, when the bishops in communion with the pope, though ministering throughout the world, agree on a doctrine of faith and morals, that doctrine is infallibly taught. This exercise of infallible teaching authority is called "ordinary universal magisterium."[42] Obviously it would be difficult to compile a list of such doctrines, but it would include a number of beliefs that have never been defined. Such beliefs would include that God is merciful, and that it is wrong to murder for personal gain. A less trivial example would be the immorality of artificial contraception, though Catholic theologians and ethicists debate whether this is infallibly taught as part of the ordinary universal magisterium. Second, when bishops gather in ecumenical councils in communion with the pope and define a doctrine of faith or morals, the bishops teach infallibly. This exercise of infallible teaching authority, called "extraordinary universal magisterium," would include doctrines like the Trinity, the hypostatic union of natures in Christ, and even papal infallibility.[43]

Next, *Lumen Gentium* reaffirms the doctrine of papal infallibility defined in *Pastor Aeternus*. Since the statement closely follows *Pastor Aeternus,* it will not be quoted in full. Attention should be given, though, to the first and last sentences, which are new.

This infallibility, however, with which the divine redeemer willed his church to be endowed in defining doctrine concerning faith or morals, extends just as far as the deposit of divine revelation that is to be guarded as sacred and faithfully expounded.[44]

41. *Lumen Gentium* 25, in Pelikan and Hotchkiss, p. 597.
42. Dionne, *The Papacy and the Church*, p. 21.
43. Dionne, *The Papacy and the Church*, p. 20.
44. *Lumen Gentium* 25, in Pelikan and Hotchkiss, p. 597.

Francis Sullivan explains this statement as follows:

> In this sentence we find first a generic description of the object of
> infallibility as "doctrine of faith and morals"; this is then distin-
> guished into a *primary object:* "the deposit of revelation," and a
> *secondary object,* which . . . is intended by the clause: "which must
> be religiously guarded and faithfully expounded."[45]

This interpretation follows the one given in the declaration *Mysterium
Ecclesiae,* which was issued by the Sacred Congregation for the Doctrine
of the Faith on June 24, 1973. "According to Catholic doctrine, the infallibility of the Church's Magisterium extends not only to the deposit of
faith but also to those matters without which that deposit cannot be
rightly preserved and expounded."[46] Therefore the infallibility of the
magisterium extends not only to the primary object of infallibility, a
truth revealed by God, but also the secondary object of infallibility,
which Dionne defines as "a truth which in itself is not revealed but so
closely connected with revealed truth that to call into question the former logically entails calling into question the revealed truth itself."[47]

In Catholic theology, the primary object of infallibility refers to
those truths revealed in sacred scripture and sacred tradition, which together make up the deposit of revelation. The secondary object of infallibility is more complex, and Sullivan gives the following as examples of
what truths this category might include: (1) the condemnation of propositions that oppose revealed truth, (2) propositions that necessarily
follow from revealed truths but are not themselves revealed, (3) historical facts that are not revealed but are closely connected with the exercise of the church's teaching office, such as the ecumenicity of a council, (4) the solemn canonization of saints, and (5) the natural moral
law.[48] Of these, the natural moral law is most controversial, and

---

45. Sullivan, *Magisterium,* p. 127.

46. *Mysterium Ecclesiae* 3, in United States Catholic Conference, *The Küng Dialogue: A Documentation of the efforts of The Congregation for the Doctrine of the Faith and
of The Conference of German Bishops to achieve an appropriate clarification of the controversial views of Dr. Hans Küng* (Washington, DC: United States Catholic Conference,
1980), p. 192. *Mysterium Ecclesiae* is discussed further in chapter 6.

47. Dionne, *The Papacy and the Church,* p. 23.

48. Sullivan, *Magisterium,* pp. 135ff.

Sullivan discusses it in more detail. What does and does not constitute the secondary object of infallibility is unclear and disputed in Catholic theology.

The last sentence we will examine from *Lumen Gentium*, which concludes the paragraph that reaffirms *Pastor Aeternus*, states,

> The assent of the church, however, can never fail to be given to these definitions on account of the activity of the same Holy Spirit, by which the whole flock of Christ is preserved in the unity of faith and makes progress.[49]

While *Pastor Aeternus* maintains that *ex cathedra* definitions are infallible "of themselves, and not by the consent of the church," *Lumen Gentium* stresses that the assent of the church cannot fail to be given to *ex cathedra* definitions. In other words, an authentic *ex cathedra* definition will always receive the assent of the faithful. This is the case because the same Holy Spirit that gifts the pope with the charism of infallibility also dwells in the church. This last sentence was no doubt intended to clarify and qualify the *ex sese* clause from *Pastor Aeternus*, but it does raise a number of interesting questions. At the beginning of section 25, the faithful are encouraged to acknowledge and assent to the teaching authority of the church. At the end of the section, the assent of the faithful is viewed as a confirmation of *ex cathedra* definitions. These potentially conflicting statements from *Lumen Gentium* could occasion great struggle for the sincere believer who disagreed with an infallible definition of the church.

The Marian Dogmas

Catholic theologians disagree over what constitutes an *ex cathedra* definition and what the church has infallibly taught. However, there is wide consensus that the two Marian dogmas, the immaculate conception of the Blessed Virgin and the assumption of the Blessed Virgin, are infallible, *ex cathedra* definitions. Further, we have already seen the important part the proclamation of the immaculate conception played in the even-

49. *Lumen Gentium* 25, in Pelikan and Hotchkiss, p. 598.

tual definition of papal infallibility. While an extended discussion of the two Marian dogmas would go beyond the scope of this work, it will be helpful to introduce them.[50] Most Protestants do not affirm the Marian dogmas because of the lack of biblical support for these doctrines.

The dogma of the immaculate conception of the Blessed Virgin expresses the belief that Mary, although conceived in the normal manner, was born without the stain of original sin. As stated earlier, the impetus for the doctrine came from the laity. The popular desire for the definition grew throughout the nineteenth century, fueled in large part by apparitions of the Blessed Virgin. The most important of these occurred in 1830 to Catherine Labouré, a French Sister of Charity, who saw a vision of Mary with the inscription "conceived without sin." This vision led to the casting of a "Miraculous Medal" which was worn by millions of people in the nineteenth century, and the popularization of the prayer, "O Mary conceived without sin, pray for us who have recourse to thee." In May 1845, the American bishops declared Mary Immaculate the patroness of the United States.[51]

Of course, the doctrine has a long history that extends well beyond the nineteenth century. Several of the early Fathers affirmed the unique holiness of Mary, the "new Eve," and believed she was free from actual sin. While Augustine affirmed the sanctity of Mary, he denied the immaculate conception, maintaining that anyone conceived by intercourse was stained with original sin. The belief in the immaculate conception grew in popularity through the liturgical feast of the Conception of Mary, which was first celebrated in the East in the late seventh century, and was later celebrated in the West, especially in England, in the eleventh century. The earliest defense of the feast and the doctrine comes from the English monk Eadmer, an associate of Anselm, in 1060. However, the doctrine was opposed by a weighty list of medieval theological giants, including Bernard of Clairvaux, Bonaventure, Albert the Great, and Thomas Aquinas. The opponents of the doctrine were concerned that, since Mary was conceived by intercourse, she could not be exempt from original sin. More importantly, if she were free from origi-

---

50. For a more detailed introduction to the Marian dogmas, see Frederick M. Jelly, *Madonna: Mary in the Catholic Tradition,* enlarged ed. (Huntington, IN: Our Sunday Visitor Publishing, 1986).

51. Chadwick, *A History of the Popes: 1830-1914,* pp. 119-20; and Jelly, *Madonna: Mary in the Catholic Tradition,* p. 114.

nal and actual sin she would stand outside the universal redemptive work of Christ. The Dominicans maintained the position of Albert and Thomas and were strong opponents of the doctrine. However, the Franciscan John Duns Scotus would later answer the Dominican critics by proposing that Mary's redemption was a preservative redemption. Her freedom from contracting original and actual sin was based on the redeeming work of Christ, but in her case it was preservative and kept her from sin. Thus Mary participated in Christ's redemption, though in a unique way. Duns Scotus' proposal was influential in resolving the major theological difficulty of the immaculate conception and thus assisted in the popularization of the doctrine.[52]

The immaculate conception of the Blessed Virgin was solemnly proclaimed by Pope Pius IX in *Ineffabilis Deus* on December 8, 1854, followed by an anathema:

> [W]e . . . declare, pronounce, and define that the doctrine which holds that the Blessed Virgin Mary, at the first instant of her conception, by a singular privilege and grace of the omnipotent God, in consideration of the merits of Jesus Christ, the Savior of mankind, was preserved free from all stain of original sin, has been revealed by God, and therefore is to be firmly and constantly believed by all the faithful.[53]

1. *Ineffabilis Deus* states that Mary was preserved free from all stain of original sin "at the first instant of her conception." Thus she was preserved from original sin as well as actual sin from the beginning of her existence as a human person.

2. The immaculate conception is a "singular privilege and grace" enjoyed by Mary alone. While others have been sanctified in the womb, such as Jeremiah and John the Baptist, they were only exempted from mortal sin.[54] Mary alone is exempt from original sin and actual sin.

3. The immaculate conception is "in consideration of the merits of Jesus Christ." Thus, following the idea of preservative redemption first

---

52. Jelly, *Madonna: Mary in the Catholic Tradition*, pp. 107-13; Hales, *Pio Nono*, p. 153.

53. *Ineffabilis Deus*, in Pelikan and Hotchkiss, p. 290.

54. Jeremiah 1:5 and Luke 1:15 are offered as support for this teaching.

proposed by Duns Scotus, Mary is truly redeemed by Jesus, but in a most perfect and anticipatory manner.

The dogma of the immaculate conception is not explicitly taught in scripture, though it is argued that the doctrine is implicit in scripture. Three passages are typically appealed to as support for the doctrine.

> I will put enmity between you and the woman, and between your offspring and hers; he will strike your head and you will strike his heel.[55]

This passage refers to God's curse of the serpent in Eden. It is used by Catholic theologians to present Mary as the "new Eve," who would give birth to the offspring who would crush Satan. The image of Mary as the "new Eve," to complement the biblical image of Christ as the "new Adam,"[56] was popular among the early Fathers and was an important source of later speculations regarding Mary.

> And [the angel Gabriel] came to [Mary] and said, "Greetings, favored one! The Lord is with you."[57]

> And Elizabeth was filled with the Holy Spirit and exclaimed with a loud cry, "Blessed are you among women, and blessed is the fruit of your womb."[58]

Here Mary is presented as favored and blessed because of the child she carries, though the biblical text does not affirm the full doctrine defined by Pius IX.

Today most Catholic theologians argue that the immaculate conception is implicit in these biblical texts in some manner, and that over time the doctrine developed and became explicit, especially in the *sensus fidelium,* the beliefs and devotion of the faithful who are guided by the Holy Spirit. As Jelly summarizes his position,

---

55. Genesis 3:15, NRSV.
56. See Romans 5:12ff.
57. Luke 1:28, NRSV.
58. Luke 1:42b-43, NRSV.

We Roman Catholics believe that precisely what the Magisterium judges to have developed authentically from the Scriptures in the living Tradition of the whole Church is truly a dogma of our faith, a doctrine somehow formally revealed by God, even though only implicitly. It is not as though we were reading something into *(eisegesis)* the sacred Scriptures, but it is truly inspired there, even though not in the actual intention of the original author.[59]

Interestingly enough, Jelly concedes that the Marian dogmas were not part of the original intention of the biblical authors.

The definition of the assumption of the Blessed Virgin was similar to that of the immaculate conception. The stimulus for the doctrine came from the faithful, and after consulting with bishops throughout the world and receiving strong affirmation for the doctrine, Paul XII defined the assumption of the Blessed Virgin on November 1, 1950. The doctrine can be traced back to the late sixth century in the East, when the Emperor Mauricius Flavius announced that the liturgical feast of Mary's Dormition would be celebrated annually. Soon afterwards the feast was understood to celebrate not just Mary's death, but her assumption as well. The feast was adopted by Rome in the late seventh century, and from the beginning of its celebration in the West the feast focused on Mary's bodily assumption.[60]

Like the immaculate conception, there is no explicit biblical witness to the assumption of Mary. The doctrine is claimed to be implicit, though, in the same texts we saw earlier in connection with the immaculate conception. One additional text is used in support of Mary's assumption.

A great portent appeared in heaven: a woman clothed with the sun, with the moon under her feet, and on her head a crown of twelve stars.[61]

While most biblical scholars concur that this text from Revelation refers to both Israel and the church, Catholics argue that it could also re-

---

59. Jelly, *Madonna: Mary in the Catholic Tradition*, p. 107.
60. Jelly, *Madonna: Mary in the Catholic Tradition*, p. 122.
61. Revelation 12:1, NRSV.

fer to Mary as the most perfect representative of the people of God and as the woman who gave birth to the savior.[62] Like the immaculate conception, the belief in the assumption developed over time and was confirmed in the sensus fidelium.

Historically, the assumption of the Blessed Virgin received much less opposition than the immaculate conception. The primary issues regarding the assumption are whether Mary died, was buried, and experienced bodily corruption. The definition of Pius XII left these questions open, though there is a long tradition that Mary did die and was buried.

The assumption of Mary was defined in the apostolic constitution *Munificentissimus Deus,* followed by an anathema.

> [W]e pronounce, declare, and define it to be a divinely revealed dogma: that the Immaculate Mother of God, the Ever-Virgin Mary, having completed the course of her earthly life, was assumed body and soul into heavenly glory.[63]

1. The definition begins with a summary of the traditional dogmas about Mary, including her immaculate conception, the title *Theotokos* or "God-bearer,"[64] and her perpetual virginity before, during, and after the birth of Jesus.[65]

2. The phrase "having completed the course of her earthly life" is intentionally vague regarding the death, burial, and corruption of Mary's body. Further, unlike the definition of the immaculate conception, the assumption is not necessarily unique to Mary. These questions are left open for further discussion.

3. The passive verb "was assumed" is used to emphasize that Mary, unlike Christ, did not "ascend" into heaven by her own power but rather was assumed by the power of God. Christ, as the divine Son of God, ascended into heaven.

---

62. See Revelation 12:5.

63. *Munificentissimus Deus* 44, in Pelikan and Hotchkiss, p. 536.

64. This title was maintained at the councils of Ephesus (431) and Chalcedon (451), although here the debate was primarily over christology.

65. The perpetual virginity of Mary was first taught in the apocryphal Protoevangelium of James, which appears to date from the second century.

4. Mary was assumed "body and soul." Her complete person was assumed, not just her soul or spirit alone.

Both Marian dogmas were reaffirmed at Vatican II. However, it is significant that, by a vote of 1114 to 1074, the dogmas were treated in *Lumen Gentium,* the dogmatic decree on the church, and not in a separate decree on mariology. The Blessed Virgin is therefore treated as a type of the church and the most perfect representative of the church.[66] Further, the dogmatic decree on ecumenism, *Unitatis Redintegratio,* spoke of an "order or 'hierarchy' of truths" that are taught in the Catholic Church.[67] Therefore, although the Marian dogmas have been infallibly defined, these doctrines are not considered to be as central to the gospel as some others, such as the doctrine of the Trinity and the bodily resurrection of Christ.

To summarize, a number of factors were involved in defining papal infallibility at Vatican I. An obvious concern for many bishops was to support the pope at a time when his political and spiritual authority was under severe attack. With the intention of buttressing papal authority, and in light of debates that go back at least as far as the Protestant Reformation, Vatican I defined a religious epistemology that made the pope an infallible belief-producing mechanism in the Catholic Church. Further, the pope has functioned in this epistemic capacity on at least two occasions, in the definition of the two Marian dogmas. This work questions whether the pope's spiritual authority and influence are dependent upon him being the final piece of a complex epistemology. However, before this suggestion can be seriously entertained, we must consider the fate of *Pastor Aeternus* as an epistemic proposal in the work of four prominent Catholic theologians.

---

66. *Lumen Gentium* 63-65, in Pelikan and Hotchkiss, pp. 631-33.
67. *Unitatis Redintegratio* 11, in Pelikan and Hotchkiss, p. 643.

CHAPTER 3

Maximal Infallibility:
Henry Edward Cardinal Manning

The first view of papal infallibility to be considered is the maximal position of Henry Edward Cardinal Manning. In chapter 4 we will examine the moderate position of John Henry Cardinal Newman. Manning and Newman make an interesting pair who, though they shared many similar experiences, disagreed markedly on the issue of papal infallibility. The continued fascination in Manning and Newman is evident in the publication of David Newsome's *The Convert Cardinals,* a study of these two Anglican converts who were elevated to the Sacred College of Cardinals and who had a profound influence on Roman Catholic theology. As Newsome notes, though, Manning is typically depicted as "too bad to be wholly credible," while Newman is portrayed as "rather too good to be true."[1]

It is widely acknowledged that the reputation of Manning suffered immensely from the work of his original biographer, E. S. Purcell, as well as from the long-delayed defense of his reputation by Catholic scholars. The unscrupulous schemes employed by Purcell in the production of his book cannot be told here.[2] It is sufficient to note that the two-volume biography,[3] which portrayed Manning as a conniving, overly-ambitious, and domineering ecclesiastic, sold quite well. Lytton

1. David Newsome, *The Convert Cardinals: John Henry Newman and Henry Edward Manning* (London: John Murray, 1993), p. 21.
2. The story is told by Robert Gray in *Cardinal Manning: A Biography* (London: Weidenfeld & Nicolson, 1985), pp. 3ff.
3. E. S. Purcell, *Life of Cardinal Manning,* 2 vols. (London: Macmillan & Co., 1896).

Strachey, who relied heavily on Purcell's work, further popularized this picture of Manning in the first "portrait" of his seedy book, *Eminent Victorians*.[4] It was not until 1921, twenty-five years after the publication of Purcell's work and primarily as a response to Strachey, that a thorough defense of Manning appeared by Shane Leslie.[5]

The popular image of Manning is hard to square with the spontaneous outpouring of emotion displayed by his Catholic fold following his death. *The Times,* which was hardly sympathetic to Manning, described the crowds that came to visit his body as "difficult to estimate, and not easy to exaggerate."[6] Perhaps this inconsistency can be attributed to the fact that Manning was primarily a man of action, and only secondarily a man of thought. His social vision of the church, which included tireless efforts in public life and a deep concern for the poor and the working class, anticipated the various socialist visions of Christianity in the twentieth century.[7] But Manning was an intellectual, and it was the combination of his practical skills and his deep intellectual concerns that made him one of the primary leaders behind the definition of papal infallibility at Vatican I. In Manning's thought one finds a rigorous presentation of maximal infallibility from a key nineteenth-century leader who viewed the definition as more than opportune.

The Life of Manning

Born on July 15, 1808, Manning was the youngest child of an affluent British family. Manning's father, William, was a Member of Parliament who made his fortune as a merchant in West India and as governor of the Bank of England. Manning grew up in an atmosphere shaped by evangelical piety. While traditionally the youngest son of wealthy families entered the service of the church, Manning aspired to a career in

4. Lytton Strachey, *Eminent Victorians* (Garden City, NY: Garden City Publishing Co., 1918).

5. Shane Leslie, *Henry Edward Manning: His Life and Labours* (London: Burns, Oates & Washbourne, Ltd., 1921).

6. As quoted by Gray, *Cardinal Manning,* p. 2.

7. An account of the public life of Manning is given by V. A. McClelland, *Cardinal Manning: His Public Life and Influence, 1865-1892* (London: Oxford University Press, 1962).

politics as a student at Oxford. These dreams were shattered, though, when William Manning lost his fortune in the banking industry while Henry was still a student. Since Manning could not enter politics after his father's disgraceful loss, for the first time in his life he seriously considered entering the ministry. The exact reasons for Manning's decision can be, and have been, debated, but it seems clear that a profound spiritual awakening was occurring in his life during this trying period. After all, there were numerous career options besides politics and ministry that were available to the talented young Manning. After completing his ministerial studies at Merton College, Oxford, Manning took Orders in the Church of England and began serving in Lavington.

Manning's evangelical sympathies grew while he was a student at Oxford. It was not until he began pastoral work at Lavington that he first questioned his religious inheritance. In his journal Manning wrote,

> The first question that rose to my mind was, What right have you to be teaching, admonishing, reforming, rebuking others? By what authority do you lift the latch of the poor man's door and enter and sit down and begin to instruct or correct him? This train of thought forced me to see that no culture or knowledge of Greek or Latin would suffice for this. That if I was not a messenger sent from God, I was an intruder and impertinent.[8]

What Manning sought, and what he perceived as a weakness of his evangelical heritage, was a theology that could ground his ministry as a legitimate ecclesial authority representing God. His journey, which would ultimately lead him to the Catholic Church, began in September 1833, with the publication of the first of the *Tracts for the Times* by John Henry Newman.

Newman, a central figure behind the Tractarian or Oxford Movement, sought to steer a course between two parties in the Church of England: the evangelical party, which stressed piety and religious enthusiasm but lacked doctrinal rigor; and the high church party, which stressed hierarchical and sacramental principles but had become too cold and formal. In fact, the Tractarians viewed themselves as restoring the original vision of the Anglican Reformation before the negative doc-

8. As quoted in Gray, *Cardinal Manning*, p. 49.

51

trinal influences of evangelical Protestantism. What Newman sought, during a time of rapid secularization, was a religious revival along the lines of evangelicalism but founded on stronger doctrinal principles. As a foundation for doctrine and authority, Newman stressed, though more enthusiastically than it had been stated before, the old Anglican principle of apostolic succession.

Apostolic succession affirms that the present-day priest has authority because Christ invested his apostles with authority. The apostles passed on this divine commission to their successors, the bishops, which in turn is passed on to priests at ordination. Apostolic succession seeks to guarantee the continuity of the church today with the apostolic church. Basing doctrine and authority in apostolic succession appealed to Manning, and though Manning was never a central leader in the movement, he was definitely persuaded by Newman and the ideals of the Tractarians.

Initially the Tractarians, especially Newman, were adamantly opposed to the Catholic Church. The apostolic church must convey the apostolic doctrine found in the earliest Church Fathers, and the Catholic Church, especially at Trent, defined too many doctrinal revisions and additions. Manning agreed that the Catholic Church taught doctrines not found in the primitive church. Further, he found papal pretensions and claims to infallibility absurd and dangerous. In one of his sermons Manning declared, "It is plain, that the meaning of a mute document, if it be tied to follow the utterance of a *living* voice which shall claim the supreme right of interpretation, must vary with its living expositor. And in this lies the real danger of the Catholic doctrine of papal infallibility." In the same sermon, Manning argued, "It is the assumption of supremacy on earth, and of freedom from all controlling authority in religion that makes the Church of Rome and the modern school unteachable and wilful."[9]

The Tractarians were equally opposed to the sixteenth-century Reformers and the principle of private judgment in scriptural interpretation. Private interpretation of scripture leads to doctrinal confusion, while faith is a deposit that is passed on in the church and preserved by the Holy Spirit. The Tractarians proposed that scripture must be interpreted in light of the tradition of the early church. What the Tractar-

9. Gray, *Cardinal Manning*, pp. 73, 74.

ians, and Manning, soon came to realize was that tradition too must be interpreted, and this inevitably rested on private judgment. Thus the system the Tractarians were devising only took the problem of private interpretation one step back from scripture alone to scripture and tradition. The desire for doctrinal and interpretive certainty and a system that could avoid the problem of private judgment was a key factor in the conversion of Newman and Manning.

It should be noted that a number of other factors were also at play in the conversions of Newman and Manning. For example, both developed a growing appreciation for and fascination with the devotional practices of the Catholic Church and how these practices facilitated spiritual development. Both remained celibate, and Newman in particular believed that, ideally, the priesthood should not marry.[10] The Tractarians hoped that the Church of England would eventually incorporate these practices as well. In Manning's case, the conversion of a number of close friends and relatives, including Newman, inevitably played some role in his own decision to convert. But Newman and Manning were wrestling with different intellectual issues and different practical concerns. Newman announced and sought to justify his conversion in his classic work, *An Essay on the Development of Doctrine.*[11] As the title suggests, Newman was looking for a system that could account for legitimate developments in Christian doctrine, many of which were responses to heretical proposals, that he observed in his historical studies. Manning dismissed the central argument for doctrinal development in Newman's *Essay,* though years later Manning admitted that the book "opened my eyes to one fact, namely that I had laid down only half the subject. I had found the *Rule,* but not the *Judge.* It was evident that to put Scripture and Antiquity into the hands of the individual is as much Private judgment as to put Scripture alone."[12] It would take Manning another five years, during which time he endured serious health problems undoubtedly related to inner turmoil, before his conversion was complete.

10. Manning married at the beginning of his ministry in Lavington, but after the early death of his wife he remained single for the rest of his ministry in the Church of England.

11. John Henry Newman, *An Essay on the Development of Christian Doctrine* (Notre Dame: University of Notre Dame Press, 1990).

12. As quoted in James Pereiro, *Cardinal Manning: An Intellectual Biography* (Oxford: Clarendon Press, 1998), pp. 68, 69.

The event that immediately led to Manning's conversion was the G. E. Gorham decision of 1850. Before the Gorham case, Manning grew increasingly aware of the problem of Erastianism, or the primacy of the state over the church in ecclesiastical matters, in the Church of England. In 1847 Lord John Russell's nomination of Renn Dickson Hampden as Bishop of Hereford caused a great stir among Anglican leaders, including Manning, who deemed Hampden's theology as heterodox. The case ended, though, when the persons leading the charge against Hampden failed to produce clear evidence of his heterodoxy. In the Gorham case, however, there was a clear doctrinal issue at stake. Henry Phillpotts, Bishop of Exeter, refused to appoint Gorham as parish priest of Bramford Speke because Gorham denied the doctrine of baptismal regeneration. While a church court upheld the decision of Phillpotts, Gorham appealed to the Judicial Committee of the British government's Privy Council, which reversed the church ruling. The Erastianism of the Church of England, and the Gorham decision in particular, had a profound effect upon Manning. Years later he wrote, "The violation of the doctrine of Baptism was of less gravity to me than the violation of the divine office of the Church by the supremacy of the Crown in council."[13] By this time, the assumed supremacy of the Catholic Church as the final court of appeal in religious matters was no longer a problem for Manning as it had been earlier in his career. In fact, it was a principle to be defended at all costs lest the state seek to control and govern the church.

On April 6, 1851, Manning was received into the Catholic Church. It is here that characterizations of Manning as a power-driven ecclesiastic are seriously called into question. In the Church of England Manning had powerful connections and was clearly a figure on the rise.[14] He had no reason to suspect that he would become Archbishop of Westminster in 1865 and be made a Cardinal in 1875. Instead, he expected to face many of the same difficulties that plagued Newman after his conversion, especially the suspicion of Catholics toward outsiders and newcomers. The fact is that Manning was a brilliant diplomat and administrator, and Catholic officials recognized this just as Anglican officials had before. Further, it is hard, if not impossible, to doubt that Manning

13. As quoted in Newsome, *The Convert Cardinals*, p. 182.
14. Newsome provides clear evidence of this on pp. 143-45.

was sincere in his beliefs, even if these beliefs happened to coincide with the Ultramontanism that was promoted by Pius IX.

But a significant change did take place in Manning after his conversion to Catholicism. No longer did he find himself in a system of compromise and uncertainty. Gray describes this change well.

> In submitting to Rome Manning for ever put behind him profitless and paralyzing internal debate. He called his conversion his last act of reason and his first act of faith; he meant, not that he had ceased to use his reason, but that reason would henceforth be the servant of dogma received through faith. There need be no more questions; the answers were all determined in Rome. Manning was perfectly adapted to maintain such a position. His mind was efficient to the point of genius, and he never showed any disposition to pursue speculative problems into labyrinths of ambiguity. What he demanded from theology was a clearing of the decks for action; once in the fight his capacity and dispatch were unrivalled.[15]

It is in this light that Manning's ceaseless activity, passion for the infallibility definition, and questionable tactics, at the Vatican council and beyond, should be evaluated.

This is not the place to rehearse Manning's extensive social activity as Archbishop of Westminster, culminating in the resolution of the London Dock Strike in 1889. However, Manning's socialist policies do call into question one popular stereotype of the supporters of papal infallibility. As James Pereiro observes, "The identification of absolutist monarchical principles as the key to understanding the minds of those who supported the doctrine of papal infallibility, if valid at all, is certainly not applicable to Manning." He further notes that, for Manning, "the Church and human society were founded on different principles, although both had as their end man's good. The divine structure of the Church need not necessarily be the ideal model for human society, but neither was human society the ideal model for the Church."[16] This point is important to keep in mind because, for Manning, the key issue behind papal infallibility was not monarchical principles but doctrinal

---

15. Gray, *Cardinal Manning*, p. 149.
16. Pereiro, *Cardinal Manning: An Intellectual Biography*, pp. 337, 338.

certainty and legitimate authority. Manning enjoyed a long and active life right up to his death in 1892.

Significant Theological Themes

Two themes in Manning's thought are crucial to understanding his theology in general and his conception of papal infallibility in particular. The first is his ecclesiology, and the second is his strong foundationalism in epistemology. These two themes are interrelated for Manning, and both incorporate other theological doctrines, especially pneumatology. Further, these two themes enjoy a close similarity in Manning's Anglican and Catholic works.

In his Catholic work *The Temporal Mission of the Holy Ghost,* Manning states his desire "to undo, as far as I may, the errors into which I unconsciously fell [as an Anglican]."[17] He lists only three errors, and these are helpful for understanding both the similarities and dissimilarities of his thought as an Anglican and Catholic. First, in his work *The Rule of Faith,* he "erroneously maintained that the old and true rule of faith is Scripture and antiquity, and I rejected as new and untenable two other rules of faith, — first, the private judgment of the individual; and secondly, the interpretations of the living church."[18] As a Catholic, of course, he upheld the interpretations of the living church. Second, concerning his book *The Unity of the Church* he states,

> But while I thought that the unity of the Church is organic and moral — that the organic unity consists in succession, hierarchy, and valid sacrament, and the moral in the communion of charity among all members of particular churches, and all the churches in Catholic unity, I erroneously thought that this moral unity might be permanently suspended, and even lost, while the organic unity remained intact, and that unity of communion belongs only to the perfection, not to the intrinsic essence of the Church.[19]

17. Henry Edward Manning, *The Temporal Mission of the Holy Ghost; or, Reason and Revelation* (New York: D. Appleton, 1866), p. 42.
18. Manning, *The Temporal Mission of the Holy Ghost,* p. 43.
19. Manning, *The Temporal Mission of the Holy Ghost,* p. 43.

As a Catholic, Manning opposed the Anglican branch theory of unity, which held that the Catholic, Orthodox, and Anglican churches were all apostolic churches. Now he insisted that there cannot be "organic" unity without "moral" unity. The one church confessed in the Nicene Creed must display a visible unity. Third, observing the conflicts between the papacy and the English government in a sermon preached at Oxford, he said, "It would seem to be the will of heaven that the dominion of the Roman Pontificate may never be again set up in this Church and realm."[20] These three issues were common disagreements between Anglicans and Catholics, and while Manning embraced the Catholic side upon his conversion, Pereiro correctly observes that

> the main line of his ideas on the matter of infallibility can be found in his Anglican writings and letters. As a Catholic, he may have completed them in some respects, particularly in what refers to the infallibility of the Pope, but the main arguments remained the same: the living presence of the Holy Spirit in the Church, the reality of the Mystical body of Christ, and the infallibility of the Church consequent to that presence. These themes were part of his original vision, and were to remain with him for the rest of his life.[21]

Manning's ecclesiology anticipated Vatican II by conceiving the church, not in cold institutional or juridical terms, but as the mystical body of Christ. The church is Christ's mystical body because of the indwelling of the Holy Spirit, who exercises both a sanctifying and a teaching work in the church. Even as an Anglican Manning believed that, because of the work of the Holy Spirit, the church enjoys infallibility in discerning truth and excluding error. As a Catholic, of course, Manning located the infallible work of the Holy Spirit in the magisterium, particularly the pope. Manning considered it a heresy, and a Trinitarian one at that, to deny the infallibility of the church, for this was to deny the ongoing activity of the Holy Spirit.[22]

Because the Holy Spirit exercises a continual teaching office in the

---

20. Manning, *The Temporal Mission of the Holy Ghost*, pp. 43-44.
21. Pereiro, *Cardinal Manning: An Intellectual Biography*, pp. 118-19.
22. Manning, *The Temporal Mission of the Holy Ghost*, pp. 83ff.

church, the church can be assured of the preservation and immutability of its doctrines. Therefore, Manning maintained that "the doctrines of the Church in all ages are primative [sic]."[23] Here Manning rejected Newman's theory of doctrinal development. Newman clearly admitted that the doctrines of the church had changed, though these changes were legitimate developments. Manning argued that

> The Church has guarded the doctrine of the Apostles, by Divine assistance, with unerring fidelity. The articles of the faith are to-day the same in number as in the beginning. The explicit definition of their implicit meaning has expanded from age to age, as the everchanging denials and perversions of the world have demanded new definitions of the ancient truth.[24]

By defining a doctrine, the church makes explicit what is already implicit in the faith, but the faith of the church never changes. Although Manning used an analogy found in Newman's book, comparing the church to an acorn which grows into an oak tree, Manning held that the beliefs of the church "have been unfolded into more explicit enunciation by a more precise intellectual conception and a more exact verbal expression, but they are the same in all their identity."[25] Manning pointed to this immutability of the Catholic faith, and the unity that resulted, as a proof of the divinity of the Catholic Church. In a debate with the atheist Robert Ingersoll, Manning emphasized the "internal unity of intellect and will" of the Catholic Church and argued "diversities and contradictions generated by all human systems prove the absence of Divine authority. Variations or contradictions are proof of the absence of a Divine mission to mankind."[26]

Manning and Newman differed considerably on the importance of the temporal power of the pope. For Newman the loss of the papal lands was not a cause for great alarm. Manning, with the Gorham decision undoubtedly in mind, strongly supported the defense of the Papal State

---

23. Manning, *The Temporal Mission of the Holy Ghost*, p. 227.

24. Henry Edward Manning and Robert G. Ingersoll, *Rome or Reason? A Series of Articles Contributed to the North American Review* (New York: C. P. Farrell, 1914), pp. 341-42.

25. Manning, *The Temporal Mission of the Holy Ghost*, pp. 224, 225.

26. Manning and Ingersoll, *Rome or Reason*, p. 313.

and viewed the stance of Newman as disloyalty to Rome. Manning was afraid that, without the temporal power, the pope would simply become another Archbishop of Canterbury who had to answer to another sovereign. Unless the pope was free from the domain of another sovereign, his divine mission of preserving the gospel and serving as pastor of all Christians would be hindered. Manning argued, "[The temporal power] is the condition by which Divine Providence has secured the liberty of the person and of the office of the Vicar of Christ, and of his supreme and independent direction of all civil powers in matters which fall within the Divine law."[27] However, once Rome finally fell to Victor Emmanuel in 1870, Manning's views softened and he was far more pragmatic than Pius IX and, later, Leo XIII. Manning encouraged a settlement that would acknowledge the legitimacy of the new Italian government while protecting the independence of the pope.[28]

In chapter 2 we saw the rapid secularization and anti-Christian forces that characterized the nineteenth century. These trends led Manning to affirm the importance of an authoritative church established on popular support. David Newsome observes that, during the *Kulturkampf* of German liberalism which actively opposed the Catholic Church, Manning grew in his conviction that "an authoritative church, far from being a tyranny, was actually the true protector of the people, who can be so vulnerable to the exploitation of secular forces."[29] An infallible pope serves as a bulwark protecting civilization against exaggerated nationalism and liberalism.[30] Therefore Manning believed that an authoritative church does not hinder humanity's quest for truth and freedom, but is rather the necessary condition for it.

A second important theme in Manning's thought is his strong foundationalism in epistemology. Manning opposed the skepticism that appeared to make objective truth in general, and knowledge of divine revelation in particular, inaccessible. Instead he maintained that knowledge is attainable, and unless a belief is certain, it is not knowledge. Manning argued that knowledge must be both objectively certain,

27. Henry Edward Manning, *The Centenary of Saint Peter and the General Council: A Pastoral Letter to the Clergy* (London: Longmans, 1867), p. 94.

28. Newsome, *The Convert Cardinals*, pp. 225ff.

29. Newsome, *The Convert Cardinals*, p. 341.

30. Henry Edward Manning, *The Oecumenical Council and the Infallibility of the Roman Pontiff: A Pastoral Letter to the Clergy*, 2nd ed. (London: Longmans, 1869), p. 52.

"that the proofs of that truth are either self-evident, or so clear as to exclude all doubt," and subjectively certain, "that we are inwardly convinced, by the application of our reason to the matter before us, of the sufficiency of the evidence to prove the truth of it."[31]

Since religious faith is a form of knowledge, faith too must be certain. In a letter to Robert Wilberforce, Manning said, "Surely divine truth is susceptible, within the limits of revelation, of an expression and a proof as exact as the inductive sciences."[32] While arguments based on probability or weighing evidence may suffice in the natural realm, properly speaking these arguments do not provide knowledge and they did not impress Manning in matters of faith. Instead, he insisted, "Where faith is, doubt cannot be; and where doubt is, faith ceases to be."[33] In particular Manning lists four truths of the faith that "constitute a proof the certainty of which exceeds that of any other moral truth I know." These truths are (1) the existence of God, (2) the revelation of God, (3) that this divine revelation is given in Christianity, and (4) that Christianity is preserved in Catholicism. These truths are not "a chain of probabilities, depending the one upon the other, but each one morally certain in itself."[34]

However, Manning held that faith is not attained by reasoned arguments. Instead, faith is a divine gift, an infused supernatural grace, which comes from God and is grounded in God. The Holy Spirit is the basis of both the objective certainty of divine revelation, and the subjective certainty of human faith. The gift of faith granted by God is the same today as that granted in the primitive church, and the doctrines of the church are handed down generation after generation by apostolic succession. In an Anglican sermon Manning stressed, "this divine gift, as it was, at the first, not discovered but received, so it has been, not critically proved, from age to age, by intellect, not gathered by inductions or by the instruments of moral reasoning, but preserved and handed on by faith."[35]

While reason cannot discover or prove the Christian faith, it does have a proper function to play in coming to faith. Private judgment is

31. As quoted in Pereiro, *Cardinal Manning: An Intellectual Biography,* p. 120.
32. As quoted in Gray, *Cardinal Manning,* p. 103.
33. Manning, *The Oecumenical Council,* p. 50.
34. Manning, *The Temporal Mission of the Holy Ghost,* pp. 32, 33.
35. As quoted by Pereiro, *Cardinal Manning: An Intellectual Biography,* p. 95.

able to discern the reasonable evidence for the Christian faith and for an infallible teaching office in the church. But reason is unable to provide the certainty that comes from faith. Once reason is confronted with the truth of the Catholic faith, there must be an act of submission to divine authority and an acceptance of faith by the human will. Though faith is a gift, it depends on the cooperation of the human will to be effective.[36]

To summarize, Manning held that knowledge is certain, and faith is certain knowledge because it is rooted in God and is a gift from God. Human reason is necessary to discern the credibility of the Christian faith, but ultimately an act of will is necessary to accept faith. Once accepted, faith is as certain as any knowledge. Manning held that reason "leads us to the feet of a Divine Teacher; but henceforward His voice, and not our balancing of probabilities, will be the formal motive of our faith. . . . My faith terminates no longer in a cumulus of probabilities gathered from the past, but upon the veracity of a Divine Person guiding me with His presence."[37]

On the issue of religious knowledge, then, Manning identifies two basic principles: divine faith and rationalism. One either accepts the divine gift of faith, or one proceeds by human criticism, "disguise it as you may in texts of Scripture, or in patristic learning, or in skeptical history, or rationalistic interpretation, the tendency of which is always to wider formulas and diminished truth, to comprehension of communion, and loss of faith."[38] In Manning's dichotomy, all systems that reject the Catholic faith are inevitably rationalism, where "Reason is the supreme and spontaneous source of religious knowledge."[39] Obviously rationalism appears in various degrees. Some make reason the sole foundation of religious knowledge; others make reason the judge of revelation; and still others reject elements of the full Christian heritage because these elements do not agree with their assumed principles, whatever these principles may be. Regardless of the form in which rationalism appears, it is based on reason and pride, and it resists the certain knowledge that comes from the acceptance of, and submission to, the divine gift of faith.

36. Pereiro, *Cardinal Manning: An Intellectual Biography*, pp. 94, 95, 173.
37. As quoted in Pereiro, *Cardinal Manning: An Intellectual Biography*, p. 178.
38. As quoted in Pereiro, *Cardinal Manning: An Intellectual Biography*, p. 198.
39. Manning, *The Temporal Mission of the Holy Ghost*, pp. 24, 25.

It is the habit of submitting to teaching authority, not reliance on reason, that distinguishes the Catholic spirit. This aspect of Manning's thought sheds light on why he so vehemently opposed Newman's desire to establish a Catholic college at Oxford. Manning's concern was not simply that Catholic students would be surrounded by Protestant intellectuals, but that Catholic students would be immersed in an environment that diametrically opposed the development of a healthy Catholic disposition. In a sermon Manning outlined the five characteristics of "the Catholic spirit": (1) "a loving submission to the Church," (2) "devotion to the saints," (3) "deference to theologians," (4) "fear and suspicion of novelty," and (5) "mistrust of self." Manning said,

> A Catholic student will be confident wheresoever the Church has spoken, or the consent of Saints or of theologians goes before him; but when he is left to himself he will have a wholesome mistrust of his own opinions. . . . Confidence in our own light is a virtue out of the Catholic unity, but a vice within it. It is the maximum of certainty to those who have no divine and infallible teacher; it is the minimum to those who are guided by the Church of God.[40]

Another important example of Manning's epistemology is his attitude toward critical historical research. Conflict arose within Catholicism when scholars like Döllinger in Germany and Acton in England began to promote the use of critical historical study to examine the doctrines of the Catholic faith. In Manning's eyes, the use of historical research to judge the content of the faith was an example of the rationalism he had abandoned in the Church of England. The proposal of the critical historians was a direct challenge to the supernatural nature of the gift of faith and the divine authority of the church. But Manning's ultimate concern was whether the doctrinal authority of the church would be subjected to the findings of historical research, which is simply another fallible human endeavor that often reaches indefinite conclusions. He argued, "How can we know what antiquity was except through the Church? No individual, no number of individuals, can go back through eighteen hundred years to reach the doctrines of antiquity."[41]

40. As quoted in Pereiro, *Cardinal Manning: An Intellectual Biography*, pp. 230-32.
41. Manning, *The Temporal Mission of the Holy Ghost*, p. 227.

Manning was adamant that the doctrinal authority of the church did not depend on the findings of historians. He insisted, "no difficulties of human history can prevail against [the church]," and asked, "Are we to understand . . . that the rule of faith is to be tested by history, not history by the rule of faith?"[42]

The methods of the historians betrayed a fundamental misunderstanding of the immutability of doctrine and the church as a living witness of the past. Manning argued, "The Church is a living history of the past. It is the page of history still existing, open before his eyes. Antiquity to the Catholic is not a thing gone by; it is here, still present."[43] In another place he states,

> But perhaps it may be asked: "If you reject history and antiquity, how can you know what was revealed before, you say, history and antiquity existed?" I answer: The enunciation of the faith by the living Church of this hour, is the maximum of evidence, both natural and supernatural, as to the *fact* and the *contents* of the original revelation.[44]

The church alone, as the mystical body of Christ through the indwelling of the Holy Spirit, enjoys infallibility and the perfect preservation of its doctrine. And therefore the church alone can judge the proper meaning of scripture and antiquity.

Papal Infallibility

Manning is a good representative of maximal infallibility. As noted in chapter 2, Manning played a significant role in the First Vatican Coun-

---

42. Henry Edward Manning, *The Vatican Council and Its Definitions: A Pastoral Letter to the Clergy* (New York: D. & J. Sadlier, 1871), p. 127. A more recent example of this same argument can be found in Alfons M. Stickler's review of Brian Tierney's book *Origins of Papal Infallibility, 1150-1350*. See "Papal Infallibility — A Thirteenth-Century Invention? Reflections on a Recent Book," *Catholic Historical Review* 60, no. 3 (October 1974): 427-41. A continued exchange between Tierney and Stickler was published in *Catholic Historical Review* 61, no. 2 (April 1975): 265-79.

43. As quoted in Pereiro, *Cardinal Manning: An Intellectual Biography*, p. 209.

44. Manning, *The Temporal Mission of the Holy Ghost*, p. 205.

cil. He was part of the congregation *de postulatis,* which determined which matters would be discussed at the council, and the congregation *de fide,* which drafted the final resolutions to be voted on at the council. Further, Manning was an outspoken leader of the Ultramontane party and actively pushed for the infallibility definition. Manning is often accused of attempting to manipulate the council. While this is not the place to fully assess these claims, it does seem fair to say that, on balance, some of Manning's actions at the council were questionable. At the same time, though, the inopportunists and opponents of papal infallibility were involved in similar tactics as well. It appears, then, that both Manning and his opponents were engaged in "the stuff of politics," and Manning, a diplomatic genius for sure, was the victor.

Manning passionately pursued the infallibility definition because he believed it was a necessary doctrine for his age. Manning considered the rejection of the divine authority of the church, which he saw in the Reformation and ultimately in the denial of the supernatural altogether, as the primary evil of the modern age. Because of the rejection of the divine, and therefore infallible, teaching authority of the church, humankind reaped doubt and uncertainty. He states, "If I were asked to say what is the chief intellectual malady of England and of the world at this day, I should say, ubiquitous, universal doubt, an uncertainty which came in like a flood after the rejection of the Divine certainty of faith."[45] The Protestant and unbelieving world had been able to avoid the divine certainty of the faith because there was significant disagreement within Catholicism on the nature of the church's infallibility. Thus for over two centuries the reply, "What is the use of infallibility if you do not know where it resides?" had enabled the modern world to elude the Catholic position.[46] The infallibility definition was needed because it was part of the immutable tradition of the church, it was denied in the modern world, and division on this point within the Catholic Church was no longer admissible.[47]

For Manning, the infallibility of the church resides in her head, the pope. Manning argued that "the denial of the infallibility of the head of

45. Henry Edward Manning, *The Vatican Decrees in Their Bearing on Civil Allegiance* (New York: Catholic Publication Society, 1875), p. 163.
46. Manning, *The Centenary of St. Peter and the General Council,* pp. 55-56.
47. Manning, *The Vatican Council and Its Definitions,* pp. 41ff.

the Christian Church is the first position of vantage to assail the infallibility of the Church as a whole, and therefore to assail the divine certainty of Christianity altogether."[48] Denying papal infallibility inevitably leads down the slippery slope of rejecting the Christian faith altogether. Therefore, papal infallibility is one of the foundations of the faith that must be defended at all costs. Manning argued that, either there is a supreme judge who is infallible, or humanity is afloat in a sea of private judgment and uncertainty. Either one accepts the divine certainty of faith, or one is left with the principle of rationalism. Manning's conception of papal infallibility in stark "either/or" terms is evident in the following striking quotation: "Of two things one at least: either Christianity is divinely preserved, or it is not. If it be divinely preserved, we have a divine certainty of faith. If it be not divinely preserved, its custody and its certainty now are alike human, and we have no divine certainty that what we believe was divinely revealed."[49] The contrast for Manning is simple: either God has preserved Christianity and we can have a "divine certainty of faith," or Christianity has not been preserved.

As a member of the congregation *de fide,* Manning played a key role in composing the final draft of *Pastor Aeternus.* His reading of the document was also much broader than many who followed him. We will examine his interpretation of four key terms from the definition of papal infallibility.

1. The pope is infallible when he speaks *ex cathedra.* Before the council, Manning proposed as requirements for an *ex cathedra* definition that "the doctrinal acts be published by the Pontiff, as Universal Teacher, with the intention of requiring the assent of the Church."[50] This is obviously a broad definition that includes many papal documents addressed to the whole church over a seemingly limitless range of subjects.

Manning maintained a broad interpretation of *ex cathedra* after the council, though within the language of the infallibility definition. He states, "The Pontiff speaks *ex cathedra* when, and only when, he speaks as the Pastor and Doctor of all Christians. By this, all acts of the Pontiff

---

48. Henry Edward Manning, *The True Story of the Vatican Council* (London: Henry S. King & Co., 1877), pp. 112-13.

49. Manning, *The True Story of the Vatican Council,* p. 181.

50. Manning, *The Oecumenical Council,* p. 61.

as a private person, or a private doctor, or as a local Bishop, or as sovereign of a state, are excluded."[51] In a response to Gladstone, Manning illustrates his understanding of *ex cathedra* by stating that infallibility extends to all papal bulls past and future.[52]

Manning dreamed of a church that speaks "for ever by a divine voice, not intermittently by General Councils, but always by the voice of its head."[53] Frequent *ex cathedra* definitions would ensure the divine certainty of the faith in the minds of the faithful. But Manning was well aware that other understandings of *ex cathedra* existed, and that such confusion over *ex cathedra* only led to doubt and the evasion of Catholic truth by Protestants and unbelievers. To counter this concern, Manning stressed that only the legislator can interpret the law. Thus, only the pope can decide which definitions are *ex cathedra,* and which definitions are not.[54]

2. *Pastor Aeternus* states that the pope is infallible when he "speaks *ex cathedra,* that is . . . he defines a doctrine concerning faith or morals to be held by the whole church." We need to examine Manning's interpretation of the word "define," for this word could exclude Manning's maximal position if interpreted too narrowly. After the council, Manning's pastoral letter instructed that *definienda* "signifies the final decision by which any matter of faith and morals is put into a doctrinal form."[55] But he taught that the word "define" extends beyond the "forensic and narrow sense" to include the "wide and common sense," that is, any authoritative ruling of a disputed question. Manning believed that "all censures, whether for heresy or with a note less than heresy, are doctrinal definitions in faith and morals."[56] Thus Manning interprets "define" in a broad manner in accordance with his maximal position.

3. Manning used the language of "faith or morals" before the council, but again he proposed a broad understanding of this limiting phrase. Manning states,

---

51. Manning, *The Vatican Council and Its Definitions*, p. 64.
52. Manning, *The Vatican Decrees in Their Bearing on Civil Allegiance*, p. 21.
53. Manning, *The True Story of the Vatican Council*, p. 205.
54. Manning, *The True Story of the Vatican Council*, p. 188.
55. Manning, *The Vatican Council and Its Definitions*, p. 94.
56. Manning, *The Vatican Council and Its Definitions*, pp. 93-94, 95.

> The infallibility of the Head of the Church extends to the whole
> matter of revelation, that is, to the Divine truth and the Divine law,
> and to all those facts or truths which are in contact with faith and
> morals. The definitions of the Church include truths of the natu-
> ral order, and the revelation of supernatural truth is in contact
> with natural ethics, politics, and philosophy.[57]

After the council, Manning maintained his previous understanding of
"faith or morals." Since infallibility extends to both interpreting the
content of divine revelation and excluding that which opposes divine
revelation, the church has "an infallible assistance in discerning and in
proscribing false philosophies and false science." This includes "the
condemnation of heretical texts . . . and also, censures, both greater and
less, those, for instance, of heresy and of error, because of their contrariety to faith; those also of temerity, scandal, and the like, because of
their contrariety to morals at least."[58]

Manning acknowledged that the council did not precisely define the
meaning of "faith or morals," and that the issue was an open theological question.[59] It appears, then, that once again a door was left open to
uncertainty and doubt. However, in a response to Gladstone, Manning
argues, "It is a formula well known, perfectly clear, sufficiently precise
for our spiritual and moral life. . . . questions will always be raised by
those who love contention against the Catholic church more than they
love either faith or morals."[60] In the following chapters it will become
clear that, despite Manning's insistence to the contrary, the meaning of
"faith or morals," as well as *"ex cathedra"* and "define," is not at all obvious in Catholic theology.

4. As a member of the congregation *de fide,* Manning exercised significant influence on the composition of *Pastor Aeternus.* His most important contribution was the addition of the phrase *ex sese non autem
ex consensu ecclesiae* to the final draft. The intention of the clause was
to put an end to Gallicanism since *ex cathedra* definitions are infallible "of themselves, and not by the consent of the church," or apart

---

57. Manning, *The Temporal Mission of the Holy Ghost,* p. 96.
58. Manning, *The Vatican Council and Its Definitions,* p. 73.
59. Manning, *The True Story of the Vatican Council,* p. 191.
60. Manning, *The Vatican Decrees in Their Bearing on Civil Allegiance,* pp. 34-35.

from the approval of a council. For Manning, the *ex sese* clause stresses that "the teacher is not infallible because the taught believe his teaching. They believe his teaching to be true because they believe their teacher to be infallible."[61] Thus the definitions of the pope are irreformable since the council is not a higher court of appeal. Apart from his efforts in defining papal infallibility, the addition of the *ex sese* clause in *Pastor Aeternus* was one of Manning's greatest achievements at the council.

An examination of Manning's position helps to evaluate the popular claim that, although the inopportunists did not prevent the definition of papal infallibility at Vatican I, they did succeed in qualifying the extravagant views of the Ultramontanes. For example, after noting Manning's fond memories of Vatican I in his old age, Newsome suggests,

> Perhaps memory had allowed him to believe that it was more of a triumph than it actually was. The principle had been won: infallibility had been defined. But when it came down to the details of the definition, the outcome was less than Manning had really hoped for. No longer could he, or anyone else, talk about *Quanta cura* and the Syllabus as having infallible authority. So circumscribed were the conditions governing an *ex cathedra* infallible pronouncement that Manning was not to see in his lifetime either Pius IX or his successor Leo XIII exercise his divinely confirmed right.[62]

This statement needs to be qualified. Newsome is correct that the council sought a more restrictive definition than Manning envisioned. At Vatican I, Bishop Gasser's official statement interpreting *Pastor Aeternus* limited *ex cathedra* definitions to solemn cases where the pope sought to pass a definitive sentence.[63] But what constitutes a solemn,

---

61. Manning, *The True Story of the Vatican Council*, p. 189.

62. Newsome, *The Convert Cardinals*, p. 281.

63. An English translation of key parts of Gasser's comments are found in J. Robert Dionne, *The Papacy and the Church: A Study of Praxis and Reception in Ecumenical Perspective* (New York: Philosophical Library, 1987), pp. 31-32. However, Dionne goes on to discuss the ongoing controversy of the intention of these statements, which confirms that the council did not exclude Manning's maximal infallibility, or at least did not do so effectively.

definitive sentence is still open to interpretation, and Manning continued to promote a broad interpretation of the definition.[64]

As illustrated above, Manning used many of the limiting terms of the definition — *ex cathedra*, define, faith or morals — before Vatican I, and he continued to use them after Vatican I in the same manner. There is nothing in *Pastor Aeternus* itself that restricted Manning's maximal position. Rather, Pereiro is correct in noting that "it was the intention of the Council not to exclude — explicitly or implicitly — from the range of papal infallibility a wider range of pontifical acts. The question was left open."[65] Whether or not Manning witnessed the infallible work of the pope again in his lifetime is open to what one considers to be infallible *ex cathedra* definitions. Manning held a maximal view both before and after the council.

Newsome is also mistaken about Manning's view of the Syllabus of Errors. Manning definitely held that the Syllabus was infallible before the council. While the Syllabus was never brought up during the council because the council adjourned early, the Syllabus would have been discussed if the council had continued. There is nothing to suggest that Manning no longer considered the Syllabus to be infallible. In fact, he maintained that the "hated Syllabus will have its justification. The Syllabus which condemned Atheism and revolution would have saved society."[66] According to Manning's maximal view, which he maintained after the Vatican council, the Syllabus qualified as an infallible papal definition.

There is a better reason why talk of the Syllabus became rare after the Vatican council. Two "errors" of the Syllabus, propositions 75 and 76, affirmed the necessity of the temporal power, but the Vatican council adjourned because of the invasion of Rome and the loss of the Papal State. Manning was one of the first defenders of the temporal power to realize that the battle for the Papal State was over, and he would no longer defend the temporal power as Pius IX and his successors continued to do. It is more likely that Manning and others stopped talking about

---

64. See Pereiro, *Cardinal Manning: An Intellectual Biography*, pp. 305-6 and Manning, *The Vatican Council and Its Definitions*, pp. 92-96.

65. Pereiro, *Cardinal Manning: An Intellectual Biography*, p. 311.

66. Manning, *The Vatican Council and Its Definitions*, p. 165. Another positive quotation on the Syllabus from Manning is given in W. E. Gladstone, *The Vatican Decrees in Their Bearing on Civil Allegiance* (London: John Murray, 1874), p. 54.

the Syllabus because it maintained positions that were no longer tenable, not because of a restrictive definition of papal infallibility. And Manning still believed that the Syllabus would one day be justified.

Manning had every right to recall his days at the Vatican council with fond memories. Manning succeeded in passing papal infallibility at the council, and though he may have wished that the definition followed his own maximal view more intentionally, there is nothing in the definition that restricted his view. The one position that was excluded was Gallicanism, due primarily to Manning's introduction of the *ex sese* clause before the final draft. If Manning's maximal position failed, it was not because of *Pastor Aeternus* and the work of the inopportunists at the council, though they may have tried. Rather, Manning's position became less popular because it became increasingly harder to maintain.

In *The Vatican Council and Its Definitions,* Manning discussed a formula which, though not defined, had become popular — the "personal, separate, independent, and absolute infallibility." An examination of this formula will provide further insight into Manning's position. Manning held that infallibility is a personal charism of the pope as a public person, and is not attached simply to the Roman See in general, as the Gallicans maintained. The personal nature of infallibility, though, does not refer to the pope as a private doctor, but as the successor of Peter in his official role as universal teacher.[67] To avoid confusing the personal infallibility with the private actions of the pope, Manning later distinguished the "official" infallibility of the pope from the "personal" infallibility. The adjective "official" stressed that the quality was not inherent in the private person, but in the office of the pope as universal teacher. Manning states,

> Infallibility is not a quality inherent in any person, but an assistance attached to an office. . . . It is an assistance of the Holy Ghost whereby Peter's faith was kept from failing either in the act of believing or in the object of belief, and through Peter the same assistance attaches to the office he bore, so that his successor in like manner shall be kept from departing from the traditions of faith committed to his custody.[68]

67. Manning, *The Vatican Council and Its Definitions,* p. 119.
68. Manning, *The True Story of the Vatican Council,* pp. 179-80.

Thus Manning's basic position on the "personal" or "official" infallibility remained the same, though his terminology changed.

The infallibility of the pope is "separate" in the sense that it is unique or distinct. The pope is a unique or distinct subject of infallibility who depends only on the assistance of the Holy Spirit, not the episcopate, in the exercise of his teaching authority. While the term "separate" could easily be misinterpreted to imply that the pope is disconnected from the episcopate, it would be a grave mistake to do so. Manning was emphatic that the unity between the pope and the episcopate could never be dissolved, just as the head cannot exist apart from the body. In a similar vein, the infallibility of the pope is "independent" in that it does not depend on the church, but depends on the assistance of the Holy Spirit.[69] Together the characteristics "separate" and "independent" are essentially another way to state Manning's interpretation of the *ex sese* clause in *Pastor Aeternus.*

While the infallibility of the pope is "separate" and "independent" of the church, the question remains whether the episcopate receives its authority, and the infallibility it enjoys in council, from the pope or directly from Christ. Manning held that the episcopate receives its authority and infallibility from the pope. On this point, Manning emphasized the providential way in which, at the council, the issue of papal infallibility was treated before the issue of the church. In doing so, the council treated the relationship between the pope and the episcopate in the same way Jesus did when he conferred the primacy on Peter. He states,

> Our Divine Lord first chose Cephas, and invested him with the primacy over the Apostles. Upon this Rock all were built, and from him the whole unity and authority of the Church took its rise. To Peter alone first was given the plentitude of jurisdiction and of infallible authority. Afterwards, the gift of the Holy Ghost was shared with him by all the Apostles. From him and through him, therefore, all began.[70]

Manning, though, notes that this issue was left open at Vatican I. "The definition does not decide the question whether the infallibility of the

69. Manning, *The Vatican Council and Its Definitions,* p. 119.
70. Manning, *The Vatican Council and Its Definitions,* p. 58. See also Manning, *The Oecumenical Council,* p. 141.

Church is derived from him or through him. But it does decide that his infallibility is not derived from the Church, nor through the Church."[71] Manning's position here was rejected at Vatican II, which decreed that the episcopate receives its authority directly from Christ.

The infallibility of the pope is "absolute" in that there is no higher court of appeal on issues of faith or morals. No ecclesiastical council, and equally important, no state authority, can overrule a papal definition.[72] Given his experience with the Gorham decision, Manning held this characteristic of papal infallibility especially dear.

Manning believed that the doctrine of the church was immutable, and the beliefs of the Catholic Church in all times are the same as the beliefs of the primitive church. Thus, he maintained that the church had always held the doctrine of papal infallibility. The Vatican decrees are an "old truth" and "no new dogma."[73] To support the antiquity of papal infallibility, especially against the charge that the doctrine is absent from scripture, Manning argued that the doctrine is found in the seven sacraments even before the writing of the New Testament. The sacrament of orders assumes a hierarchy in the church.[74] Of course, many question whether the seven sacraments are found in the New Testament and early church history, especially as they are understood in Catholic theology. Manning also argued,

> We are told that in the New Testament there is to be read no successor of St. Peter, no vicar of Jesus Christ. But before the New Testament was collected and diffused, all the world recognized one pastor as chief over all, reigning in the place of Peter from his See in Rome.[75]

Again, many seriously doubt that the Bishop of Rome was understood as the infallible teacher of all Christians during the canonization of the New Testament. But for Manning, it is simply an issue of whether one proceeds by divine, infallible faith, which is based on God's gift and is

71. Manning, *The Vatican Council and Its Definitions*, p. 96.
72. Manning, *The Vatican Council and Its Definitions*, p. 119.
73. Manning, *The Vatican Decrees in Their Bearing on Civil Allegiance*, p. 10.
74. Manning, *The Temporal Mission of the Holy Ghost*, pp. 184-85.
75. Manning, *The Temporal Mission of the Holy Ghost*, p. 190.

preserved in the church; or by rationalism, which is based on fallible and uncertain human efforts.

Manning rejected theories of doctrinal development and instead held that there are three basic stages by which an ancient truth is defined in the church. The first stage is "simple belief," where the truth is held in faith by the church. Over time, though, the faith of the church is challenged, and this leads to a period of "analysis." The period of challenge and analysis, which often takes centuries, is resolved by an act of "definition."[76] Manning held that papal infallibility was part of the simple faith of the primitive church, and that this truth was first challenged by the rise of Gallicanism and the Council of Constance in the fourteenth and fifteenth centuries. He maintained that,

> from the beginning of Christianity down to the times immediately preceding the Council of Constance — that is, for fourteen hundred years — the doctrine of the stability of the faith of Peter in his See and in his Successor was in possession, by the immemorial and universal tradition of the Church.[77]

Manning viewed Gallicanism as "no more than a transient and modern opinion which arose in France" and as a "royal theology," similar to the Statutes of Henry VIII in England.[78] Of course, the act of definition against Gallicanism occurred at the Vatican council.

The Council of Constance does present a special problem, though. Usually reckoned as the sixteenth general council of the church, Constance ended the Great Schism, deposed two competing papal rivals and accepted the resignation of a third, and elected Martin V as the new pope. During its fifth session, Constance decreed a conciliar position, which puts the papacy under the council and therefore directly contradicts the *ex sese* clause of *Pastor Aeternus.* Without the conciliar position, the council would not have been able to depose the three competing claimants to the papacy. Manning addresses this problem by suggesting that, since a legitimate pope did not preside over the early sessions of Constance, those sessions

76. Manning, *The Oecumenical Council,* p. 64.
77. Manning, *The Oecumenical Council,* pp. 66-67.
78. Manning, *The Centenary of St. Peter,* p. 41.

were null from the beginning, from the nullity of the assembly, the irregularity of the voting, as well as the heterodoxy of the subject matter. They were protested against as soon as read, and let to pass, not only because opposition was vain, but because their passing was, *ipso facto,* void of effect.[79]

For Manning, Constance was not an ecumenical council, at least not until the thirty-fifth session. Of course, without the earlier sessions, there would have been no one pope to preside over the closing sessions.

Manning's treatment of Honorius is also instructive. The case of Pope Honorius was discussed at the Vatican council because he was condemned for his monothelite christology by ecumenical councils and subsequent popes. A standard response to this problem is that Honorius's heretical statements were not infallible *ex cathedra* statements. However, Manning's maximal interpretation of *ex cathedra* makes this defense less plausible. Manning's position is that the case against Pope Honorius is controversial and open to different interpretations. In fact, Honorius may eventually be cleared of personal heresy by future historical research.[80] Clearly Manning is in a difficult position here, as other popes and ecumenical councils declared Honorius a heretic. Either Honorius was in error on a matter substantial enough to command the attention of later popes and councils, or these later popes and councils were in error.

Manning believed papal infallibility was essential not only for preserving the doctrine of the church, but also the unity of the church. He stressed that "the supreme privilege of infallibility in the head is the divinely ordained means to sustain for ever the unity of the Universal Church in communion, faith, and doctrine." Further, in keeping with his position on the immutability of doctrine, Manning maintained that the infallibility of the church and the pope is a divine fact "on which the unity of the Church has depended from the beginning."[81] Without the infallible doctrinal jurisdiction of the magisterium, the unity of the church is unattainable.

While it might be argued that the doctrine of papal infallibility has en-

79. Manning, *The Oecumenical Council,* p. 95.
80. Manning, *The Vatican Council and Its Definitions,* p. 123.
81. Manning, *The Vatican Council and Its Definitions,* pp. 118, 119.

couraged unity in the Catholic Church, it could also be argued that it has contributed to division and discouraged reunion with Orthodox and Protestant churches. Manning, however, was against attempts at reunion that diluted Catholic doctrine. Even before the Vatican council and the definition of papal infallibility, he stated, "The Primacy of honor, but 'not of jurisdiction,' among a plurality of divided Churches, is an illusion which disappears when the true and divine unity of the kingdom which cannot be divided against itself rises into view."[82] Rather, truth must come before unity, for without truth there can be no unity.[83]

Manning hoped, and earnestly believed, papal infallibility would be an effective missionary tool that would appeal to Protestants in England. The doctrine defiantly professes certainty in an age of doubt and skepticism, and ended the intra-Catholic debate that allowed Protestants to avoid the full heritage of Catholic doctrine. In a speech given at the Vatican council, Manning made known his view that papal infallibility would not hinder reunion with Protestants, but would appeal to Protestants and help restore them to the Catholic fold. In a pastoral letter written before the Vatican council, Manning acknowledged that among Protestants there is "a strong traditional belief in many great Christian verities, which, though undermined and menaced, are still here and revered piously by multitudes." He goes on to state, "It is certain, also, that upon a multitude of minds who are wavering and doubtful, seeking for a foundation on which to rest, and an authority to which to listen, the voice of a General Council will have great power."[84]

Analysis

A number of issues factored into Manning's conversion to Catholicism and his efforts to define papal infallibility, including concerns over the legitimation of ecclesial authority and Erastianism. Clearly, though, epistemic issues were important to Manning as well. His strong foundationalism, which includes stringent standards for knowledge and a desire for epistemic certainty, is typical of classic modernism. For

82. Manning, *The Temporal Mission of the Holy Ghost,* p. 48.
83. Manning, *The True Story of the Vatican Council,* pp. 182-83.
84. Manning, *The Centenary of St. Peter and the General Council,* pp. 89, 90.

Manning, knowledge must be "self-evident, or so clear as to exclude all doubt," and the inductive sciences are offered as a model for certain knowledge.

This strong foundationalism, though, has been subject to devastating critique recently. For one, the epistemic standards of strong foundationalism are far too high. Using Manning's proposal as an example, there are many things that we treat as knowledge that are not self-evident or beyond all doubt, such as belief in the reliability of sense perception and memory unless there are good reasons to question these belief-producing mechanisms. Second, Manning's proposal that knowledge must be self-evident or beyond all doubt is self-defeating, since the proposal itself is neither self-evident nor beyond all doubt. Third, Manning's model for epistemic certainty, the inductive sciences, has been found to be less than certain. For instance, philosopher of science Thomas Kuhn argues that the inductive sciences are theory driven like other disciplines that are often viewed as less certain, such as the social sciences.[85] While researchers gather facts from empirical observation and experimentation, this data must be interpreted, and there is no way to offer hard proof of the adequacy of the resulting theories. Kuhn calls widely accepted theories paradigms. Over time, though, paradigm shifts can occur when paradigms are questioned and rejected, as illustrated by the Copernican revolution. In many respects, Manning's strong foundationalism is highly suspect as an epistemic proposal.

The weakness of Manning's epistemology is further illustrated when we turn to the issue of religious knowledge. Manning obviously holds methodist commitments in epistemology as an attempt to secure certainty and has a strong epistemic conception of ecclesial canons. He paints a stark contrast: either God has preserved Christianity and we have a "divine certainty of faith," or we do not have religious certainty and Christianity has not been preserved. This certainty is not attained by an inerrant scripture, nor by scripture and tradition, since such proposals rest on private judgment. Rather, epistemic certainty is attained by an infallible pope who is able to discern the meaning of scripture and tradition for the church today. The fortunes of Manning's epistemic method did not fare well, though.

85. Thomas S. Kuhn, *The Structure of Scientific Revolutions* (Chicago: University of Chicago Press, 1962).

As an Anglican, Manning came to realize that the Tractarian principle of scripture and antiquity only took the problem of epistemology one step back from the *sola scriptura* principle of evangelical Protestantism. What Manning did not realize was that papal infallibility was simply another step back in the same epistemic direction. Papal pronouncements come in texts, whether written or oral, and these too must be interpreted using private judgment. W. E. Gladstone, the British statesman and devout Anglican, realized this early on.

> These are written definitions. What are they but another Scripture? What right of interpreting this other Scripture is granted to the Church at large, more than of the real and greater Scripture? Here is surely, in its perfection, the petition for bread, answered by the gift of a stone.[86]

An example of the problem is seen in the fate of *Pastor Aeternus* itself. The terms of the definition, especially *ex cathedra* and "faith or morals," were given numerous interpretations by Catholic theologians. We have seen how Manning, one of the drafters of the document, maintained a maximal position after the council. As will be seen in the following chapters, other more moderate interpretations appeared as well. Gladstone, and numerous other Protestants, recognized the problem of interpretation immediately. He argued that

> there is no established or accepted definition of the phrase *ex cathedra,* and [the Catholic individual] has no power to obtain one, and no guide to direct him in his choice among some twelve theories on the subject, which, it is said, are bandied to and fro among Roman theologians, except the despised and discarded agency of his private judgment.[87]

A similar problem is the identification of infallible pronouncements, which arise from contested interpretations of *ex cathedra* and "faith or morals" among other places. While Manning held a maximal

---

86. W. E. Gladstone, *Vaticanism: An Answer to Replies and Reproofs* (London: John Murray, 1875), p. 99.

87. Gladstone, *The Vatican Decrees in Their Bearing on Civil Allegiance,* pp. 34-35.

interpretation of these terms that would have viewed a large number of papal pronouncements as infallible, his moderate opponents disagreed. Lytton Strachey, in his mock portrayal of Manning, ridiculed,

> How was it to be determined, for instance, which particular Papal decisions did in fact come within the scope of the definition? Who was to decide what was or was not a matter of faith or morals? Or precisely *when* the Roman Pontiff was speaking *ex cathedra?* Was the famous Syllabus Errorum, for example, issued *ex cathedra* or not? Grave theologians have never been able to make up their minds. Yet to admit doubts in such matters as these is surely dangerous.[88]

Gladstone and Strachey make important points that should not be lost in their rhetorical banter. Instead of solving the problem of identifying and interpreting Christian beliefs, papal infallibility only pushes the problem one step back. Private judgment inevitably comes into play. Manning's maximal interpretation of papal infallibility simply cannot bring the epistemic certainty he desired.

As a proposal in religious epistemology, Manning's maximal infallibility led to numerous substantial difficulties. Manning's maximal interpretation of *ex cathedra* was problematic, which is especially clear in the case of Pope Honorius. While proponents of moderate infallibility could argue that Honorius was not speaking *ex cathedra,* this option was not readily available to maximalists like Manning. Thus Manning proposed that the case against Honorius was debated among scholars, and Honorius may not have been a heretic after all. A. J. A. Gratry clearly saw the implications of Manning's position.

> Archbishop Manning is here exposed to an actual peril. If I can believe his words, he resists openly and utterly three Councils. He knows, as well as we do, all the writings of those Councils which condemn Honorius as a heretic. What does he set against them? The letters themselves of Honorius. Archbishop Manning, if I can believe my eyes, appears to invite the readers, to whom his Mandement is addressed, to judge for themselves these letters,

88. Strachey, *Eminent Victorians*, p. 107.

burnt as heretical by the VIth council, but which, happily, have come down to us to prove the orthodoxy of the excommunicated Pope.[89]

Ironically, in order to maintain his position of maximal infallibility, Manning asks his readers to use their private judgment and overrule the decisions of three ecumenical councils. Gratry draws out the implications of Manning's position: Manning has exposed himself to excommunication since he is defending a heretic.[90] More importantly for our purposes, Manning's maximal infallibility faces a real dilemma: either Honorius made a grave doctrinal error, or subsequent popes and councils were in error to condemn him.

Other problems arise from the traditional Catholic belief in the immutability of doctrine, which Manning defended. For example, it is hard to take seriously Manning's insistence that papal infallibility was held before the writing of the New Testament in the seven sacraments of grace. Further, the definition of the immaculate conception by Pius IX and *Pastor Aeternus* at the Vatican Council clearly displayed doctrinal advance within Catholicism, Manning's insistence to the contrary notwithstanding. As will be further illustrated in the next chapter, such doctrinal advances led to the demise of doctrinal immutability and the emergence of theories of doctrinal development.

Whenever historical difficulties arose against maximal infallibility, Manning's standard defense was to question the certainty of historical research. Manning is correct that historical research is theory-driven, and in some instances it is pursued with anti-supernatural presuppositions.[91] But, as we have already suggested, the tenuous nature of historical investigation is no reason to reject altogether the epistemic resources that historical investigation can provide. Poor historical reconstructions, as well as anti-supernatural presuppositions, can be questioned without abandoning historical research.

Manning's disregard of history made it easier for him to idealize absolute papal authority. Ignoring the checkered past of the papacy,

89. Auguste Joseph Alphonse Gratry, *Papal Infallibility Untenable: Three Letters*, 1st American ed. (Hartford: Church Press, 1870), p. 9.

90. Gratry, *Papal Infallibility Untenable*, p. 10.

91. A classic example is Ernst Troeltsch, "Historical and Dogmatic Method in Theology," in *Religion in History* (Minneapolis: Fortress Press, 1991), pp. 11-32.

Manning argued that uncertainty and despair were ushered in with the Reformation, especially during the Enlightenment. An authoritative papacy was the protector of the masses against the ravages of modernity. The atheist Robert Ingersoll, though, replied with his own historical recollection. After recounting in graphic detail the crimes of the papacy during the height of its influence, he stated,

> Nothing was left but ignorance, bigotry, intolerance, credulity, the Inquisition, the seven sacraments and the seven deadly sins. And yet a Cardinal of the nineteenth century, living in the land of Shakespeare, regrets the change that has been wrought by the intellectual efforts, by the discoveries, by the inventions and heroism of three hundred years.[92]

No doubt the truth lies between the two idealized portraits offered by Manning and Ingersoll. Nonetheless, Manning's one-sided reading of history obscured real problems that were inherent in his position.

Manning responded to problems with maximal infallibility by making the pope the final judge in religious matters. If a question arises whether a definition is *ex cathedra* or within the bounds of "faith or morals," the pope provides the final ruling. Terms that are supposed to serve a limiting function serve no such function at all, especially since "morals" can include almost any area of human life. Thus Manning's maximal infallibility is essentially a form of absolutism that is impervious to outside critique. Gladstone, for one, was highly concerned with this danger, though as a British statesman his chief concern was whether papal allegiance would impede the authority of state rulers over Catholic subjects.[93] Likewise, Sheridan Gilley describes Manning's maximal infallibility as "one of those closed thought systems made so unpopular by Karl Popper and by Fascism and Communism in this century."[94]

Even in Manning's own ministry, maximal infallibility proved to be inadequate. Robert Gray tells how, in April 1888, Leo XIII issued a sud-

92. Manning and Ingersoll, *Rome or Reason*, p. 375.

93. See, e.g., Gladstone, *Vaticanism*, p. 99.

94. Sheridan Gilley, "Manning: The Catholic Writings," in *By Whose Authority? Newman, Manning, and the Magisterium*, ed. by V. Alan McClelland (Bath: Downside Abbey, 1996), p. 248.

den decree against the Irish "Plan of Campaign" against landlords, which was a social policy that Manning supported. Two years later Manning wrote,

> The Decree of Leo XIII was absolutely true, just, and useful. But in the abstract. The condition of Ireland is abnormal. The Decree contemplates facts which do not exist. . . . Pontiffs have no infallibility in the world of facts, except only dogmatic. The Plan of Campaign is not a dogmatic fact, and it is one thing to declare that all legal agreements are binding, and another to say that all agreements in Ireland are legal.[95]

In his comments on this event, Gray states, "It is never wise to jump too quickly to conclusions, but it rather looks as though Manning may have been saying that the Pope had made a mistake."[96] Gray is correct that we should not jump to conclusions too quickly, because Manning would not have viewed this incident as evidence against the infallibility definition. It is not even clear that this incident caused Manning to rethink the appropriate limits of papal infallibility. What we do see, however, is the inadequacy of Manning's epistemic vision. Papal infallibility is supposed to bring certainty and bypass private judgment, but here Manning's private judgment is involved in a complex process of assessing a moral situation, determining the limitations of the pope's infallibility in this particular situation, and offering an interpretation of the papal decree that evades its clear intention. Here even Manning did not follow the consequences of his own epistemic proposal.

Manning's dream for the infallibility definition and the inherent problems with maximal infallibility are summarized well by Eamon Duffy.

> No controversy in the first thousand years of Christianity had been settled merely by papal fiat: even Leo I's Tome had been adopted by a general council. Agreement on the truth in early Christianity had emerged by convergence, consensus, debate, painful and costly processes which took decades and even centuries to crystal-

---

95. As quoted in Gray, *Cardinal Manning,* p. 293.
96. Gray, *Cardinal Manning,* p. 293.

lize. Manning and his associates wanted history without tears, a living oracle who could short-circuit human limitation. They wanted to confront the uncertainties of their age with instant assurance, revelation on tap.[97]

Manning did not view infallible papal pronouncements as "revelation on tap," but he did see papal infallibility as bringing epistemic certainty in an uncertain age. Duffy is right, though, that ecumenical agreement and the defense of Christian truth has always been a far more complex affair than Manning's epistemology allowed.

Manning argued that epistemic certainty was necessary for the preservation of Christian doctrine. Given the problems with his maximal infallibility, it appears his presupposition was incorrect. "Divine certainty of faith" or the failure of Christ's promises to preserve the church are not the only options. Since this is the case, another presupposition of Manning should be questioned, namely that epistemic certainty is necessary to maintain unity in the church. Again, if epistemic certainty and unqualified disunity are the only options, the church must settle for ecumenical division as well as continuing division within Christian traditions. As with his epistemic criteria, we should question whether Manning's standards for unity — "internal unity of intellect and will" — are too high as well. Manning gives an ideal view of Catholic unity that ignores vibrant internal disagreements, many of which are healthy for the life of the church. Even the Catholic Church cannot meet Manning's criteria for unity.

However, Manning is correct to argue that unity cannot exist apart from shared doctrinal commitments. While unity includes more than common truth claims, it cannot include less. In this work, the theism found in the canonical heritage of the undivided church is offered as a substantial basis for shared doctrinal commitments, and thus for ecumenical unity. This unity is not an "internal unity of intellect and will," but a unity based on a substantial vision of God, the human situation, and salvation.

It is hard to see how Manning's other concerns with ecclesial authority, including the question of the legitimation of ecclesial authority

---

97. Eamon Duffy, *Saints and Sinners: A History of the Popes,* 2nd ed. (New Haven: Yale University Press, 2001), pp. 231-32.

and the issue of Erastianism, are connected to papal infallibility. While these are real concerns that can be addressed in numerous ways, these issues of authority are not dependent on the pope or the Catholic Church functioning as an infallible belief-producing mechanism.

Manning's dream never came to pass. The infallibility definition did not bring about the conversion of Protestant England. Rather, the inopportunists were correct that papal infallibility would hinder ecumenical relations between Catholic, Orthodox, and Protestant Christians. Because of the inherent inadequacies of maximal infallibility, and not because of the success of the inopportunists at Vatican I *per se,* many Catholic theologians would abandon maximal infallibility, as well as doctrinal immutability, by the time of Vatican II. In the next two chapters moderate versions of infallibility will be examined that have become prevalent in contemporary Catholic thought.

CHAPTER 4

Moderate Infallibility:
John Henry Cardinal Newman

The moderate position of John Henry Newman is the second view of papal infallibility to be considered.[1] While Newman was a popular figure in nineteenth-century England, the Ultramontanes viewed him with suspicion, and rightly so since he opposed extreme Ultramontanism and maximal infallibility whenever a good opportunity presented itself. A creative thinker who viewed himself more as a controversialist than a theologian, Newman believed that the value of his work would be best judged after his life. Newman's prediction proved true. As recent biographer Sheridan Gilley observes,

> Indeed, it was Newman's understanding of the Vatican decrees which in the years after his death was tacitly received by the Church; and it is generally accepted now that papal infallibility has been unambiguously exercised only twice in the modern period, in defining the Marian doctrines of the Immaculate Conception in 1854 and of the Assumption in 1950.[2]

1. Newman classified himself, along with Bishop Joseph Fessler, as a "Minimizer," though he felt the term was a derogatory one. See his *Letter to the Duke of Norfolk* in *Newman and Gladstone: The Vatican Decrees,* ed. Alvan Ryan (Notre Dame: University of Notre Dame Press, 1962), p. 184. This work follows J. Robert Dionne, who calls positions like Newman's "moderate" and uses the label "minimalist" for Roman Catholics who reject papal infallibility. Thus Dionne classifies Döllinger as a minimalist. See *The Papacy and the Church: A Study of Praxis and Reception in Ecumenical Perspective* (New York: Philosophical Library, 1987), pp. 30-31.
2. Sheridan Gilley, *Newman and His Age* (London: Darton, Longman & Todd, 1990), p. 378.

Further, it is common to suggest that, while Vatican I was Manning's council, Vatican II was Newman's.[3] Newman was undoubtedly significant for later Roman Catholic theology, though it is debated how much he influenced the Vatican II decrees, especially *Lumen Gentium.*

Part of Newman's enduring success stems from the fact that, unlike Manning, Newman benefited from a series of sympathetic biographers, beginning with Wilfred Ward and continuing to the present with Ian Ker, Gilley, and Frank M. Turner.[4] In fact, Newman's biographers border on panegyric. Further, Newman himself wrote an intellectual autobiography, a classic of the genre, entitled *Apologia Pro Vita Sua.*[5] The warmth and vulnerability that pervade this work have won Newman many admirers. Of course, Newman continues to attract biographers and admirers because his work itself is so rich and suggestive. As Nicholas Lash warns, "To summarize Newman's thought is, notoriously, to distort it."[6] While the same could be said of the other three theologians, it applies to none more than Newman.

The Life of Newman

John Henry Newman was born in London on February 21, 1801. His early life has striking similarities to Manning's. Newman's father, John, was involved in the banking business, though not at the same level as Manning's father.[7] And John Newman's bank was forced to close its doors as well, in Newman's case at the end of the Napoleonic Wars in 1816. The collapse of his father's bank was a crucial time in young John Henry's life,

3. See, for instance, David Newsome, *The Convert Cardinals* (London: John Murray, 1993), p. 364.

4. Wilfred Ward, *The Life of John Henry, Cardinal Newman, Based on His Private Journals and Correspondence* (London: Longmans, Green & Co., 1912); Ian Ker, *John Henry Newman: A Biography* (Oxford: Clarendon Press, 1988); Sheridan Gilley, *Newman and His Age.* Frank M. Turner, *John Henry Newman: The Challenge to Evangelical Religion* (New Haven: Yale University Press, 2002). Other major biographers include Meriol Trevor and Charles Stephen Dessain.

5. John Henry Newman, *Apologia Pro Vita Sua* (London: Oxford University Press, 1964).

6. Nicholas Lash, *Newman on Development* (Shepherdstown, WV: Patmos Press, 1975), p. 153.

7. Newsome, *The Convert Cardinals,* pp. 23-25.

and though he was raised in the Church of England, it was this event that led to his embracing Christianity. In his autobiography, Newman recalls, "I was brought up from a child to take great delight in reading the Bible; but I had no formed religious convictions till I was fifteen. Of course I had a perfect knowledge of Catechism."[8] Early in his newfound Christian faith Newman embraced a form of evangelicalism. However, he never had a conversion experience like that emphasized by evangelicals at the time. At the age of 16 he began his studies at Trinity College, Oxford, and quickly excelled as a student, though he was painfully shy in college and throughout life. He decided to forgo law, which his father hoped he would study, to pursue theology and a career in the church. In 1822, on his first attempt, Newman was elected a fellow at Oriel College, "at that time the object of ambition of all rising men in Oxford, and attainable only by those who had the highest academical pretensions."[9]

Newman went through no less than three religious conversions during his lifetime. The first was his conversion to an evangelical form of Christianity during his teenage years. This in turn gave way to his mature Anglican position. Newman's evangelical convictions faded while he was at Oxford. As early as 1824 he found himself rejecting key evangelical doctrines, such as the doctrine of imputed righteousness in favor of baptismal regeneration, and the emphasis on a conversion experience. During this time he also began to adopt a number of views that would later characterize his position as a leader of the Tractarian, or Oxford, Movement. He developed a love for the Church Fathers and patristic literature; he viewed the church as a substantive, institutional body; he affirmed the importance of apostolic succession; and he rejected Erastian views of church polity, which elevate the state over the church in ecclesiastical matters. Further, he was introduced to Bishop Butler's *Analogy of Religion,* which persuaded him of the analogy between the works of God in nature and those revealed in divine revelation, and the importance of converging probabilities for achieving epistemic certitude in matters of faith. However, in 1827 Newman admitted that he was "drifting in the direction of the Liberalism of the day" before being "rudely awakened from my dream."[10] Liberalism became the position

8. Newman, *Apologia Pro Vita Sua,* p. 1.
9. Quoted in Ker, *John Henry Newman,* pp. 15-16.
10. Newman, *Apologia Pro Vita Sua,* p. 14.

that Newman most resisted, and he was certain that any form of Protestantism, with its appeal to private judgment, would be unable to withstand such a formidable opponent of the orthodox Christian faith. In fact, Newman argued that liberalism was simply a consistent application of the Protestant principle.

In 1833 Newman joined a movement to oppose liberalizing tendencies in the Church of England. Soon the group was called the Tractarian Movement, named after a series of polemical works, the *Tracts for the Times,* which Newman contributed to and edited. The Tractarian Movement presented an "apostolical" position that was an alternative to evangelical and high church, or "high and dry," positions against liberalism. In *Apologia Pro Vita Sua,* Newman lists three propositions "about which I was so confident" during this time.

> First was the principle of dogma: my battle was with liberalism; by liberalism I mean the anti-dogmatic principle and its developments. . . .
>
> Secondly, I was confident in the truth of a certain definite religious teaching . . . viz. that there was a visible Church, with sacraments and rites which are the channels of invisible grace. I thought that this was the doctrine of Scripture, of the early Church, and of the Anglican Church. . . .
>
> But now, as to the third point on which I stood in 1833, and which I have utterly renounced and trampled upon since, — my then view of the Church of Rome.[11]

While Newman vehemently opposed the Protestant principle, he equally opposed the Catholic Church, viewing the pope as the Antichrist. David Newsome observes,

> It is sometimes forgotten how deep was Newman's detestation of the Roman Church in the early days of the Oxford Movement, and how — of all its leading spirits — he must have seemed the least likely to fall victim to either argument or blandishment on behalf of the Roman claims.[12]

11. Newman, *Apologia Pro Vita Sua,* pp. 50-53.
12. Newsome, *The Convert Cardinals,* p. 134.

Newman and the Tractarians saw themselves, and the Church of England, as representing a true *via media* between Protestantism, which tends to subtract from the apostolic faith, and Roman Catholicism, which tends to add to the apostolic faith. Antiquity, or the consent of the Church Fathers, was the principle that supported the *via media*. Newman maintained that private judgment, while it could readily distort scripture, could not so easily misinterpret antiquity. The Protestant error, then, was the appeal to *sola scriptura,* while the Roman Catholic error was the appeal to the authority of the church over that of antiquity.[13]

Over time, the Tractarian appeal to antiquity gave way for Newman. For one, Newman, like Manning, came to realize that antiquity was also subject to the shortcomings of private judgment, and this realization "created a sort of distrust of my theory altogether."[14] Further, Newman became concerned that the *via media* was "unreal"; that is, it represented an intellectual option, but was not a "real" option that could be identified with a living Christian body in history. In 1839, while studying the history of the Monophysites, Newman was struck by an analogy between contemporary Anglicans and Protestants, and the Monophysites of the fifth century. He writes, "I saw my face in that mirror, and I was a Monophysite. The Church of the *Via Media* was in the position of the Oriental communion, Rome was where she now is; and the Protestants were the Eutychians." He continues,

> It was difficult to make out how the Eutychians or Monophysites were heretics, unless Protestants and Anglicans were heretics also; difficult to find arguments against the Tridentine Fathers, which did not tell against the Fathers of Chalcedon; difficult to condemn the Popes of the sixteenth century, without condemning the Popes of the fifth. The drama of religion, and the combat of truth and error, were ever one and the same. The principles and proceeding of the Church now, were those of the Church then; the principles and proceedings of heretics then, were those of Protestants now. I found it so, — almost fearfully. . . .[15]

13. Ker, *John Henry Newman,* pp. 142, 143. Newman deals extensively with these themes in *The Via Media of the Anglican Church,* ed. H. D. Weidner (Oxford: Clarendon Press, 1990).

14. Newman, *Apologia Pro Vita Sua,* p. 117.

15. Newman, *Apologia Pro Vita Sua,* pp. 118, 119.

Newman saw an analogy between the Monophysites and present-day Anglicans and Protestants, though the specific issues of controversy were different. Soon afterwards, the words of St. Augustine against the Donatists were brought to Newman's attention: *"Securus judicat orbis terrarum."*[16] Newman felt these words applied not only to the Donatists, but to the Monophysites as well. The private opinions of individuals or Christian sects, usually defended by an appeal to scripture or tradition, were no match for the doctrinal decisions of the universal church. "[These words] decided ecclesiastical questions on a simpler rule than that of Antiquity; nay, St. Augustine was one of the prime oracles of Antiquity; here then Antiquity was deciding against itself."[17]

By now Newman found himself drifting toward Roman Catholicism. However, although he could no longer affirm the *via media,* he found no firm evidence that the Church of England was in heresy. He still rejected, and even despised, the abuses and excesses of Rome. Thus, he felt an obligation to remain in the Church of England and try to reform her from within. But between July and November of 1841, Newman received "three blows which broke me."[18] First, as he worked on a translation of St. Athanasius, Newman was confronted with the same analogy that haunted him earlier during his study of the Monophysites. "I saw clearly, that in the history of Arianism, the pure Arians were the Protestants, the semi-Arians were the Anglicans, and that Rome was what it was then. The truth lay, not with the *Via Media,* but with what was called 'the extreme party.'"[19]

Second, Anglican bishops began to bring charges against Newman over his controversial Tract 90, published in February of that year. In Tract 90, the last of the *Tracts for the Times,* Newman gave a "Catholic" interpretation of the Thirty-Nine Articles. The concerned bishops argued that Newman had clearly misrepresented the intention of the Thirty-Nine Articles, and that he was leading the Anglican Church toward Catholicism. Newman, though, argued that "whereas it is usual at this day to make the particular *belief of their writers* their true interpretation, I would make the *belief of the Catholic* Church such."[20]

16. "Let him who is secure judge the world."
17. Newman, *Apologia Pro Vita Sua,* pp. 120, 121.
18. Newman, *Apologia Pro Vita Sua,* p. 144.
19. Newman, *Apologia Pro Vita Sua,* p. 144.
20. Quoted in Ker, *John Henry Newman,* p. 220. The italics are in the original.

While Newman felt he had a duty to reform the Anglican Church, it became evident that the bishops did not share his vision of a more "Catholic" Anglicanism.

Third, Newman adamantly opposed the efforts of the Anglican Church and the Prussian government to establish a bishopric in Jerusalem. For one, the Anglican Church "was not only forbidding any sympathy or concurrence with the Church of Rome, but it actually was courting an intercommunion with Protestant Prussia and the heresy of the Orientals," the latter of which included Monophysites and Nestorians.[21] Further, "The Jerusalem Bishopric was the ultimate condemnation of the old theory of the Via Media: — if its establishment did nothing else, at least it demolished the sacredness of diocesan rights. If England could be in Palestine, Rome might be in England."[22] By the end of the year, Newman was "on my death-bed, as regards my membership with the Anglican Church."[23]

Still, Newman had a long road ahead of him before he would finally convert to Roman Catholicism in 1845. As he considered the marks of the church found in the Nicene Creed, he reasoned that, while the Church of Rome best displayed the note of catholicity, the Anglican Church best displayed the note of sanctity. Further, Newman states, "I felt some of my old objections against Rome as strongly as ever. I had no right, I had no leave, to act against my conscience. That was a higher rule than any argument about the Notes of the Church."[24] In March of 1843 Newman retired from his ecclesiastical duties and entered lay communion. While he began to believe that the Anglican Church was in schism, he confessed, "I could not go to Rome, while I thought what I did of the devotions she sanctioned to the Blessed Virgin and the Saints."[25] Obviously, the journey Newman traveled was a tortuous one.

A breakthrough came as Newman considered the idea of doctrinal development in the church. Rather than conceiving the Christian faith in static terms, Newman proposed that God may have intended for the divine revelation given in Jesus Christ to develop over time in the Spirit-led church. Such a possibility would account for the absence of fully de-

---

21. Newman, *Apologia Pro Vita Sua*, p. 148.
22. Newman, *Apologia Pro Vita Sua*, p. 155.
23. Newman, *Apologia Pro Vita Sua*, p. 153.
24. Newman, *Apologia Pro Vita Sua*, p. 156.
25. Newman, *Apologia Pro Vita Sua*, p. 192.

veloped Catholic doctrines in antiquity, including her devotion to Mary and the saints. At the same time, Newman began to question why the Anglican Church accepted some councils but not others, and why they accepted some Catholic doctrines but not papal supremacy. As Ker observes, "He thus found himself in the position that he 'must either believe all or none.'"[26] Newman came to the conclusion "that there was no medium, in true philosophy, between Atheism and Catholicity, and that a perfectly consistent mind, under those circumstances in which it finds itself here below, must embrace either the one or the other."[27] A similar sentiment was expressed in a private letter written during this time: "And this most serious feeling is growing on me; viz. that the reasons for which I believe as much as our system teaches, *must* lead me to believe more, and that not to believe more is to fall back into skepticism."[28]

On the basis of accumulated probabilities — by which Newman held that, in religious matters, a believer attains certitude — Newman came to believe that the Anglican Church was in schism, that Christian doctrines had developed, and that the doctrines of the Catholic Church were the true developments. However, Newman had deceived himself before, and he was concerned lest he had done so again. He decided to write a book explaining the reason for his new convictions. If, after writing the book, he still had not changed his mind, he would ask for acceptance into the Catholic Church. The result, *An Essay on the Development of Christian Doctrine,* is a remarkably innovative work that has had a profound influence on Catholic theology.[29] We will examine the themes of this work more carefully later in this chapter. On October 9, 1845, as *Essay* was preparing for publication, Newman was received into the Catholic Church by Father Dominic Barberi. In *Apologia* he writes that, since he became a Catholic, "I have been in perfect peace and contentment; I never have had one doubt. . . . Nor had I any trouble about receiving those additional articles, which are not found in the Anglican Creed."[30]

While Newman's religious theories and conversion alleviated his

26. Ker, *John Henry Newman,* p. 292.
27. Newman, *Apologia Pro Vita Sua,* p. 206.
28. Newman, *Apologia Pro Vita Sua,* p. 238. The italics are Newman's.
29. John Henry Newman, *An Essay on the Development of Christian Doctrine* (Notre Dame: University of Notre Dame Press, 1990).
30. Newman, *Apologia Pro Vita Sua,* p. 247.

epistemic worries, they raised suspicions among his new ecclesiastical superiors and academic colleagues in the Catholic Church. It is easy to appreciate these suspicions. While most Catholics believed that the doctrines of the Catholic Church were immutable, a recent innovative convert suggested that these doctrines had developed over time under the guidance of the Holy Spirit. Stephen Prickett aptly describes the situation: "[*Essay*] was written in limbo, defending the claims of a Church he did not belong to with the weapons of the Church that had abandoned him."[31] In effect, Newman converted to a conception of the Catholic Church that he himself created. That, over time, he brought many Catholics over to his position is evidence of his genius. In the meantime, his ecclesiastical superiors and academic colleagues were puzzled by this influential Englishman who was now part of their fold. It was assumed that Newman needed further education to be initiated into the Roman way of doing things, so he spent time studying in Rome after his conversion.

Newman articulated a number of positions that were frowned upon by his ecclesiastical superiors. For example, Newman's belief that the infallibility of the church fundamentally resided in the *consensus fidelium* did not sit well with his Ultramontane superiors who would eventually promote papal infallibility at Vatican I. His indifferent attitude toward the temporal power of the pope was viewed by many Catholics as disloyalty. In 1864 Newman's desire to establish a Catholic college at Oxford was opposed and barred by Archbishop Manning, who felt that an Oxford education, especially under Newman's oversight, would corrupt Catholic youth. For much of his Catholic career as an Oratorian in Birmingham, Newman did not feel he was properly appreciated or used by his new church.

While as an Anglican Newman opposed devotion to the Blessed Virgin, as a Catholic he greeted with enthusiasm the definition of her immaculate conception. To Newman, the definition of this doctrine in 1854 confirmed his theory of doctrinal development. The immaculate conception was a definition that was difficult to prove from scripture and early tradition, and it had taken the church approximately eight centuries to reach a definite position on the doctrine. Thus the immaculate conception, which critics defamed as new, was a prime example

31. Quoted in Newsome, *The Convert Cardinals*, p. 166.

of how doctrines develop over time in the church under the guidance of the Spirit.[32]

Newman was less enthusiastic about Vatican I and the rumors that circulated regarding the effort to define papal infallibility. While Newman received several invitations to attend the council as a theological advisor from the likes of Bishops Ullathorne and Dupanloup, as well as an invitation to be a consultant on one of the conciliar commissions, he declined all such offers and insisted he was too busy working on his next book, *A Grammar of Assent*.[33] During this time Newman repeatedly stated that he held papal infallibility as a "theological opinion," but not as an article of faith. He believed the doctrine was too new. It had not had enough time to develop adequately. Further, the doctrine would hinder well-intentioned Protestants from converting to Catholicism. The extent of his opposition became public when a private letter to Bishop Ullathorne was leaked to the press. It is worth quoting the letter at length.

> When we are all at rest, and have no doubts, and at least practically, not to say doctrinally, hold the Holy Father to be infallible, suddenly there is thunder in the clear sky, and we are told to prepare for something we know not what to try our faith we know not how. No impending danger is to be averted, but a great difficulty is to be created. Is this the proper work for an Ecumenical Council? As to myself personally, please God, I do not expect any trial at all; but I cannot help suffering with the various souls which are suffering, and I look with anxiety at the prospect of having to defend decisions, which may be not difficult to my private judgment, but may be most difficult to maintain logically in the face of historical facts. What have we done to be treated, as the faithful never were treated before? When has definition of doctrine de fide been a luxury of devotion, and not a stern painful necessity? Why should an aggressive insolent faction be allowed to "make the heart of the just to mourn, whom the Lord hath not made sorrowful"?[34]

32. See Newman, *Apologia Pro Vita Sua,* pp. 263-66.

33. John Henry Newman, *A Grammar of Assent* (New York: Longmans, Green & Co., 1947).

34. Quoted in Ker, *John Henry Newman,* pp. 651-52.

While Newman did accept the definition of papal infallibility, he despised the tactics and attitudes of the extreme Ultramontanes at the council. In private letters he wrote, "The definition of July involved the dethronement of September"; and "I cannot think thunder and lightning a mark of approbation . . . and a sudden destruction of the Pope's temporal power does not seem a sign of approval either."[35] Nevertheless, Newman believed that the council was free. On the whole, Newman was pleased with the moderation of the definition, and he looked for a future council to address any unresolved issues resulting from the definition of papal infallibility.

Before and after the council Newman corresponded with many who struggled with the definition of papal infallibility. This number included Catholics, of course, but also Anglicans considering conversion. Newman would not make a detailed, public statement on papal infallibility until the publication of the *Letter to the Duke of Norfolk* in January 1875.[36] The occasion for this work was W. E. Gladstone's celebrated attack against maximal infallibility, *Vatican Decrees in Their Bearing on Civil Allegiance.* Gladstone's work was the opportunity Newman was looking for. It allowed him to respond to Protestants like Gladstone, but it also provided an opportunity to respond indirectly to the extreme Ultramontanes, some of whom were Newman's ecclesiastical superiors. In fact, since the work contained several pointed attacks against extreme Ultramontanes, some Roman officials wanted Newman censured. However, Ullathorne and Manning, the latter of whom was made a Cardinal in March of that year, dissuaded them from this course of action. Given that Manning was one of the objects of Newman's indirect attacks, his support of Newman speaks much for his character, or at least his political sensibilities. Many English Catholics and Anglicans applauded and embraced Newman's work. Like the work of the German bishop Joseph Fessler, Newman's *Letter* was an influential early presentation of moderate infallibility.

The *Letter* was Newman's last major publication. In January 1879, Newman was made a Cardinal by Pope Leo XIII, the successor of

35. Quoted in Gilley, *Newman and His Age,* p. 369.
36. John Henry Newman, *Letter to the Duke of Norfolk,* in *Newman and Gladstone: The Vatican Decrees,* ed. Alvan Ryan (Notre Dame: University of Notre Dame Press, 1962).

Pius IX. Newman rightly saw this as a vindication of his life and work as a Catholic. While he remained mentally sharp until his death, his physical health began to fail in the mid-1880s, and he died of pneumonia on August 11, 1890.

Significant Theological Themes

Before turning to Newman's view of papal infallibility, two related themes need to be introduced: his proposal for doctrinal development and his weak foundationalism in epistemology. The idea of doctrinal development has become a key part of contemporary moderate articulations of papal infallibility. Jaroslav Pelikan calls Newman's *Essay* "the almost inevitable starting point for an investigation of development of doctrine."[37] Paul Misner notes that the *Essay* has been "of unsurpassed importance for subsequent Roman Catholic theology."[38] The significance of Newman's *Essay* and the theory of doctrinal development will become clear later in this chapter and in subsequent chapters.

Newman begins the *Essay* by describing his theory of doctrinal development as "undoubtedly an hypothesis to account for a difficulty."[39] As Newman studied the history of the early church, he encountered a problem. Both Anglicans and Roman Catholics maintained doctrines that evidenced change, such as episcopal government, infant baptism, and even the doctrine of the Trinity. Newman's theory is an attempt to understand the permanent identity of the Christian faith in light of the doctrinal changes that have occurred during the church's 1800 years of existence. It is helpful to distinguish Newman's proposal from two other positions that were held by Catholic theologians at the time. One was the Gallican tradition as represented by J. B. Bossuet. Bossuet maintained that Catholic doctrines do not change, but are further explicated and clarified over time to distinguish the unchanging faith of the church from various heresies. Another position was the Spanish tradition, which also insisted that Catholic doctrines do not change. This

---

37. Quoted in Lash, *Newman and His Age,* p. 2.

38. Paul Misner, *Papacy and Development: Newman and the Primacy of the Pope* (Leiden: E. J. Brill, 1976), p. 3.

39. John Henry Newman, *An Essay on the Development of Christian Doctrine* (Notre Dame: University of Notre Dame Press, 1990), p. 30.

tradition, though, held that later doctrines can be logically deduced from earlier beliefs and doctrines.[40] Unlike these two positions, Newman argued that Christian doctrines do indeed change, or develop, over time within the Spirit-led church. Further, these developments are more than a clarification of what was already believed, or the outcome of logical deduction. As Owen Chadwick states, "Newman thought that, when heresy appears, the mind of the Church has to be *discovered* by meditation, discussion, dialectic, until a definition is made: and so 'after a difficult childhood, a new dogma is born.'"[41] Gilley observes that "the theory converted the stock objection to Rome, that Rome had changed, into a presumptive argument in her favor."[42]

Newman summarizes his theory of doctrinal development as follows:

> [T]hat the increase and expansion of the Christian Creed and Ritual, and the variations which have attended the process in the case of individual writers and Churches, are the necessary attendants on any philosophy or polity which takes possession of the intellect and heart, and has had any wide or extended dominion; that, from the nature of the human mind, time is necessary for the full comprehension and perfection of great ideas; and that the highest and most wonderful truth, though communicated to the world once for all by inspired teachers, could not be comprehended all at once by the recipients, but, as being received and transmitted by minds not inspired and through media which were human, have required only the longer time and deeper thought for their full elucidation.[43]

For Newman, Christianity is a fact of human history that impresses an idea of itself on the mind of believers. Here Newman follows John Locke's epistemology, where knowledge is attained through ideas that come from sense experience. Newman argues that Christianity is a great system of thought much like Platonism or Stoicism. Like all great

40. Owen Chadwick, *From Bossuet to Newman: The Idea of Doctrinal Development* (Cambridge: Cambridge University Press, 1957), p. 149 and chaps. 1-2.

41. Chadwick, *From Bossuet to Newman*, p. 183.

42. Gilley, *Newman and His Age*, p. 230.

43. Newman, *Essay on the Development of Christian Doctrine*, pp. 29-30.

systems of thought, Christianity is a vital, living idea, and time is needed to comprehend and work through its full implications. Newman insists,

> It is indeed sometimes said that the stream is clearest near the spring. Whatever use may fairly be made of this image, it does not apply to the history of a philosophy or belief, which on the contrary is more equable, and purer, and stronger, when its bed has become deep, and broad, and full.[44]

Newman continues, "here below to live is to change, and to be perfect is to have changed often."[45] All great ideas that take control of the human mind grow and develop over time, and Christianity is no different.

Newman lists a number of types of development that Christianity has experienced during its history. There are political developments in the organization and structure of the church. There are logical developments in the growth of the doctrines. There are historical developments that mold the opinion of the church concerning certain persons or events. There are ethical developments that impact the way the church lives and worships. And there are metaphysical developments that make explicit the system of thought underlying the various doctrines held implicitly. Newman gives the following example that briefly illustrates each type of development.

> Taking the Incarnation as its central doctrine, the Episcopate, as taught by St. Ignatius, will be an instance of political development, the *Theotokos* of logical, the determination of the date of our Lord's birth of historical, the Holy Eucharist of moral, and the Athanasian Creed of metaphysical.[46]

In addition to legitimate developments, there are also false developments or corruptions that arise in the history of an idea. The various heresies that have been rejected by the church are examples of corruptions of Christianity.

---

44. Newman, *Essay on the Development of Christian Doctrine,* p. 40.
45. Newman, *Essay on the Development of Christian Doctrine,* p. 40.
46. Newman, *Essay on the Development of Christian Doctrine,* p. 54.

On the basis of antecedent probability, Newman argued that (1) development of doctrine is to be expected in Christianity, (2) an infallible authority is to be expected to facilitate the development of Christianity, and (3) the development of doctrine that has occurred under the guidance of popes and councils in the Catholic Church is the probable fulfillment of the first two expectations. Before looking specifically at his arguments, we should first consider Newman's use of antecedent probability. Newman believed that the historian must bring certain assumptions "antecedently" to the study of the evidence, or facts, of history. Such assumptions make historical research possible. At the same time, the research of the historian confirms, refutes, or modifies the antecedent assumptions that are brought to the evidence.[47] Newman held that his theory of doctrinal development was antecedently probable and was confirmed by historical evidence.

Why, then, should doctrinal development be expected in Christianity? Newman argued that scripture, as a deposit of divine revelation, was incomplete and left unanswered too many important questions for one not to expect development. For example, what religious duties are required of parents on behalf of their children, and how do Christians receive forgiveness of post-baptismal sin? Newman found the answer to these questions in the later developments of infant baptism and penance.[48] But Newman found evidence of development in scripture as well. An important example is the development of the messianic idea in both the Old and New Testaments.[49] Since such important developments occur within scripture, the Spirit-led church can continue to expect similar developments today.

Newman proposed that, if it is part of the divine plan for the idea of Christianity to develop over time, it is also antecedently probable that God would provide an external authority to discern true developments from corruptions. This need, he maintained, is met in the doctrine of the infallibility of the church.[50] Christianity is in need of an infallible developing authority because

47. Lash, *Newman and His Age,* pp. 20ff.; Chadwick, *From Bossuet to Newman,* p. 138.

48. Newman, *Essay on the Development of Christian Doctrine,* pp. 60, 61.

49. Newman, *Essay on the Development of Christian Doctrine,* pp. 64ff.

50. Newman, *Essay on the Development of Christian Doctrine,* p. 78.

Christianity . . . is a revelation which comes to us as a revelation, as a whole, objectively, and with a profession of infallibility; and the only question to be determined relates to the matter of the revelation. If then there are certain great truths, or duties, or ob-servances, naturally and legitimately resulting from the doc-trines originally professed, it is but reasonable to include these true results in the idea of the revelation itself, to consider them parts of it, and if the revelation be not only true, but guaranteed as true, to anticipate that they too will come under the privilege of that guarantee.[51]

Since the developments of Christianity are an outgrowth of the original deposit of divine revelation, developments should also enjoy the same guarantee of truth as the original deposit of divine revelation. But throughout history, up to the present time, opinions have abounded over the true meaning of revelation and its proper developments. This variety of opinions points to the antecedent probability of an infallible developing authority.

Finally, Newman asked if an infallible developing authority, the need for which is demonstrated by antecedent probability, can be found any-where in history. The answer, of course, is Yes, in the Catholic Church. Newman argued that "if there must be and are in fact developments in Christianity, the doctrines propounded by successive Popes and Coun-cils, through so many ages, are they."[52] The result of Newman's inquiry, then, is an all-or-nothing situation where one must either accept all the developments of Catholicism to have authentic Christianity, or one must settle for a corruption. For Newman, there are no systems of thought comparable to Trent, only objections to particular doctrines found in Trent. "You must either accept the whole or reject the whole; at-tenuation does but enfeeble, and amputation mutilate."[53]

Newman offers several examples of development, including those that Protestants would affirm, such as the canon of the New Testament and the *homoousion,* and those that only Catholics would affirm, such as papal supremacy. His point, of course, is to show the similarities be-

51. Newman, *Essay on the Development of Christian Doctrine,* pp. 79-80.
52. Newman, *Essay on the Development of Christian Doctrine,* p. 96.
53. Newman, *Essay on the Development of Christian Doctrine,* p. 94.

tween developments that Protestants accept and those they do not. With papal supremacy, for instance, Newman admits that the doctrine cannot be found in the earliest Christian documents. However, he argues that the papacy was not needed as this time, and would not be needed until the church reached a certain size and prominence. Nonetheless, there is good antecedent probability of a "Popedom." Newman states, "It is the absolute need of a monarchical power in the Church which is our ground for anticipating it. A political body cannot exist without government, and the larger is the body the more concentrated the government must be."[54] So, the antecedent probability of the papacy, together with the actual state of the church as it developed through history, support the doctrine of papal supremacy. In addition, Newman highlights the biblical texts traditionally used to support the papacy. However, instead of arguing that these texts demonstrate the early existence of the papacy, he calls these texts "promises" and "prophecies" that do not describe what is but anticipate what will be.[55]

In the second part of the *Essay,* Newman presents seven notes that are supposed to help distinguish legitimate developments from illegitimate corruptions.[56] These notes will not detain us here, primarily because, as Owen Chadwick observes, these are tests "which convinced no one and which [Newman] himself once admitted to be incapable of performing their ostensible purpose."[57] We should pause to observe, though, the significance of Newman's theory for subsequent Catholic theology. For Catholics who accept his proposal, the debate over papal infallibility no longer hinges on whether the doctrine can be found in scripture or the early church. This is not to say that Newman's approach is non-historical, for history and the development of Christianity through time are crucial for Newman. But a doctrine can be new and still be authentic if it is accepted by the infallible Catholic Church as a genuine development.

A second theme that needs to be introduced is Newman's weak

---

54. Newman, *Essay on the Development of Christian Doctrine,* p. 154.

55. Newman, *Essay on the Development of Christian Doctrine,* p. 156.

56. These seven notes of the genuine development of an idea are "preservation of its type," "continuity of its principles," "its power of assimilation," "its logical sequence," "anticipation of its future," "conservative action upon its past," and "its chronic vigour."

57. Chadwick, *From Bossuet to Newman,* p. 143.

foundationalism in epistemology.[58] Newman differed from Manning and traditional scholastic theology in that he did not confine rationality to what can be demonstrated by formal proof or syllogistic argument. While Manning held that Christian doctrine could be proven and precisely expressed in a manner similar to the inductive sciences, Newman thought such approaches were inadequate. However, Newman still wanted to maintain the status of religious beliefs as knowledge claims and account for the certainty with which religious beliefs are held. To accomplish this, he insisted that different types of reasoning are appropriate for different areas of investigation. With Aristotle, Newman agreed that moral arguments differ from mathematical arguments. Since mathematical arguments can be demonstrated by formal proof, they can attain a greater certainty than moral arguments. However, following Bishop Butler, Newman maintained that moral arguments, as well as theological and political arguments, can be based on accumulated probabilities. These accumulated probabilities, none of which amounts to a formal proof when taken alone, can come close to proof when taken together and can lead to certitude. Newman gives a helpful analogy: "The best illustration . . . is that of a *cable* which is made up of a number of separate threads, each feeble, yet together as sufficient as an iron rod."[59]

Faith, though, was never simply a matter of reason for Newman. While reason can test and verify faith, it usually is not the basis of faith. The illiterate peasant can have true religious and moral knowledge even if he cannot adequately explain why he believes the things he does. Likewise, the educated professional may be aware of evidences for God's existence and still reject theistic belief because she does not desire to submit to God. Thus Newman made room in his religious epistemology for the subjective element of human decisions. Three elements are especially important in Newman's articulation of this subjective element. First, Newman emphasized the role of conscience for religious and moral decision-making. Newman viewed conscience as a faculty

58. The key primary sources here are Newman's Anglican work *Fifteen Sermons Preached Before the University of Oxford* (London: Longmans, Green & Co., 1898); and his mature Catholic statement, *A Grammar of Assent*. My summary is indebted to Gilley, *Newman and His Age*, pp. 356-62, and Ker, *John Henry Newman*, pp. 258-69, 637-50.

59. As quoted in Ker, pp. 620-21. Newman further explains that the iron rod "represents mathematical or strict demonstration."

given by God that provides dependable religious and moral knowledge. Conscience, though, can be cultivated or seared by the moral and intellectual behavior of the individual. Second, Newman stressed the importance of *phronesis,* or practical judgment, for making religious and moral decisions. In *A Grammar of Assent,* Newman called this judgment the "illative sense," which he defined as "right judgment in ratiocination."[60] Since religious and moral arguments are not based on formal proofs but accumulated probabilities, such judgment is required when deciding between positions on religious and moral issues. Third, as suggested above, Newman maintained that the epistemic and moral virtue of the individual does matter in religious and moral decision-making. Intentional immoral actions can sear the conscience of the individual, and epistemic dishonesty can lead to distorted judgment. Newman believed that virtue was more important than evidence for accepting faith. Further, he stressed that, ultimately, faith only comes by divine grace.

Newman took the subjective side of religious epistemology seriously. However, he also sought to avoid a relativism that views religious and moral propositions as mere opinions rather than knowledge claims. Here we again see his interaction with Locke's epistemology, which distinguishes knowledge claims that can be held with certainty from opinions that should be held with varying degrees of assent. In the *Grammar,* Newman described religious and moral propositions as assertions for which one can reach certitude. The terms "assertion" and "certitude" need further clarification. Newman begins the *Grammar* by distinguishing three types of propositions that correspond to three different acts or mental states: there are questions that arise from doubt, conclusions that result from inference and argument, and assertions that are based on assent. Religious propositions are the latter, that is, they are assertions based on assent. Assent is the volitional, unconditional acceptance of a proposition as true, and certitude is one type of assent. Newman describes certitude as a mental state with three characteristics: "that it follows on investigation and proof, that it is accompanied by a specific sense of intellectual satisfaction and repose, and that it is irreversible."[61] Certitude is based on rational grounds, though

60. Newman, *Grammar of Assent,* p. 260.
61. Newman, *Grammar of Assent,* p. 196.

it may or may not follow from strict logic or a formal proof. Further, certitude is permanent and indefectible. If one loses a conviction, one was never certain of it. Therefore, even though religious assertions do not rest on strict proof, one can still be certain of them.

Newman's discussion of certitude helped him answer an early Protestant critique of papal infallibility. The doctrine of papal infallibility is supposed to secure religious certainty. However, Protestants argued that the doctrine is of little use since fallible individuals have to decide whether or not the pope is infallible. Therefore, religious certainty cannot be attained unless every person is infallible. Newman answered this objection by distinguishing certitude and infallibility. He states,

> A certitude is directed to this or that particular proposition; it is not a faculty or gift, but a disposition of mind relatively to a definite case which is before me. Infallibility, on the contrary, is just that which certitude is not; it *is* a faculty or gift, and relates, not to some one truth in particular, but to all possible propositions in a given subject-matter.[62]

Newman argued that an individual can be certain about a particular proposition without possessing the gift of infallibility. For example, a student can remember for certain what she had for lunch without having an infallible memory. Further, all Christians can be certain that God is infallible although Christians are not infallible. In the same way, Catholics can be certain that the pope is infallible without all Catholics being infallible.[63]

However, Newman made another important observation about certitude that is crucial. A certitude may be true or false. That is, one can be certain in one's mind about a proposition, and the proposition still be false. Early on, the possibility of false certitudes was seen as the Achilles' heel of the *Grammar*. Ker observes,

---

62. Newman, *Grammar of Assent*, p. 170.

63. Newman's argument here is fundamentally correct and affirms the particularism advocated in this work. However, this argument does not deal with the critique that papal infallibility cannot bring epistemic certainty since one still has to identify and interpret papal pronouncements.

Where non-Christian (as opposed to high Anglican) critics joined forces with the Catholic reviewers was in criticizing the failure to provide a theory of truth which would enable true certitudes to be distinguished from false certitudes. Newman was well aware that this was the weak point of the book; but it was not exactly a failure, since he had not even attempted to provide one.[64]

So, while Newman showed how Catholics could be certain of papal infallibility without all Catholics being infallible, his theory includes the possibility that Catholics could be certain and wrong. As Ker notes, this conclusion left many unsatisfied.

Papal Infallibility

Since Newman lived during the definition of papal infallibility, and since his opposition of the doctrine turned to acceptance, one would expect a certain amount of development in his thinking on the subject. However, there is also significant continuity in Newman's view of infallibility. As a Catholic, Newman always maintained the infallibility of the Catholic Church. Before Vatican I, he believed that papal infallibility was a theological opinion that could be held as probable, but not a doctrine to be held with certainty. While it is an oversimplification, it is accurate to say that, after Vatican I, Newman simply transferred papal infallibility from the category of theological opinion to doctrine, and interpreted the doctrine in light of his prior conviction of the infallibility of the church. To trace these themes, we will begin with his treatment of the infallibility of the church in *Apologia Pro Vita Sua,* written before Vatican I in 1864. Then we will consider his sustained treatment of papal infallibility in *Letter to the Duke of Norfolk,* written after Vatican I in 1875. In addition, the personal correspondence of Newman provides insight into his thought in the crucial period between these two major works.[65]

---

64. Ker, *John Henry Newman,* p. 638.

65. The best treatment of Newman's view of papal infallibility is John R. Page, *What Will Dr. Newman Do? John Henry Newman and Papal Infallibility, 1865-1875* (Collegeville, MN: Liturgical Press, 1994). Page has provided an invaluable service espe-

In *Apologia* Newman gives a helpful illustration of the epistemic role of the infallibility of the Catholic Church.

> People say that the doctrine of Transubstantiation is difficult to believe; I did not believe the doctrine till I was a Catholic. I had no difficulty in believing it, as soon as I believed that the Catholic Roman Church was the oracle of God, and that she had declared this doctrine to be part of the original revelation.[66]

Once Newman accepted the infallibility of the church and converted to Catholicism, his belief in the church as "an oracle of God" took priority over particular beliefs he might hold as theological opinion.[67] When the church declares a doctrine as dogma, it can be held with certainty. Another example is the doctrine of the immaculate conception of the Blessed Virgin. Once the church declared this doctrine to be *de fide,* it was held with certainty by the Catholic faithful. While it might be argued that belief in the infallibility of the church interferes with freedom of thought, this is exactly why Newman thinks the infallibility of the church is so important. Private judgment is untrustworthy, and human reason needs restraints to keep it from heresy or even atheism. On one hand, the infallibility of the church is an opponent of reason because it provides intellectual boundaries. However, since such boundaries are needed for the proper exercise of reason, the infallibility of the church is actually an ally of reason.[68]

Newman stressed that, at the writing of *Apologia,* the exact seat of infallibility has not been established, though the normal seat of infallibility is the pope in ecumenical council.[69] Further, the infallibility of the church has important limitations. The church is infallible only in matters of faith, and not in "secular matters," unless such secular matters

---

cially in his treatment of the personal correspondence between *Apologia* and *Letter.* Another helpful collection of Newman's writings on infallibility is J. Derek Holmes, ed., *The Theological Papers of John Henry Newman on Biblical Inspiration and on Infallibility* (Oxford: Clarendon Press, 1979).

66. Newman, *Apologia Pro Vita Sua,* p. 248.

67. William Abraham calls this type of belief a "threshold concept." See William J. Abraham, *Crossing the Threshold of Divine Revelation* (Grand Rapids: Eerdmans, 2006).

68. Newman, *Apologia Pro Vita Sua,* pp. 254-62.

69. Newman, *Apologia Pro Vita Sua,* p. 266.

touch on issues of religion. But even in matters of faith, the infallibility of the church has conditions. The church cannot define a dogma that is contrary to "the great truths of the moral law, of natural religion, and of Apostolic faith." Instead, "It must not go beyond them, and it must ever appeal to them. Both its subject matter, and its articles in that subject matter, are fixed. And it must ever profess to be guided by Scripture and tradition."[70] Those in the church who possess infallibility are not infallible in all of their proceedings, but only when solemnly deciding an issue of faith. Newman's discussion of infallibility in *Apologia* does not locate infallibility solely in the papacy, but it does anticipate the conditions found in *Pastor Aeternus.*

Before and during the Vatican council, Newman opposed the definition of papal infallibility as inopportune. For one thing, he felt the doctrine was too modern to be defined. The church had not had enough time to carefully consider the implications of the doctrine and to formulate it properly. He felt the doctrine was a hasty reaction to growing secularization and the pope's dwindling temporal power, and he did not want the church to rush to a definitive position.[71] Further, he felt the definition was inopportune because of the struggles of numerous Catholics, and potential Anglican converts, who confided in him through personal correspondence. Both before and after the Vatican council, Newman acted as a spiritual advisor to many who wrestled with the viability of papal infallibility. For these reasons, Newman saw the potential definition of papal infallibility as a great danger for the church.

Beyond the issue of opportunity, Newman had doubts about the truth of the definition, though these doubts were not insurmountable. Regarding the cases of Vigilius and Honorius, Newman wrote in a personal letter that, "taking the history by itself I should say that it told very strongly against the Pope's infallibility though I don't think it actually disproves it."[72] In another private letter he describes papal infallibility "as being pious to hold or agreeable to general sentiment. But if I am asked to defend it logically and prove it — I don't profess to be able — and I don't expect it will ever be made an article of faith."[73] Newman

70. Newman, *Apologia Pro Vita Sua,* p. 263.
71. Page, *What Will Dr. Newman Do?* pp. 29, 83, 91, 109.
72. Quoted in Page, *What Will Dr. Newman Do?* p. 63.
73. Quoted in Page, *What Will Dr. Newman Do?* p. 78.

maintained his belief that papal infallibility would never be defined until it finally happened.

While the Catholic Newman always upheld the infallibility of the church, he felt the ultimate authority in the church was the general Catholic population, the *consensus fidelium*. As the definition of papal infallibility loomed nearer, Newman wrote a telling private letter that states his views on the locus of infallibility and anticipates his response to the definition.

> But any declaration of the Pope's, if he were ruled infallible, would require explanation in the concrete in *another way* also — not only as to its application, but its interpretation. As lawyers explain acts of Parliament, so theologians have ever explained the dicta of Popes and Councils — and that explanation, when received generally, is the true Catholic doctrine. Hence I have never been able to see myself that the ultimate decision rests with any but the general Catholic intelligence. And so I understand it to be implied in the "Securus iudicat orbis terrarum."[74]

Earlier, in notes he prepared for Ignatius Ryder's debate with W. G. Ward, Newman wrote that the *Schola Theologium* "*determines* BOTH *the proof* that a pronouncement is infallible or not, *and also* what the meaning of the pronouncement is."[75] So, since the general Catholic population, and especially the theologians, both identify and interpret infallible statements, there is a real sense that the *consensus fidelium* is the ultimate locus of the church's infallibility. As Ker correctly observes, "The insistence on the reception by the whole Church of the definitive judgements of Councils and Popes, including in particular their interpretation by the theologians, was to form the keynote of Newman's own theology of infallibility in the months and years ahead."[76]

One irony of the Vatican council is that Newman's proposal for doc-

---

74. Quoted in Page, *What Will Dr. Newman Do?* p. 99.

75. Holmes, ed., *The Theological Papers of John Henry Newman,* p. 147. Italics and capitalization JHN.

76. Ker, *John Henry Newman,* p. 634. This theme is treated more fully in John Henry Newman, *On Consulting the Faithful in Matters of Doctrine* (London: Collins, 1986), and in Samuel D. Femiano, *Infallibility of the Laity: The Legacy of Newman* (New York: Herder & Herder, 1967).

trinal development was used by some Ultramontanes to support the definition of papal infallibility. In a private letter to Newman, Bishop Moriarty, in attendance at the council, wrote,

> Strange to say, if ever this definition comes you will have contributed much towards it. Your treatise on development has given the key. A Cardinal said the other day — "We must give up the first ten centuries, but the infallibility is an obvious development of the supremacy."[77]

Needless to say, Newman was not fond of this application of his theory. In his reply to Moriarty, he explained, "Of course I do not allow, as your Eminent friend seemed to think, that *anything* is a development; there are right developments and wrong ones. . . . nor do I think with your friend that infallibility follows on Supremacy — yet I hold the principle of development."[78] Once papal infallibility was defined, though, Newman eventually viewed the definition as a legitimate development.

Newman was disappointed with the actions and attitudes of the Ultramontanes at the Vatican council. Nonetheless, he disagreed with Döllinger's claim that the intrigues of the Ultramontanes annul the definition. In a letter to Döllinger he wrote, "I suppose in all Councils there has been intrigue, violence, management, because the truth is held in earthen vessals [*sic*]. But God over rules."[79] Rather than criticize the council, Newman gave a positive spin to the proceedings and saw the definition as a victory for the inopportunists. In a private letter, Newman wrote, "I saw the Definition yesterday and am pleased at its moderation, that is, if the doctrine in question is to be defined at all. The terms used are vague and comprehensive; and, personally, I have no difficulty in admitting it."[80] Newman was especially pleased that the definition did not specify which papal acts are infallible, in particular the Syllabus of Errors. Rather, the definition allowed for discussion on the identity and interpretation of infallible definitions. As for any excesses in the definition, Newman was confident that such would be clarified in the future. In a private letter he wrote,

77. Quoted in Page, *What Will Dr. Newman Do?* p. 95.
78. Quoted in Page, *What Will Dr. Newman Do?* p. 96.
79. Quoted in Gilley, *Newman and His Age*, p. 368.
80. Quoted in Gilley, *Newman and His Age*, p. 126.

I know that a violent reckless party, had it its will, would at this moment define that the Pope's powers need no safeguards, no explanations — but there is a limit to the triumph of the tyrannical — Let us be patient, let us have faith, and a new Pope, and a reassembled Council may trim the boat.[81]

Such hopes are the reason many view Vatican II as Newman's council.

Even though the definition had been passed, one question still remained: Is the definition authorized by an ecumenical council? Newman's concern here was different from Döllinger's. For Newman, it was crucial that the minority bishops at the council accept the definition. Further, it was necessary that the Catholic faithful embrace the definition. This concern goes back to Newman's understanding of the infallibility of the church and his insistence that the ultimate guarantor of truth is the general acceptance of the church, the *securus judicat orbis terrarum.* As time passed, it became clear that the doctrine had indeed met this essential condition. However, Newman's advice to those struggling with the doctrine during this time is interesting. In a private letter, he writes, "'Your duty lies in observing two conditions, both of them in your power — first make an act of faith, in *all* that the Holy Church teachers [*sic*] — and secondly, as regards this particular doctrine, turn away from any doubt which rises in your mind about its truth.'"[82] The problem, of course, is that if all the faithful with doubts accept Newman's advice, the faithful no longer function as a real check on papal and conciliar definitions.

It was nearly five years after Vatican I before Newman published *Letter,* his definitive treatment of papal infallibility. The delay can be attributed to a number of reasons. For one, he needed adequate time to formulate his own position regarding the definition. But more importantly, he did not want to agitate the extreme Ultramontanes who were his ecclesiastical superiors. We have already seen how Newman used the opportunity provided by Gladstone's polemical work against the extreme Ultramontanes to present his own position. Newman's response to Gladstone allowed him to criticize maximal infallibility while publicly defending the Catholic Church.

---

81. Quoted in Page, *What Will Dr. Newman Do?* pp. 186-87.
82. Quoted in Page, *What Will Dr. Newman Do?* p. 132.

Gladstone questioned whether Catholics can be trustworthy subjects of the state due to their allegiance to a pope who claims infallibility. Newman's *Letter* began with a direct response to this concern. Newman argued that the tension between the church and the state is an ancient issue, and the church has always rejected unqualified allegiance to the state. In fact, the Catholic Church is the only true heir of the ancient church, since both the Anglican and Orthodox churches are subject to the state.[83] Next, Newman appealed to the idea of development to argue that papal claims to allegiance are legitimate. After quoting Matthew 16:18-19 and referring to it as a "prophecy and promise" that has been fulfilled over time, Newman argued, "That which in substance was possessed by the Nicene Hierarchy, that the Pope claims now."[84] In Newman's judgment, the prerogatives of the Catholic Church under papal authority are hers "partly by the direct endowment of her Divine Master, and partly as being a legitimate outcome of that endowment."[85] However, his appeal to development here was criticized by many of his ecclesiastical superiors. They argued that papal prerogatives were possessed by the bishop of Rome from the beginning of the church in Peter, and were given entirely by direct endowment from Christ.

Papal prerogatives, though, do not mean the pope is never wrong and cannot be resisted. In fact, the pope cannot be infallible in political matters since such issues fall outside the purview of the gospel and are not matters of "faith or morals." The key question, then, is who should the Catholic obey in cases of conflict, the civil authority or the pope? Newman answered,

> [I]t is my *rule,* both to obey the one and to obey the other, but that there is no rule in this world without exceptions, and if either the Pope or the Queen demanded of me an "Absolute Obligation," he or she would be transgressing the laws of human nature and human society. I give an absolute obedience to neither. Further, if

83. Newman, *Letter to the Duke of Norfolk,* pp. 91-92. Of course, a number of Protestant churches had rejected the union of church and state, but these do not enter into Newman's discussion. Such churches would be criticized by Newman as not offering a substantive, institutional ecclesiology.
84. Newman, *Letter to the Duke of Norfolk,* p. 99.
85. Newman, *Letter to the Duke of Norfolk,* p. 100.

ever this double allegiance pulled me in contrary ways, which in this age of the world I think it never will, then I should decide according to the particular case, which is beyond all rule, and must be decided on its own merits. I should look to see what theologians could do for me, what the Bishops and clergy around me, what my confessor; what friends whom I revered: and if, after all, I could not take their view of the matter, then I must rule myself by my own judgment and my own conscience. But all this is hypothetical and unreal.[86]

While his response may appear to revert to the Protestant appeal to private judgment, Newman insists that it differs because he appeals to private judgment only in extraordinary situations, not in ordinary situations as Protestants do.

Newman's appeal to private judgment in extraordinary situations leads to his discussion of conscience. Conscience is the ethical law of God implanted in the heart and mind of humanity. While the promptings of conscience are not always right, conscience still commands obedience because it is the voice of God in the creature, though it is distinct from revelation. Through proper training and experience, one's conscience can be further nourished and formed. Newman wrote,

> Conscience is the aboriginal Vicar of Christ, a prophet in its informations, a monarch in its peremptoriness, a priest in its blessings and anathemas, and, even though the eternal priesthood throughout the Church could cease to be, in it the sacerdotal principle would remain and would have a sway.[87]

While the natural religion of conscience must be assisted and completed by divine revelation, nonetheless, "The Pope, who comes of Revelation, has no jurisdiction over Nature."[88]

However, Newman makes several important qualifications here. First, "conscience is not a judgment upon any speculative truth, any ab-

---

86. Newman, *Letter to the Duke of Norfolk*, p. 125, italics JHN. The last statement is especially interesting given that, while the situation may be "hypothetical and unreal" in Newman's own life, it has definitely been a "real" issue Catholics have had to face.

87. Newman, *Letter to the Duke of Norfolk*, p. 129.

88. Newman, *Letter to the Duke of Norfolk*, p. 193.

stract doctrine, but bears immediately on conduct, on something to be done or not done." Second, and closely related,

> a collision is possible between [conscience] and the Pope's authority only when the Pope legislates, or gives particular orders, and the like. But a Pope is not infallible in his laws, nor in his commands, nor in his acts of state, nor in his administration, nor in his public policy. Let it be observed that the Vatican Council has left him just as it found him here.[89]

So, while it is possible for conscience and the pope to conflict over "practical" issues, such matters are not part of the pope's infallibility. Conscience will not conflict with the pope in matters of "speculative truth" and "doctrine," where the pope exercises infallibility. Newman ends this section with his memorable quotation: "Certainly, if I am obliged to bring religion into after-dinner toasts, . . . I shall drink, — to the Pope, if you please, — still, to Conscience first, and to the Pope afterwards."[90]

After his discussion of conscience, Newman takes up the 1864 papal encyclical *Quanta Cura* and especially the attached Syllabus of Errors. Newman argues that, while many close to the pope contend that the Syllabus is infallible, infallible utterances are rare and the Syllabus is clearly not one of them. The Syllabus cannot be infallible since it was composed by a high-ranking ecclesial official instead of the pope himself. In fact, the Syllabus does not even enjoy the same status as the encyclical to which it was attached. Further, the Syllabus has suffered from misinterpretation, as many neglect to consult the original references of the propositions. Therefore, the Syllabus, properly interpreted, should be received *prima facie* by an act of obedience, but not with the assent of faith. Newman ends his discussion of the Syllabus with a not-so-subtle stab at the extreme Ultramontanes.

> Now, the Rock of St. Peter on its summit enjoys a pure and serene atmosphere, but there is a great deal of Roman *malaria* at the foot of it. While the Holy Father was in great earnestness and charity

89. Newman, *Letter to the Duke of Norfolk,* p. 134.
90. Newman, *Letter to the Duke of Norfolk,* p. 138.

addressing the Catholic world by his Cardinal Minister, there were circles of light-minded men in his city who were laying bets with each other whether the Syllabus would "make a row in Europe" or not.[91]

The final sections of the *Letter* deal with the Vatican council and the definition of papal infallibility. Regarding the Vatican council, Newman felt it important to clarify his own position, especially since his private letter to Ullathorne had been published and the media had made much of his disapproval of the council. Here Newman distanced himself from Döllinger and quoted some key sections from his private letters that show his approval of the definition.

Next, Newman addressed Gladstone's concern that, in the Catholic Church,

> more and more have the assertions of continuous uniformity of doctrine receded into scarcely penetrable shadow. More and more have another series of assertions, of a living authority, ever ready to open, adopt, and shape Christian doctrine according to the times, taken their place.[92]

Gladstone gave two examples of novel doctrines, the definitions of the immaculate conception and papal infallibility. Newman, though, argued that Catholics have a different view of history, and a different way of approaching history, than Gladstone, Döllinger, and most Protestants. Newman's concern is that these persons "seem to me to expect from History more than History can furnish, and to have too little confidence in the Divine Promise and Providence as guiding and determining those enunciations."[93] Newman insisted that historical evidence can never thoroughly prove or disprove a doctrine of the church. Further, as is the case in the interpretation of scripture, private judgment is not a reliable guide in the interpretation of history. Instead of relying on private interpretation, the Catholic looks to the church's use of history and "other informants also, Scripture, Tradition, the ecclesiastical

91. Newman, *Letter to the Duke of Norfolk,* p. 166.
92. Quoted in *Letter to the Duke of Norfolk,* p. 174.
93. Newman, *Letter to the Duke of Norfolk,* p. 176.

sense, or φρόνημα, and a subtle ratiocinative power, which in its origin is a divine gift."[94] The church believes many things that are beyond the discoveries of history or reason, but these doctrines are firmly held because "Revelation has declared them by means of that high ecclesiastical *Magisterium* which is their legitimate exponent."[95] Since the Catholic assents to the infallibility of the church, specific doctrines are necessarily justified once they are defined and received by the church.

Regarding the specific doctrines of the immaculate conception and papal infallibility, Newman agreed that doctrinal development has occurred. Even if one believes there is not enough historical evidence in favor of the doctrine before the definition, as Newman did with the doctrine of papal infallibility, the fact that the doctrine is defined by the church overcomes and resolves any historical difficulties. Newman made a similar argument concerning the case of Pope Honorius. Since the church has defined that the pope is infallible in his *ex cathedra* definitions, one can be assured that Honorius's monothelite teachings did not proceed from his infallibility.[96] When a doctrine is defined, historical difficulties are properly interpreted and resolved in light of the infallible definition.

As Newman turned to the definition of papal infallibility, he was careful to place the infallibility of the pope within the context of the church's infallibility, and the infallibility of the church within the context of the Christian faith as a product of divine revelation. The Christian faith comes from divine revelation, and God has seen fit to preserve this revelation in the church. To this end, God has given the church a supernatural guidance to lead the church into truth and to secure it from error. The pope's infallibility is similar to and a part of the infallibility of the church.

Newman explained that, according to *Pastor Aeternus,* any infallible pronouncement of the pope must be proclaimed to the church *ex cathedra.* To meet the requirements of *ex cathedra,* the pope must speak, first, as a "Universal Teacher"; second, "in the name and with the authority of the Apostles"; third, "on a point of faith and morals";

94. Newman, *Letter to the Duke of Norfolk,* p. 177.
95. Newman, *Letter to the Duke of Norfolk,* p. 178.
96. Newman, *Letter to the Duke of Norfolk,* p. 179. Later, on pp. 180-81, Newman also argues that, since Honorius's letters are previous to a council's definition, they are not a final decision and therefore are not infallible.

and fourth, "with the purpose of binding every member of the Church to accept and believe his decision."[97] Therefore, the pope is not infallible in conversations, in interpreting scripture and tradition, or in stating his own opinion, because in these instances the pope does not speak *ex cathedra.* If the pope makes a solemn judgment on an issue that does not affect Christian doctrine, then the pope is not infallible. Here Newman gave the example of the condemnation of "Galileo's Copernicanism," which cannot be infallible "unless the earth's immobility has a 'necessary connexion with some dogmatic truth,' which the present bearing of the Holy See towards that philosophy virtually denies."[98] In Newman's moderate infallibility, the requirements of *Pastor Aeternus* severely limit when the pope speaks *ex cathedra.*

Newman clearly distinguished the inspiration of the apostles and the *assistentia* of infallibility given to the church. The former refers to the giving of divine revelation through the apostles, which is a unique event. The latter is the gift of guarding and preserving the original revelation. So, the charism given to the church, and the pope, is "no direct suggestion of divine truth, but simply an external guardianship, keeping them off from error." Further, since the process of defining doctrine is a human affair open to error, "what Providence has guaranteed is only this, that there should be no error in the final step, in the resulting definition or dogma."[99]

Another limitation of infallible papal definitions is that the definition must come from the Apostolic *depositum* found in scripture and tradition. Newman was well aware that this limitation is problematic, since the pope himself is the ultimate judge of whether his definition is found in scripture and tradition. He candidly observed,

> A Protestant will object indeed that, after [the pope's] distinctly asserting that the Immaculate Conception and the Papal Infallibility are in Scripture and Tradition, this safeguard against erroneous definitions is not worth much, nor do I say that it is one of the most effective. . . .[100]

97. Newman, *Letter to the Duke of Norfolk,* p. 187.
98. Newman, *Letter to the Duke of Norfolk,* p. 188.
99. Newman, *Letter to the Duke of Norfolk,* p. 189.
100. Newman, *Letter to the Duke of Norfolk,* p. 190.

Nonetheless, since the definition must be related to the Apostolic *depositum,* there are basic limits to what a pope or ecumenical council can define.

In a similar manner, papal definitions on morals must come from "the Moral law, that primary revelation to us from God." For this reason,

> If the Pope prescribed lying or revenge, his command would simply go for nothing, as if he had not issued it, because he has no power over the Moral Law. If he forbade his flock to eat but vegetable food, or to dress in a particular fashion (questions of decency and modesty not coming into the question), he would in like manner be going beyond his province, because such a rule does not relate to a matter in itself good or bad.[101]

When the pope does define a matter of morals, he must address the whole world on an issue that is necessary for salvation. Newman believed,

> Nearly all that either oracle [the pope or the Catholic church] has done in this respect, has been to condemn such propositions as in a moral point of view are false, or dangerous, or rash; and these condemnations, beside being such as in fact, will be found to command the assent of most men, as soon as heard, do not necessarily go so far as to present any positive statements of universal acceptance.[102]

Universal moral teachings, if they exist at all, are rare and less controversial than dogmatic statements.

Newman argued for "that principle of minimizing so necessary, as I think, for a wise and cautious theology," though he submitted himself "to the opinion of divines more learned than I can pretend to be myself."[103] Newman observed that infallible definitions come in two forms: statements of truth and condemnations of error. But the church must be careful when running to conclusions regarding infallible definitions. He argued,

101. Newman, *Letter to the Duke of Norfolk,* p. 191.
102. Newman, *Letter to the Duke of Norfolk,* p. 192.
103. Newman, *Letter to the Duke of Norfolk,* p. 192.

Theologians employ themselves in determining what precisely it is that is condemned in that thesis or treatise; and doubtless in most cases they do so with success; but that determination is not *de fide;* all that is of faith is that there is in that thesis itself, which is noted, heresy or error, or other peccant matter, as the case may be. . . . But . . . instances frequently occur, when it is successfully maintained by some new writer, that the Pope's act does not imply what it has seemed to imply, and questions which seemed to be closed, are after a course of years re-opened. In discussions such as these, there is a real exercise of private judgment, and an allowable one; the act of faith, which cannot be superseded or trifled with, being, I repeat, the unreserved acceptance that the thesis in question is heretical, or erroneous in faith. . . .[104]

Here we see Newman's emphasis on the importance of the *Schola Theologium.* Infallible propositions are necessarily general statements, and great care must be exercised when applying them to specific situations and issues.

In his conclusion, Newman stressed that infallible definitions are rare. And, one more time, he took a shot at the extreme Ultramontanes: "Still the fact remains, that there has been of late years a fierce and intolerant temper abroad, which scorns and virtually tramples on the little ones of Christ."[105] Newman's conclusion reminds us that, while his position is now widely accepted, such was not the case when he first presented it.

Analysis

Newman's restrictive interpretation of the conditions of *Pastor Aeternus* and his proposal for doctrinal development save him from many of the problems faced by Manning and the proponents of maximal infallibility. For instance, in the case of Pope Honorius, Newman can simply argue that Honorius was not speaking *ex cathedra* in his monothelite letters. And since doctrines develop over time, papal infallibility does not

104. Newman, *Letter to the Duke of Norfolk,* p. 193.
105. Newman, *Letter to the Duke of Norfolk,* p. 197.

need to appear in scripture or the patristic church. In fact, by Newman's lifetime there had likely been only one exercise of strictly papal infallibility in the history of the church, the definition of the dogma of the immaculate conception of the Blessed Virgin Mary. Concerns about the antiquity of the Marian dogma can also be addressed by appealing to the theory of doctrinal development. In many ways, Newman's moderate infallibility is better able to address epistemic problems that arise from *Pastor Aeternus* than Manning's maximal infallibility.

Further, the suggestive insights of Newman's weak foundationalism anticipate a number of current proposals in religious epistemology. For example, Newman stressed the importance of accumulated probabilities for knowledge claims, as well as the importance of *phronesis,* or "the illative sense," for adjudicating cumulative cases. He held the principle of "proper epistemic fit" by distinguishing various fields of knowledge, such as mathematics and ethics, and acknowledging the different types of arguments needed to justify beliefs in these various fields. He treated conscience as a "reliable belief-producing mechanism," at least in the field of morality. His discussion of epistemic and moral virtue for attaining knowledge has recently been emphasized by virtue epistemologists. Further, his stress on conscience and virtue led him to reject the need of justification for knowledge, which is maintained by proponents of externalism today. All of these aspects of Newman's religious epistemology are attractive, and the importance of Newman's work here continues to be recognized.

However, Newman continued to maintain a strong epistemic conception of the Christian faith and ecclesial canons. In the *Essay,* he views the Christian faith as a great philosophy like Platonism or Stoicism. Like these other great ideas, time is needed to fully work out the significance of Christian doctrine. As this process of discovery occurs through history, an infallible epistemic authority is needed to keep the church in the truth of divine revelation. Missing here is any concern about the soteriological nature of the Christian faith and the soteriological function of ecclesial authority.

With this strong epistemic conception of the Christian faith, Newman follows the epistemological assumptions of his time that certainty distinguishes knowledge from opinion. For instance, in the *Letter* he argues, "All sciences, except the science of Religion, have their certainty in themselves; as far as they are sciences, they consist of necessary conclusions from undeniable premises, or of phenomena manipulated into general truths by an irresistible induction."[106] He goes on to argue that in "the science of Religion," papal infallibility is needed to bring certainty of the truths of divine revelation. As we saw in chapter 3, though, Newman's view of scientific knowledge has been abandoned. The theory-driven nature of science, and the impossibility of offering hard proof for the superiority of one scientific paradigm over another, have been well recognized. Of course, this is not to say we cannot have knowledge in science. In fact, we have every reason to think that our scientific knowledge is increasing on a daily basis. But there is a tentative character to our scientific paradigms and discoveries because of their theoretical nature. Like Manning, Newman views science as the standard of certain knowledge, and he wants to treat the Christian faith as a type of science. To make the "science of Religion" epistemologically secure, he posits the need for an infallible church and an infallible pope.

Clearly Newman's proposal is deeply wedded to methodist commitments in epistemology. Before his conversion to Catholicism, Newman was troubled by the fact that the Church of England accepted some councils of the church, but not all of them. As he studied the first four ecumenical councils, he saw his own face and the face of Anglicanism in the Monophysites and semi-Arians. The Monophysites rejected the decision of the councils, and the semi-Arians tried to maintain a *via media*. In the same way, Anglicans reject some Western councils and seek to maintain a *via media*. Of course, and this is key, Anglicans officially rejected the particular doctrinal positions of the Monophysites and semi-Arians. But, for Newman, they followed the same method as the early heretics and semi-Arians, and this made Anglicanism and the *via media* suspect. Newman ultimately concluded that there is no other option besides Trent and Catholicism on one hand, and doctrinal corruption of varying degrees on the other. Ultimately, the only two options are Catholicism and skepticism. Again, we see the same stark contrast that is found in Manning.

Of course, Newman's epistemic conception of councils is problematic since there have been numerous councils in the history of the church that have defined heretical or erroneous doctrines. So Newman

106. Newman, *Letter to the Duke of Norfolk*, p. 132.

adopts an epistemic conception of the church and the pope to determine which councils should be accepted and which rejected. Once he crosses this threshold, though, he begins to accept religious beliefs that he would otherwise reject. The list of these beliefs include transubstantiation, the propriety of veneration to Mary and the saints, and the doctrine of papal infallibility itself, among others. All of this is part of his attempt to secure religious epistemic certainty.

However, there is much subtlety and ambiguity in Newman's proposal. He concedes that the pope is infallible since a church council has so decided, but he recognizes and even highlights the difficulty of identifying and interpreting infallible pronouncements. Ultimately, the *consensus fidelium,* and especially the theologians, identify and properly interpret infallible pronouncements, but the *consensus fidelium* and the theologians themselves are not infallible. As Gilley notes, Newman's moderate infallibility has a "paradoxical safeguard, that what is infallible in papal utterances is a matter of expert interpretation by the *Schola Theologorum,* the collective judgement of the body of theologians, which is not itself infallible."[107] Obviously this is a complex epistemic proposal that includes more than an infallible pope, and brings results that are definitely less than certain.

When Newman discusses other epistemic resources, he begins to make distinctions that are easily questionable. For instance, Newman holds that conscience is a reliable belief-producing mechanism in ethical, "practical" judgments, but not in doctrinal, "speculative" judgments. As such, conscience could lead one to reject a moral judgment of the pope. Newman's distinction, however, is difficult to square with the language of *Pastor Aeternus,* which affirms the infallibility of the pope not only in matters of faith but also in matters of morals. When Newman considers the condemnation of Galileo, which is a matter of speculative judgment, he stresses that the "present bearing of the Holy See" does not consider this philosophy to have a connection to the dogmatic truth of the church. But obviously, the Holy See contemporary with Galileo did make this connection. Further, Newman himself points out the problem of the apostolic *depositum* and the moral law acting as limitations on an infallible pope who is supposed to properly interpret these epistemic sources.

107. Gilley, *Newman and His Age,* p. 378.

In the end, the epistemic limitations Newman highlights do not appear to be effective resources at all.

It comes as no surprise that Newman's proposal for infallible doctrinal development is problematic as well, especially since he himself describes it as "an hypothesis to account for a difficulty." The difficulty that Newman seeks to account for is an epistemic one. Newman proposes an epistemic method, infallible doctrinal development in the church, to bring certainty so that religious beliefs can have the status of knowledge. Further, he admits the importance of antecedent probability in his historical investigation. However, as we have seen, the antecedent epistemic assumptions that Newman brings to the discussion should be questioned. We do not need to possess an infallible epistemic method before the church can be preserved in the truth of the gospel, and before we can affirm particular Christian claims.

Once we challenge the antecedent epistemic assumptions underlying the *Essay,* it is important to see how Newman's theory of doctrinal development undermines other important epistemic resources available to us, especially in the field of historical investigation. Like Manning, Newman stresses the uncertainty of historical investigation to bolster his own method for attaining religious epistemic certainty. In doing so, though, Newman gives up an important epistemic resource in favor of a flawed theory that can be, and has been, used against him by representatives of positions he opposed most. We saw how some Ultramontanes used Newman's theory of doctrinal development to argue for papal infallibility. Other Ultramontanes rejected Newman's theory because they felt it could easily lead to Liberalism. That some theological Liberals have adopted Newman's theory in an attempt to circumvent historical doctrinal positions demonstrates that these concerns are valid.[108] While Newman is correct that historical investigation has epistemic limitations, we should be hesitant to give up the important resources it offers us.[109]

---

108. See, for example, Maurice Wiles's two works *The Making of Christian Doctrine* (London: Cambridge University Press, 1967) and *The Remaking of Christian Doctrine* (London: SCM Press, 1974).

109. Other substantial discussions and critiques of the *Essay* should be noted. For example, Newman's contemporary J. B. Mozley, in *The Theory of Development: A Criticism of Dr. Newman's Essay on the Development of Christian Doctrine* (London: Rivingtons, 1878), observes that Newman's work does not account for a form of doc-

The extensive journey that Newman has taken us on does not, and cannot, reach the goal of religious epistemic certainty. At least three of his assumptions need to be rejected to free Newman from the epistemic quagmire he finds himself in: one, his epistemic conception of the Christian faith and ecclesial canons; two, his belief that epistemic certainty is necessary for knowledge; and three, his turn to methodism in epistemology to secure certainty. Further, these epistemic assumptions increase division in the church. Once we have rejected these assumptions, Newman's work in religious epistemology can be enlightening indeed. Newman's emphasis on the importance of accumulating probabilities, the importance of the "illative sense" in judging between cumulative cases, the need for reliable belief-producing mechanisms like conscience, and the importance of epistemic and moral virtue can be extended to most, if not all, of our knowledge claims. Also, we can retain his principle of proper epistemic fit and his externalism. Here we are left with some building blocks that could be, and have been, used to develop a compelling contemporary religious epistemology and that avoid some of the wrong turns of the past. Still, moderate interpretations of *Pastor Aeternus* became increasingly popular during and especially after Newman's lifetime, primarily because of the superiority of this position over maximal infallibility. In the next chapter, we will consider a contemporary proponent of moderate infallibility, Avery Cardinal Dulles.

---

trinal corruption that most concerns Protestants, that is, "corruption by excess" or "abuse in exaggeration" (pp. 34-36). Lash observes that Newman's argument from antecedent probability assumes "a preference for a particular form of political structure (monarchical), a particular conception of the notion of unity appropriate in ecclesiology . . . , and a misunderstanding of the relationship between the kingdom of God and the church in history" (p. 40). Further, Lash questions whether Newman's theory really allows scripture and tradition to function as an effective critique of the magisterium, a critique related to my own. Owen Chadwick ends his work *From Bossuet to Newman* with a pointed question: "These new doctrines, of which the Church had a feeling or inkling but of which she was not conscious — in what meaningful sense may it be asserted that these new doctrines are not 'new revelation'?" (p. 195).

CHAPTER 5

Moderate Infallibility:
Avery Cardinal Dulles

The Second Vatican Council brought a significant transition in the attitude of the Catholic Church. Instead of maintaining the defensive posture that had characterized Catholicism since the Protestant Reformation, Vatican II positioned the Catholic Church for constructive dialogue with other Christian traditions and religious faiths. In addition, the council critically examined some of the doctrinal positions of the Catholic Church, though many of the conciliar documents are intentionally vague and it is still unclear to what extent Vatican II represents a doctrinal shift.

By Vatican II the moderate position on papal infallibility had gained strength, and since the council it has become the dominant position among Catholic theologians. The work of the American Jesuit theologian Avery Cardinal Dulles will be examined as representative of the contemporary moderate position. In his autobiography, Dulles humbly makes "no claim to be a major figure [in theology]" and distinguishes himself from the "speculative brilliance of a Rahner or a Lonergan, or the erudition of a de Lubac, a von Balthasar, or a Congar."[1] While this evaluation may be appropriate, Dulles has been an influential interpreter of Vatican II and a prominent Catholic voice on the American scene. In fact, his lack of "speculative brilliance" is precisely what qualifies him as a good representative of the contemporary moderate position on papal infallibility.

---

1. Avery Dulles, *A Testimonial to Grace and Reflections on a Theological Journey* (Kansas City: Sheed & Ward, 1996), p. 143.

Further, it is fitting to follow Newman with a contemporary theologian who has a high admiration for him. It is evident that Dulles has learned much from Newman. In addition to writing a number of articles on Newman's thought, Dulles has also published a book that seeks "to survey Newman's teaching about the classical theological questions in a comprehensive and systematic way."[2] Dulles offers a contemporary moderate position with clear lines of connection to the position of Newman that we surveyed in chapter 4.

The Life of Dulles

Avery Dulles, born in Auburn, New York, on August 24, 1918, came from a prominent family with Presbyterian roots. His father, John Foster Dulles, served as Secretary of State under President Dwight Eisenhower. Having "been trained in one of the 'better' nonsectarian boarding schools of New England [Choate]," Avery Dulles went on to graduate from Harvard University in 1940. He then spent a year and a half at Harvard Law School before entering the United States Navy during World War II. Dulles converted to Roman Catholicism in the fall of 1940 during his first year of law school, and wrote an account of his conversion entitled *A Testimonial of Grace* while in the Navy.[3] Dulles's conversion differs from that of Manning and Newman in that he did not convert from another Christian tradition *per se* but from atheism.

Dulles describes the intellectual journey that led him to Catholicism in *Testimonial,* his spiritual autobiography and *apologia.* Upon entering Harvard, Dulles held, "like most of my comrades, a fairly complete but equally naïve philosophy of life, founded on a variety of popular superstitions. . . ." This philosophy of life combined the theory of evolution with a thoroughgoing materialism that "considered it a

---

2. Avery Cardinal Dulles, *Newman* (New York: Continuum, 2002), p. ix.

3. Originally published in 1946, a fiftieth-anniversary edition was published in 1996. The new edition includes an afterword that traces Dulles's career as a priest and theologian. All references to *A Testimonial of Grace* will follow the pagination of the 1996 edition titled *A Testimonial of Grace and Reflections on a Theological Journey.* Additional details of Dulles's life are filled in by T. Howland Sanks, "Avery Dulles," in *A New Handbook of Christian Theologians,* ed. Donald W. Musser and Joseph L. Price (Nashville: Abingdon Press, 1996), pp. 135-41.

proved fact that the original and uncreated reality, the sufficient cause of the whole universe, was physical matter. . . ." Despite his Presbyterian background, Dulles states, "It did not enter my mind to consider that the world owed its existence to a wise Creator, that a beneficent Providence watched over and directed it, or that the soul, as the loving work of God's hands, possessed an eternal destiny."[4] Rather, Dulles supposed that "supernatural religion was now relegated to the realm of superstition, and morality exposed in its true guise, as a sort of social contract expressive of the general desires of the community."[5] During this time Dulles took great delight in the arts and, as far as political ideas were concerned, espoused a libertarian ideal. "My Utopia was a society which gave to each the freedom to seek his own brand of happiness, and to the elite the opportunity of stealing fire from the gods."[6]

During his sophomore year at Harvard, Dulles took a general course in philosophy which,

> introducing me to the works of Aristotle and Plato, made me perceive how much sounder was their outlook on the universe than the narrow mathematicism of Descartes and Spinoza or the sterile skepticism of Hume and Kant. The modern philosophers seemed to stultify themselves by erecting enormous epistemological difficulties at the outset. The Greeks, on the other hand, without neglecting the problem of knowledge, got much further in solving the problem of being.[7]

Dulles's early readings in metaphysics challenged his materialism. But Dulles too, like the Greeks he admired, never neglected epistemology. For now, though, it was Aristotle's metaphysics that engaged Dulles and restored his confidence in human reason and the senses. Dulles became an avid reader of contemporary Aristotelians, many of whom were Catholic, such as Jacques Maritain and Étienne Gilson. Plato took Dulles further toward faith by convincing him of the objective nature of morality and virtue. Dulles gives credit to his tutor at Harvard, the Irish

---

4. Dulles, *Testimonial of Grace*, pp. 3-4.
5. Dulles, *Testimonial of Grace*, p. 5.
6. Dulles, *Testimonial of Grace*, p. 7.
7. Dulles, *Testimonial of Grace*, p. 11.

Catholic Paul Doolin, for exercising considerable influence on his thinking during his sophomore year.

Dulles admitted that a life of pursuing pleasure could not bring real happiness or lasting achievement. He states, "My philosophy failed me because it was not big enough to contain the human, let alone the heroic."[8] His political ideas were changing as well, as he now conceded that "the State should serve some higher purpose than to conform to the whims and illusions of the masses." Instead, "government should be practiced by those who had the necessary learning and experience." Rejecting the liberalism so popular at Harvard at the time, Dulles "became increasingly disposed to accept authority, not only in politics, but also in faith and morals."[9]

Dulles's conversion to theism came in February during his junior year while reading Augustine's *City of God* as an assignment in medieval history. Leaving the library, Dulles was taken by the beauty of nature and the strength of the teleological argument for the existence of God — all things reach their created end by design, not chance. The moral argument for the existence of God also captivated Dulles. He describes his early faith as a "positive natural religion" composed of a "tripartite creed, made up of the existence of the moral law, its supremacy, and its relation to the will of God."[10] While not yet a Catholic, he was convinced that God must be conceived in personal, and specifically Christian, terms. Dulles attributes his initial conversion to philosophical reflection, and it is no accident that his early teaching and writing were in the areas of philosophy and apologetics. However, Dulles notes that his belief in God was more than the result of rational demonstration from so-called proofs. He realized every proof could be doubted, and skepticism could easily set in. His own acceptance of God's existence, while rooted in reason, was based more on what he calls "intuition."[11]

It would be two more years, while Dulles was in law school, before he became a Catholic. In the meantime, he constantly studied the Gospels and wrestled with the intellectual credibility of the divinity of Christ.

8. Dulles, *Testimonial of Grace*, p. 30.
9. Dulles, *Testimonial of Grace*, pp. 32-33.
10. Dulles, *Testimonial of Grace*, pp. 39, 41.
11. Dulles, *Testimonial of Grace*, p. 47.

While he accepted the divinity of Christ as probable, "the act of faith was for me a terrible stumbling block. In a sense it seemed to be the surrender of that which I valued more than anything else: intellectual honesty. To make a subjective certainty out of an objective probability was a sacrifice of reason itself."[12] Eventually, Dulles did affirm the Christian faith, an act he attributes solely to the grace of God.

With his new faith in Christ, Dulles began to look for a church, a living institution, for guidance. He states,

> I went to Protestant churches of nearly every denomination —
> Presbyterian, Episcopalian, Methodist, Baptist, Unitarian, and
> nonsectarian. In none of these did I find what I was looking for.
> Whatever the individual differences between these sects might be,
> they were alike, in the manifestations which I saw of them, in failing to insist on the inerrancy of the doctrines which they had inherited from Christ. . . . Every member of the congregation was
> considered entitled to interpret as strictly or as loosely as he
> pleased the word of God.
>
> Christ Himself was frequently discussed on a merely human
> level. He was congratulated for His psychological insights, for His
> artful leadership, and even for His sense of humor. His Messianic
> role, on the other hand, was deliberately ignored, and the dogmatic aspects of His teaching were casually passed over.[13]

His disillusionment with Protestantism led him to a Catholic mass, which did not fare much better. Dulles criticized the elaborate ritual and external aids to worship, as well as the dry sermon and dull service. He states that "while the Protestant churches left me with a sense of mere inadequacy, the Catholic Church I found in many respects positively repellant. . . . I preferred the cold chastity of Protestant worship."[14]

While Dulles was not initially impressed with Catholic worship, he was attracted to Catholic theology. Here he found an alternative philosophical and social system that opposed the liberalism he had found so

---

12. Dulles, *Testimonial of Grace*, p. 59.
13. Dulles, *Testimonial of Grace*, p. 61.
14. Dulles, *Testimonial of Grace*, p. 64.

wanting. And as he continued to participate in Catholic worship, he found its rituals more meaningful and rich. Dulles was looking for a church that would provide clear guidance in his journey of faith and make the distant, historical Christ a living reality for him in the present. He writes,

> From my most rudimentary notions of the Church . . . I originally conceived of it as a visible and organic institution. The Protestant theory which reduced the Church to the status of a merely invisible society, consisting of the community of the elect, had no place in my thought. Such a society would not have answered the fundamental needs of which I have spoken and for which, I knew, Christ had made provision. The Church in which I was interested had certain organic functions, namely to safeguard the integrity of the faith, to spread the Gospel to all nations, to enunciate the moral law, and to administer the Sacraments.[15]

Here Dulles found himself asking, among other questions, an epistemic question similar to that of Manning and Newman: Which church is able to provide sure guidance on questions of faith and morals?

It is clear from the *Testimonial* that the young Dulles was attracted to traditional Catholic claims of Christ's direct endowment of papal authority on Peter, and through him on the succession of bishops at Rome. Further, he examined extensively the Catholic Church's claim to infallibility. He states,

> If I could find one inconsistency of dogma, one article of faith which the Church had been compelled to suppress or to retract, or one binding doctrine which was absurd in the light of reason or of natural science, I was resolved to conclude that there existed on earth no visible institution endowed with the powers which Christ had ostensibly vested in the Apostles.[16]

Dulles was satisfied that the Catholic Church had never committed herself to error, and agreed, "Surely it was a divine protection which had

---

15. Dulles, *Testimonial of Grace*, p. 82.
16. Dulles, *Testimonial of Grace*, pp. 83-84.

saved the Church through all these centuries from the human failings of princes and prelates alike."[17] He was also convinced that the Catholic Church was the indefectible church of Christ's promise to Peter. When Dulles concluded that the Catholic Church was the true church of Christ and the visible institution he was looking for, he committed himself to her and was baptized.

Obviously Dulles's faith would grow from these initial beginnings. In the afterword to the revised edition of his early autobiography, Dulles states, "In a sense I could say . . . that there is no further history of my religious opinions, since in becoming a Catholic I arrived at my real home." But, of course, he had "filled out with theological reflection what was previously a basic stance of faith. Although my faith journey was complete, my theological journeyings were just beginning."[18] After serving in the Navy, Dulles joined the Society of Jesus in 1946 and, upon completion of his novitiate, studied philosophy for three years at Woodstock College, a Jesuit institution in Maryland. After his studies at Woodstock, Dulles taught philosophy for two years at Fordham University in New York. In 1953 Dulles returned to Woodstock to take up theological studies under the guidance of Gustave Weigel. Dulles credits Weigel with introducing him to the ecumenical movement and the thought of Paul Tillich, from whom "I first learned the importance of symbol for the theology of revelation."[19] During this time Dulles also developed an interest in the *nouvelle théologie* coming out of France, a retrieval and *ressourcement* project represented by theologians like Henri de Lubac, Jean Daniélou, and Yves Congar.

Dulles was ordained to the priesthood in 1956, and after a year of spiritual and pastoral studies in Germany, he began doctoral studies at Pontifical Gregorian University in Rome. During his time in Rome, the Second Vatican Council was announced by Pope John XXIII, and Dulles became further interested in ecumenism. His dissertation, written under Jan Witte, investigated the *vestigia ecclesiae,* the "traces of the Church" outside the Catholic Church. He writes, "The conclusions of my thesis . . . seemed bold at the time, but five years later, in the light of

17. Dulles, *Testimonial of Grace,* p. 85.
18. Dulles, *Testimonial of Grace,* p. 97.
19. Dulles, *Testimonial of Grace,* p. 103.

Vatican II's Decree on Ecumenism, they had become common Catholic doctrine."[20]

After completing his doctorate, Dulles taught at Woodstock College from 1960 until the school was closed in 1974. His initial teaching and writing focused on fundamental theology and apologetics. In *Apologetics and the Biblical Christ* he challenged the "historicist apologetic" popular in the early twentieth century which "placed unquestioning confidence in the powers of scientific historical method to defend the rational basis of the Christian faith."[21] Instead he proposed a weak foundationalist approach that viewed the Gospels more as religious testimony than modern history.[22]

Upon the death of Gustave Weigel at the beginning of 1964, Dulles was charged by his Woodstock colleague John Courtney Murray to serve as "an interpreter of the Council for the benefit of Catholics in the United States."[23] While Dulles continued to work in the field of fundamental theology, specifically in the area of divine revelation, his work interpreting Vatican II moved him into ecclesiology as well. Throughout his career as a theologian, Dulles would make his main contributions in the fields of fundamental theology, ecclesiology, and ecumenism. Regarding his interpretation of the council, Dulles writes,

> In the late 1960s, seeking to make a strong case for the new directions set by Vatican II, I may have tended to exaggerate the novelty of the Council's doctrine and the shortcomings of the preconciliar period. But after 1970, as the Catholic left became more strident, and as young Catholics began to dismiss or ignore the heritage of previous centuries, I felt it necessary to put greater emphasis on continuity with the past.[24]

During the 1970s and 80s Dulles published a number of books on ecclesiology that addressed issues arising out of Vatican II. In 1971

20. Dulles, *Testimonial of Grace*, p. 106.

21. Avery Dulles, *Apologetics and the Biblical Christ* (Paramus, NJ: Newman Press, 1963), p. 6.

22. Dulles, *Apologetics and the Biblical Christ*, p. 69. See also *Testimonial of Grace*, p. 108, and Sanks, "Avery Dulles," in *A New Handbook of Christian Theologians*, p. 136.

23. Dulles, *Testimonial of Grace*, pp. 109-10.

24. Dulles, *Testimonial of Grace*, p. 110.

Dulles also became deeply involved in the United States Lutheran–Catholic dialogue, which has published statements on papal primacy, teaching authority and infallibility, and justification, among other topics.

Dulles's most popular work has been *Models of the Church*. Following his mentor Weigel, Dulles argued for a "dialogic approach" since

> the Church as a mystery could not be contained under any conceptual definition. Rather, it should be designated by a variety of images and metaphors, each of which captured certain limited aspects of the complex reality. A selective use of figures, I believed, underlay the divisions between opposed theological schools, none of which had the total truth, and none of which was totally wrong.[25]

Dulles followed a similar approach in *Models of Revelation* and *The Craft of Theology*.[26] Dulles's use of models and symbols, for which he is best known, will be examined more carefully below. In *Testimonial* he defends this approach as one that has allowed him "to retrieve what is best in the tradition, to reject one-sided opinions, and contribute to the formation of a fruitful consensus."[27]

Dulles taught at the Catholic University of America in Washington, D.C., from 1974 until his retirement in 1988. In 1988 he returned to Fordham University to occupy a university chair, a position he maintains to the present. Dulles was made a Cardinal by Pope John Paul II on February 21, 2001.

Significant Theological Themes

Avery Dulles has spent his career exploring two major areas that directly impact his position on papal infallibility: a "symbolic realist" approach to fundamental theology, and ecclesiology. We will begin with

25. Avery Dulles, *Models of the Church*, expanded ed. (New York: Image Books, 1987), was originally published in 1974. Dulles's quotation on this work is from *Testimonial of Grace*, p. 118.

26. Avery Dulles, *Models of Revelation* (Maryknoll, NY: Orbis Books, 1999), was originally published in 1983. Avery Dulles, *The Craft of Theology: From Symbol to System*, new expanded ed. (New York: Crossroad, 1995), was originally published in 1992.

27. Dulles, *Testimonial of Grace*, p. 119.

Dulles's symbolic realism, a phrase he uses to describe his basic philosophical stance. While we are particularly interested in his symbolic realist epistemology, it should be noted that this approach also includes an ontology where "reality is held to have a symbolic structure."[28] Dulles adopts this ontology from theologians like Karl Rahner and employs it in his work on ecclesiology and other theological topics. Dulles makes use of a symbolic realist epistemology to help him mediate between conflicting theological positions in contemporary theology and ecumenical dialogue.

Dulles was attracted to critical reflection on symbols early in his theological studies at Woodstock College. His early writings on doctrinal statements and infallibility show some of the convictions that led Dulles further in the direction of symbolic realism. In *Spirit, Faith, and Church* Dulles stresses the "historical relativity of all doctrinal statements" that inevitably follows since "the truth of revelation is never known in its naked absoluteness, but is always grasped within the perspectives of a sociocultural situation."[29] The theological reasons for this stance on fundamental theology are laid out further in *The Survival of Dogma,* namely, the "ineffable mystery of God," the "pilgrim status of the Church" this side of the eschaton, and "the diversity and mutual tension among the authoritative organs of revelation."[30] Because of the historical relativity of all doctrinal statements, and as a precursor to his work with models, Dulles argues that

the "word of God" is best heard when one maintains a certain critical distance from any given expression of that word. By holding a multitude of irreducibly distinct articulations in balance, one can best position himself to hear what God may be saying here and now. To recognize the historically conditioned character of every expression of faith is not to succumb to historical relativism, but rather to escape imprisonment within the relativities of any particular time and place.[31]

28. Dulles, *The Craft of Theology,* p. 20. The term "symbolic realism" also appears, among other places, in *Models of Revelation,* p. 266.

29. Wolfhart Pannenberg, Avery Dulles, S.J., and Carl E. Braaten, *Spirit, Faith, and Church* (Philadelphia: Westminster Press, 1970), p. 54.

30. Avery Dulles, *The Survival of Dogma* (New York: Crossroad, 1982), p. 87.

31. Dulles, *The Survival of Dogma,* pp. 88-89.

Further, Dulles believes that his approach leads one away from an overly epistemic conception of the faith to "the concrete imperatives of salvation" and "salvation truth."[32]

In his two most popular books, *Models of the Church* and *Models of Revelation,* Dulles continues to develop his symbolic realism by borrowing the use of models from the physical and social sciences. In *Models of the Church* Dulles lays out the major "approaches" or "types" of the church and argues that "a balanced theology of the Church must find a way of incorporating the major affirmations of each basic ecclesiological type. Each of the models calls attention to certain aspects of the Church that are less clearly brought out by the other models." Dulles elects to use the term "model" because of his belief that "the Church, like other theological realities, is a mystery. Mysteries are realities of which we cannot speak directly. If we wish to talk about them at all we must draw on analogies afforded by our experience of the world. These analogies provide models." Further, Dulles suggests,

> we cannot integrate [models] into a single synthetic vision on the level of articulate, categorical thought. In order to do justice to the various aspects of the Church, as a complex reality, we must work simultaneously with different models. By a kind of mental juggling act, we have to keep several models in the air at once.[33]

The models Dulles identifies are "the church as institution," "the church as mystical communion," "the church as sacrament," "the church as herald," "the church as servant," and, in the expanded edition, "the church as community of disciples."

Terrence Merrigan rightly observes that, while Dulles clearly intends to differentiate models from "images, metaphors, analogies, theories, types, symbols, and so forth," he does "occasionally appear to use them almost interchangeably."[34] With this in mind, Dulles proposes in *Models of the Church* that a model can be a type of "image" or "symbol." For instance, when one turns to the biblical material, a variety of images are used to describe the church. Dulles suggests,

32. Dulles, *The Survival of Dogma,* pp. 23, 119.
33. Dulles, *Models of the Church,* pp. 9-10.
34. Terrence Merrigan, "Models in the Theology of Avery Dulles: A Critical Analysis," *Bijdragen* 54 (1993): 148.

In the religious sphere, images function as symbols. That is to say, they speak to man existentially and find an echo in the inarticulate depths of his psyche. Such images communicate through their evocative power. They convey a latent meaning that is apprehended in a nonconceptual, even a subliminal, way. Symbols transform the horizons of a man's life, integrate his perception of reality, alter his scale of values, reorient his loyalties, attachments, and aspirations in a manner far exceeding the powers of abstract conceptual thought. Religious images, as used in the Bible and Christian preaching, focus our experience in a new way.[35]

Not only do religious symbols shape experience, but in order for a symbol to gain acceptance, "images must resonate with the experience of the faithful. . . . Religious experience, then, provides a vital key for the evaluation and interpretation of symbols."[36] Thus there is a dialectical relationship between symbols and religious experience — symbols shape religious experience, but they must also resonate with religious experience.

Dulles continues, "When an image is employed reflectively and critically to deepen one's theoretical understanding of a reality it becomes what is today called a 'model.'" A model can be an image, such as the church as temple, vine, or flock. But many models are more abstract than images, such as the church as institution, society, and community.[37] Models can help the theologian explain more adequately the mysteries of the Christian faith, and they can aid in the discovery of new insights. When a model becomes dominant, it becomes a "paradigm."[38]

A key issue here is how to discern and adjudicate between competing models. Dulles proposes that "we shall have to criticize each of the models in the light of all the others. We must refrain from so affirming any one of the models as to deny, even implicitly, what the others affirm."[39] Nonetheless, a primary model is inevitably adopted, and various aspects of all models are rejected. So how does the theologian, and the church, choose a primary model and discern what is lacking in the

35. Dulles, *Models of the Church*, p. 20.
36. Dulles, *Models of the Church*, p. 21.
37. Dulles, *Models of the Church*, p. 23.
38. Dulles, *Models of the Church*, p. 29.
39. Dulles, *Models of the Church*, p. 196.

various models? Here Dulles borrows from John Henry Newman's notion of ecclesial reception and argues that "theological verification depends upon a kind of corporate discernment of spirits" and "the inner enlightenment of the Holy Spirit."[40] In other places, he appeals to Newman's concept of the "illative sense" to "discern and access the force of multiple convergent signs that could not be turned into logical premises."[41]

In *Models of Revelation* Dulles develops a similar position, though Merrigan suggests that here Dulles's discussion of models "acquires a new level of sophistication."[42] Dulles describes a model as an "'organizing image' which gives a particular emphasis, enabling one to notice and interpret certain aspects of experience." Again, the use of models in theological reflection "illuminate[s] certain aspects of a reality too complex and exalted for human comprehension. . . . Revelation, as a divine mystery, surpasses all that theology can say about it."[43] This time Dulles proposes five models, "revelation as doctrine," "revelation as history," "revelation as inner experience," "revelation as dialectical presence," and "revelation as new awareness."

Although Dulles does not intend to propose a sixth, "symbolic" model of revelation, he does employ "symbolic mediation" as a "dialectical tool . . . to enrich and correct the existing models and to achieve a fruitful cross-fertilization."[44] Further, he proposes that revelation is a form of "symbolic communication" or "symbolic disclosure." Revelation, he states,

> never occurs in a purely interior experience or an unmediated encounter with God. It is always mediated through symbol — that is to say, through an externally perceived sign that works mysteriously on the human consciousness so as to suggest more than it can clearly describe or define. Revelatory symbols are those which express and mediate God's self-communication.

40. Dulles, *Models of the Church*, pp. 26, 198. See also Merrigan, "Models in the Theology of Avery Dulles," pp. 151-57.

41. Avery Dulles, *A Church to Believe In* (New York: Crossroad, 1982), p. 42.

42. Merrigan, "Models in the Theology of Avery Dulles," p. 142. Merrigan attributes this new level of sophistication to Dulles's use of Ian Barbour.

43. Dulles, *Models of Revelation*, pp. 31-32.

44. Dulles, *Models of Revelation*, p. 128.

Dulles continues to explain that "a symbol is a special type of sign to be distinguished from a mere indicator (such as the shadow on a sun dial) or a conventional cipher (such as a word or diagram). A symbol is a sign pregnant with a plentitude of meaning which is evoked rather than explicitly stated."[45] Dulles consistently argues that symbols have specific cognitive content and are not infinitely flexible — hence the "realism" of his symbolic realism — but he does believe that symbols impart greater truth than propositional statements. He argues that revelation as symbolic communication gives participatory rather than speculative knowledge, has a transforming effect, influences commitments and behaviors, and brings one to new realms of awareness beyond what is possible with discursive thought.[46]

Dulles's symbolic realist treatment of tradition has many similarities with his treatment of revelation. Before we observe these similarities, it is instructive to survey his concerns with traditional Catholic appeals to tradition apart from scripture and to consider his own position on tradition. In *Revelation and the Quest for Unity* Dulles argues that the conception of tradition as something "passed down from generation to generation by word of mouth, or at least by some channel other than the canonical Scriptures" was avoided at Vatican II and is problematic for at least three reasons:

> In the first place, it involves a *deus ex machina*. The existence of these alleged traditions cannot be verified by historical evidence, but is postulated for the sake of the argument. Secondly, the thesis is actually contrary to all probability. It is almost incredible that if the early Fathers had known all these facts they would have written so vaguely about the Sacraments, about Mary, etc. . . . Finally, even if we did grant the existence of such traditions in apostolic times, contrary to all appearances, it is most difficult to see how they could be utilized by the modern Church as doctrinal sources. A tradition cannot be a valid source unless its existence and contents can be established with some assurance.[47]

45. Dulles, *Models of Revelation*, p. 131.
46. Dulles, *Models of Revelation*, pp. 136-37.
47. Avery Dulles, *Revelation and the Quest for Unity* (Washington, DC: Corpus Books, 1968), p. 75.

For his own proposal, Dulles borrows Newman's theory of doctrinal development and argues,

> It is a firm tenet of Catholic theology that all revelation was given, at least in embryonic form, before the end of the apostolic age, but this completion of revelation does not reduce the Church to a state of inertness. On the contrary, the Church throughout the centuries has the task of meditating constantly in order to plumb the depths of the revelation already given. . . . Because we accept the principle of development, we are not compelled to seek, in the original fonts, fully formulated propositions matching every tenet of the contemporary Church. The relationship is rather that of a seed to a flower, or that of an acorn to an oak.[48]

Like Newman, Dulles argues that the Holy Spirit is the vital principle guiding the church as it develops its doctrines through history. Tradition, then, "is to be understood primarily, in an active sense, as the sacred process of handing on; secondarily, in an objective sense, as the complex of insights gained through the process."[49] When questions arise as to where and how authentic tradition can be identified, Dulles points to the institutional church, and in particular the hierarchical magisterium when infallibly judging.

In *The Reshaping of Catholicism* Dulles presents a similar view of tradition that seeks to avoid the two extremes of an "objectivist" view of tradition that is "excessively rigid, conceptual, and authoritarian," and a fluid "modernist" view that tends to divorce specific doctrinal content from divine revelation. Dulles appeals to Maurice Blondel as he presents a middle position on tradition that takes into account his symbolic realism.

> The common error of [the modernists and the dogmatists] was to identify knowledge too closely with conceptual thought and formal declaration. Since the content of the Christian faith is a mystery, it is never fully reducible to explicit statement; it always remains to some degree unspecifiable. . . .

48. Dulles, *Revelation and the Quest for Unity*, p. 76.
49. Dulles, *Revelation and the Quest for Unity*, p. 77.

Tradition, then, is the bearer of what is tacitly known and thus of what cannot be expressed in clear, unambiguous statements. . . . Tradition, for Blondel, is the church's continuing capacity to interpret, to discern, to penetrate. Far from being a confining or retrograde force, it is a power of development and expansion.[50]

Dulles gives other examples of tacit knowledge, such as knowing how to ride a bike, swim, type, or perform other skills that are hard to explain conceptually. Tradition, then, is the tacit knowledge of the church to discern and delve deeper into the symbolic communication made available in divine revelation, so as to continually present the Christian faith in ways that are appropriate for the contemporary context.

Dulles's mature position on symbolic realism is presented in *The Craft of Theology,* where he presents a "postcritical" theology that attempts to mediate between strong foundationalism and the liberal appeal to religious experience. Using George Lindbeck's famous typology, Dulles rejects "propositionalist-cognitive" and "experiential-expressive" views of doctrine and instead argues for a position similar to Lindbeck's "cultural-linguistic" view.[51] Dulles calls his position "ecclesial-transformative" and proposes that, in this view,

Revelation . . . is regarded as a real and efficacious self-communication of God, the transcendent mystery, to the believing community. The deeper insights of revelatory knowledge are imparted, not in the first instance through propositional discourse, but through participation in the life and worship of the Church.[52]

Dulles goes on to fill out this position on doctrine, arguing that from this perspective scripture and tradition

transmit the message [of revelation] less by explicit statement than by forming the imagination and affectivity of the Christian

50. Avery Dulles, *The Reshaping of Catholicism* (San Francisco: Harper & Row, 1988), pp. 77, 83-84.

51. Dulles, *The Craft of Theology,* pp. 17-18. See also George Lindbeck, *The Nature of Doctrine: Religion and Theology in a Postliberal Age* (Philadelphia: Westminster Press, 1984).

52. Dulles, *The Craft of Theology,* p. 18

community. The biblical and traditional symbols impart a tacit, lived awareness of the God who has manifested himself of old. By appropriating the symbols and "dwelling in" their meaning, new believers are able to apprehend reality, as it were, through the eyes of their predecessors in the faith.[53]

While Dulles maintains many of Lindbeck's insights, he differs from Lindbeck in that he focuses on the formative power of "biblical and traditional symbols" rather than narratives *per se*. Further, while Dulles acknowledges the lack of neutral ground when adjudicating rival religious or philosophical claims, he still proposes criteria for selecting a religious or philosophical position.[54] Therefore Dulles holds a weak foundationalist position in epistemology.

A second major theme in Dulles's writings that is significant for his position on papal infallibility is his ecclesiology. Obviously, Dulles's ecclesiology and symbolic realism are interconnected. In the first edition of *Models of the Church,* Dulles proposes that "the church as sacrament" is an especially attractive model because of its ability to integrate the strengths of the other models.[55] A sacramental view of the church also occurs throughout the documents of Vatican II. It is worth observing that the original proponents of this model, such as Karl Rahner, maintain a basic philosophical stance that is similar to Dulles's symbolic realism. In Dulles's presentation of the church as sacrament, the terms "sacrament," and especially "sign," could be replaced with Dulles's preferred notion "symbol."[56]

---

53. Dulles, *The Craft of Theology,* pp. 24-25.

54. Dulles, *The Craft of Theology,* pp. 60-61. Dulles states that, first, we eliminate "what is manifestly illusory and unhelpful." Next, we "eliminate as personally unacceptable those creeds which, in our estimation, would fail to enhance the quality of our lives." And finally, "the chief criterion for a viable religious faith is its ability, or apparent ability, to satisfy those hungers of the human spirit which cannot be satisfied apart from faith."

55. Dulles, *Models of the Church,* pp. 197-98.

56. This observation is interesting in light of Dulles's insistence that he is not proposing a new model or choosing between the models, but is simply mediating between the existing models. Yet, in his ecclesiology, Dulles is attracted to a sacramental model that has a definite leaning toward symbolic realism, and in his work on revelation he suggests that revelation has a strong symbolic character.

To understand the sacramental model of the church, it is first necessary to define a sacrament. Dulles states,

> A sacrament is, in the first place, a sign of grace. A sign could be a mere pointer to something that is absent, but a sacrament is a "full sign," a sign of something really present. . . . Beyond this, a sacrament is an efficacious sign; the sign itself produces or intensifies that of which it is a sign. Thanks to the sign, the reality signified achieves an existential depth; it emerges into solid, tangible existence.[57]

The church, while it confers the sacraments, can also be viewed as having a sacramental nature and described as a sacrament. Dulles states, "The Church therefore is in the first instance a sign. It must signify in a historically tangible form the redeeming grace of Christ." The institutional church is a visible sign that points to and makes present the grace of Christ. Again, the church as sacrament is one of five models that Dulles presents, but he does find it to be useful for blending the strengths of the other models. Further, in *Models of Revelation* Dulles points to the idea of the church as sacrament to support his proposal of revelation as symbolic communication.[58]

However, one model of the church that Dulles clearly rejects as primary is the church as institution.[59] In rejecting this model, Dulles emphasizes that he is rejecting "institutionalism," but not the church as an institution. Dulles believes this view of the church, which includes a strong hierarchical conception of authority, reached its climax during the second half of the nineteenth century, particularly at Vatican I.[60] Dulles also associates the institutional model with the "regressive method" in theology, which he describes as "utilizing the latest teaching of the magisterium as an indication of what must have been present from the beginning, since the Church at this period disclaimed any power of innovation in its teaching of revelation."[61]

In rejecting the institutional model of the church, Dulles follows the

---

57. Dulles, *Models of the Church*, p. 66.
58. Dulles, *Models of Revelation*, pp. 218-22.
59. Dulles, *Models of the Church*, p. 198.
60. Dulles, *Models of the Church*, p. 36.
61. Dulles, *Models of the Church*, p. 40.

direction of Vatican II, which sought to present a more collegial view of the church. The theme of collegiality is stressed in Dulles's presentation of the church as a "community of disciples." This model, which Dulles proposes as a "bridge model" that integrates the strengths of the other models, first appeared in *A Church to Believe In* and was later added to the expanded edition of *Models of the Church.* While the model of the church as sacrament complements Dulles's symbolic realism, the model of the church as community of disciples corresponds to a major concern in Dulles's ecclesiology: the relationship between the hierarchical magisterium and theologians.

While the hierarchical magisterium and theologians are often viewed as being in conflict with one another, Dulles questions this characterization and argues that the church, as the whole people of God, needs both. This is especially the case since, as was stressed at Vatican II, the teaching of the church does not simply flow from the magisterium down, but involves the whole people of God. Since God is the only absolute authority, ecclesial authorities are secondary and are subject to revision by other ecclesial authorities. Examples of authorities in the church, which Dulles suggests function as mutual checks and balances, include the hierarchical magisterium, scholars, charismatic leaders, and the consensus of the entire church.[62]

In *A Church to Believe In* Dulles speaks of two magisteria: an ecclesiastical magisterium that is based on juridical authority, and a teaching magisterium that depends on scholarly investigation. The idea that there is more than one magisterium is itself debated, and Dulles himself argues that the term "magisterium" as used in the current sense only goes back to the nineteenth century.[63] Still, Dulles states,

> The Church, in my opinion, needs two kinds of teacher — the official teacher, whose task is to establish the official doctrine of the Church, and the theologian, whose function is to investigate questions about faith with the tools of critical scholarship. These two classes . . . are inseparably united, reciprocally dependent, but really and irreducibly distinct.[64]

---

62. Dulles, *Survival of Dogma*, p. 84, chap. 6. Avery Dulles, *The Resilient Church* (Garden City, NY: Doubleday & Co., 1977), p. 99.

63. Dulles, *A Church to Believe In*, pp. 103, 118.

64. Dulles, *A Church to Believe In*, p. 118.

Later, he affirms "one may say that the functional specialty of the ecclesiastical magisterium is judgment; that of the theologian is understanding."[65] It should be noted that Dulles's contention for multiple authorities coincides well with his symbolic realist view of the Christian faith. Since the Christian faith is ultimately a mystery that transcends any single articulation of it, multiple authorities are needed to mine the riches of the faith and avoid reductionistic extremes.

Papal Infallibility

With this introduction to Dulles's thought, we now turn to his treatment of papal infallibility. Early on Dulles was aware of the two primary problems for conceiving the pope as an infallible belief-producing mechanism, the problems of identifying and interpreting infallible doctrines. When Dulles addresses whether a Catholic can dissent from the church's official teaching, he notes that it is not sufficient to simply distinguish fallible and infallible doctrines and insist a Catholic cannot dissent from the latter. He states,

> In the first place, there is no agreed list of irreformable decrees, and therefore the distinction does not really tell us what may, and what may not, be questioned. Secondly, the interpretation of admittedly dogmatic statements is not always clear, and thus what one person regards as the very core of the definition will seem to another to be an excessively narrow interpretation of it. Thirdly, many dogmas are as great a stumbling block to the contemporary believer as the nondogmatic statements.[66]

The problematic dogmas Dulles refers to include the Marian dogmas, transubstantiation, and papal infallibility itself. He goes on to say that "there are so few statements of unquestionably dogmatic status, that to say that they alone constitute the binding content of faith would excessively narrow down the import of Christianity."[67] In other places, Dulles

---

65. Dulles, *A Church to Believe In*, p. 125.
66. Dulles, *Spirit, Faith, and Church*, p. 53. See also *Survival of Dogma*, pp. 146-47.
67. Dulles, *Spirit, Faith, and Church*, p. 54.

pushes the problem of interpretation further and suggests that the Christian may legitimately question such key beliefs as the doctrine of the Trinity, incarnation, redemption, and resurrection when such beliefs "seem to mean something incredible." In such cases "the Christian is within his rights in withholding an assent. At best his act of faith will have to take the form of believing that the Church will be able to explain the proposition in a coherent manner."[68]

One reason scripture and dogmatic statements are so difficult to interpret is because of the symbolic nature of revelation and the need to distinguish "the truth of revelation" from "time-bound formulations."[69] In *Spirit, Faith, and Church* Dulles offers several criteria to help distinguish divine revelation from its historical casing. First, "heed should be paid to variations in literary conventions." Doctrinal statements should be subject to the same type of form criticism that biblical scholars use when interpreting scripture. For example, he believes anathemas in doctrinal statements are best understood as hyperbole and "rhetorical superlatives." Second, "An antiquated worldview, presupposed but not taught in an earlier doctrinal formulation, should not be imposed as binding doctrine." Here he goes so far as to suggest, "It is hard to predict what may happen to the currently accepted ideas of creation, inspiration, miracle, resurrection, etc. We must be prepared for revisions insofar as the traditional notions are to some extent bound up with an obsolete cosmology." Third, "Technical terms should be interpreted in terms of the systematic framework presupposed by those who used them." One example he offers is the term "transubstantiation." Fourth, "In the interpretation of Biblical and theological terms, cognizance should be taken of connotation as well as denotation." Rather than offer exact definitions for biblical and theological terms, Dulles suggests that equivalent terms and ideas be sought that better communicate to contemporary persons. He states,

> In order to find suitable equivalents, one would probably have to come at the whole problem of sin, salvation, and new life in God from a new direction. The Biblical and medieval terms are so im-

68. Dulles, *Survival of Dogma*, p. 147.
69. Dulles, *Spirit, Faith, and Church*, p. 57. See also *Survival of Dogma*, p. 197; *The Resilient Church*, p. 53; and *A Church to Believe In*, p. 142.

bedded in the context of patriarchal and feudal forms of life that they have become almost unserviceable for popular usage.

Fifth, "No doctrinal decision of the past directly solves a question that was not asked at the time." And finally, "In Holy Scripture and in authoritative doctrinal statements, one should be alert for signs of social pathology and ideology."[70]

It would seem that the "historical situationism" Dulles presents would exclude the very possibility of doctrinal infallibility. While some Catholic theologians, such as Hans Küng, maintain this, Dulles believes this is not necessarily the case so long as one holds a moderate understanding of infallibility. Dulles states,

> Infallibility does not demand that a given formulation of the truth be always and everywhere imposed, but only that it be not directly contradicted. It means that when the Church, through its highest teaching organs, defines a truth pertaining to revelation, divine providence, working through a multiplicity of channels, will preserve the Church from error. But it may well be necessary, as generations pass, to reinterpret the defined dogma in accordance with the presuppositions, thought categories, concerns, and vocabulary of a later age.[71]

Dulles's proposal for the infallibility and reformability of doctrines needs careful consideration.

First, Dulles offers a negative definition of infallibility. Instead of infallibility ensuring that the church will speak truly when meeting certain conditions, infallibility ensures that the church will be preserved from error. While "speaking truly" and "being preserved from error" could mean the same thing, Dulles intends something like the traditional understanding of indefectibility by the latter. Whenever the church makes a doctrinal decision, infallibility ensures that the church will not stray so far as to lose the truth of the gospel. When speaking of the "certain measure of infallibility" that the church does possess, Dulles states,

---

70. Dulles, *Spirit, Faith, and Church*, pp. 57-64.
71. Dulles, *The Resilient Church*, pp. 53-54.

According to the Gospels, Christ promised that the Church would last till the end of time and that the powers of death would never triumph over it; he said he would be with his apostles, or their successors, for all the centuries to come. If the Church lost sight of the essential content of God's revelation in Christ and definitely committed itself to a false understanding of the gospel, the world would be in effect deprived of the benefits of Christ's coming.[72]

In another place he affirms, "The perseverance of the Church in the truth of the gospel gives it a certain qualified infallibility, without necessarily guaranteeing every proposition set forth by the teaching authorities, even in their most solemn acts."[73] Dulles suggests that if papal infallibility were defined today, the word "infallibility" would likely not be used.

While Dulles's definition of infallibility sounds much like indefectibility, he still distinguishes the two. According to Dulles, indefectibility "means the impossibility of ceasing to exist, or, in other words, antecedently guaranteed continuation in being." However, surely a church that exists throughout time, but has lost the truth of the gospel, is no church at all. Dulles recognizes this problem and suggests "indefectibility would seem to involve a certain infallibility in belief and in preaching. . . . In preserving the Church as Church, God preserves it in the truth of the gospel."[74] So while Dulles distinguishes infallibility and indefectibility, his understanding of the two terms requires that they be interrelated.

Second, Dulles's historical situationism allows all doctrines to be reformulated, even doctrines that have been infallibly proclaimed. Dulles states,

In principle, every dogmatic statement is subject to reformulation. At times it may be sufficient to reclothe the old concepts in new words that, for all practical purposes, have the same meanings. But in other cases the consecrated formula will reflect an in-

---

72. Dulles, *The Survival of Dogma*, p. 145. See also p. 197.
73. Dulles, *Models of the Church*, p. 182.
74. Avery Dulles, "Infallibility: The Terminology," in *Teaching Authority and Infallibility in the Church: Lutherans and Catholics in Dialogue VI*, ed. Paul C. Empie, T. Austin Murphy, and Joseph A. Burgess (Minneapolis: Augsburg, 1978), p. 74.

adequate understanding. In order to bring out the deeper and divinely intended meaning, which alone is inseparable from faith, it may be necessary to discard the human concepts as well as the words of those who first framed the dogma. When men acquire new cultural conditioning and mental horizons, they have to reconceptualize their dogmas from their present point of view.[75]

In order to maintain the truth of revelation through time, doctrines may need to be recast in new words and even new concepts. Dulles also suggests that a "qualified negation" of an infallible doctrine could lead to further development.[76] However, Dulles's proposal for the reformability of doctrines would appear to run into numerous problems. For instance, does not his position directly contradict *Pastor Aeternus,* which states that infallible papal definitions are irreformable? Dulles argues that,

> In the context, the point of the definition is evidently not to affirm the fact of irreformability, but rather to identify its source — namely, the infallibility of the pope. Read against the background of the Gallican "Four Articles" of 1682, from which the term comes, "irreformable" may be taken to mean "not subject to review by any higher authority."[77]

Therefore, *Pastor Aeternus* affirms that the pope is the supreme teaching authority in the church, although papal definitions may need to be reformulated through time. But does this not lead to another problem, namely, doctrinal relativism? Here Dulles appeals to the infallibility of the Catholic Church so that, in any formulation of a given doctrine, the church will not leave the truth of the gospel and fall into heresy.[78]

Like those who held a moderate position at Vatican I, Dulles believes infallible definitions are "few and far between."[79] However, these few doctrines still pose significant challenges for ecumenical dialogue. Dulles agrees that papal infallibility and the two Marian dogmas have

---

75. Dulles, *The Survival of Dogma,* pp. 161-62.
76. Dulles, *The Survival of Dogma,* p. 198.
77. Dulles, *The Survival of Dogma,* p. 186.
78. Dulles, *The Survival of Dogma,* p. 190.
79. Dulles, *The Survival of Dogma,* p. 197.

been infallibly defined, but these doctrines are among the most contro-versial in ecumenism. To address this problem, Dulles notes that a "hi-erarchy of truths" has been recognized by the Catholic Church since the decree on ecumenism at Vatican II. While there is disagreement as to which truths are primary and which are secondary, Dulles suggests, "the primary or central truths are those that express the central mystery of God's saving work in Jesus Christ — the work that forms the princi-pal theme of the Christian kerygma as set forth in the New Testament and in the historic creeds." Other secondary truths, which are derived from the central message of the gospel, are beneficial for Christian liv-ing and should not be discarded. Nonetheless, "the secondary charac-ter of certain doctrines permits a more relaxed attitude toward them."[80] A hierarchy of truths allows papal infallibility and the Marian dogmas to be seen as secondary doctrines of the church that, though true, are not necessarily essential for the Christian faith and reconcilia-tion with other Christian groups.

Dulles has written two key articles on papal infallibility that de-serve special consideration. Both of these articles deal with papal in-fallibility as an ecumenical issue, and both explore numerous options and possibilities for the future of the papacy. In the first article, "To-ward a Renewed Papacy," Dulles observes that revisioning the papacy is a "delicate operation" in light of the teaching of Vatican I.[81] This is especially the case because Vatican I "laid such heavy emphasis on the irreformability of the divinely given structures and teachings of the Church." However, Dulles argues that dogmatic statements, includ-ing infallible ones, are subject to "hermeneutical treatment" whereby doctrines can be "reinterpreted so as to bridge the gap between the era when they were written — with its own concerns, presuppositions, conceptuality, and literary and linguistic conventions — and the inter-preter's own era, in which all of these variables will have changed." Given the reformability of all doctrine, Dulles wants "to explore the need and possibility of reinterpreting three of the key assertions of Vatican I: the divine institution of the papal office, the pope's primacy

---

80. Dulles, *The Resilient Church*, p. 56.

81. In *The Resilient Church*, pp. 113-31. This article is a revision of Avery Dulles, "Papal Authority in Roman Catholicism," in *A Pope for All Christians: An Inquiry into the Role of Peter in the Modern Church*, ed. Peter J. McCord (New York: Paulist Press, 1976), pp. 48-70.

of jurisdiction, and his infallibility."[82] We will examine each of these in turn.

According to traditional Catholic teaching, the papacy was divinely instituted by Christ and can be traced back to the apostles. It should be recalled that Dulles was attracted to this teaching as a young convert. Here, however, Dulles observes that this traditional teaching faces substantial historical difficulties. Clearly the papacy is a product of historical development, though Catholics can argue that this development was divinely intended. But if the papacy is a product of development, "this leaves open the question of a possible further development that would leave the papacy behind."[83] Instead of the divine institution of the papal office, Dulles believes a more helpful notion is that of a "Petrine function" or "Petrine ministry." Dulles suggests that,

> many New Testament passages attribute to Peter a particular responsibility for the mission and unity of the Church as a whole. This function, it is argued, is permanently necessary, for if no one is charged with the universal direction of the Church, fragmentation and anarchy cannot be avoided — a consequence to which history bears abundant witness. In theory, the Petrine function could be performed either by a single individual presiding over the whole Church or by some kind of committee, board, synod, or parliament — possibly with a "division of powers" into judicial, legislative, administrative, and the like.[84]

Such a view of the "Petrine ministry" would appear to conflict with the rejection of Gallicanism at Vatican I. But Dulles argues,

> Vatican I, which situated supreme authority in the pope, left some uncertainty regarding the relations between the papacy, the universal episcopate, and ecumenical councils (which are not necessarily mere meetings of bishops). Since this uncertainty was not fully cleared up by Vatican II, the question of the supreme direc-

---

82. Dulles, *The Resilient Church*, pp. 115-16.
83. Dulles, *The Resilient Church*, p. 118.
84. Dulles, *The Resilient Church*, pp. 118-19.

tive power in the Church still requires further discussion within the Roman Catholic communion.[85]

In fact, Dulles argues that the term "papacy" itself is unclear. While it presently refers to the pope himself, he sees no reason why, in the future, it could not refer to a constitutional form of government instead. Further, the papacy is not necessarily connected to the bishop of Rome. The papacy could be held by the bishop of another city, or could rotate among sees. Dulles suggests that "the essential would seem to be that the Petrine function should be institutionalized in some way so that there is in the government of the universal Church an effective sign and instrument of unity."[86] So while Dulles rejects the idea of the papal office as a divine institution, he embraces a "Petrine ministry" that could be flexibly understood to meet the challenges and demands of the universal church through history.

In addition to the issue of divine institution, Vatican I teaches that the pope has a primacy of jurisdiction, in addition to a primacy of honor, that is "universal, ordinary, immediate, truly episcopal, supreme, and full." This notion of jurisdiction, which comes from the Roman legal tradition, corresponds to a highly institutional understanding of the church. Dulles, though, reminds us that leadership in the church is never about political power, but service and spiritual influence. Further, the collegial vision of the Catholic Church that appears at Vatican II leads to a less legalistic and institutional understanding of papal primacy. Dulles explains, "For one member of a college to exercise jurisdiction, in a political sense, over all others would seem to destroy the fundamental equality that is the very basis of collegial relationships."[87] While the papacy, however understood, would inevitably involve primacy, Dulles maintains that such primacy is best understood in collegial and ministerial terms.

Next Dulles addresses papal infallibility, which, in Dulles's opinion, is "the most offensive of all the definitions of Vatican I." Papal infallibility is problematic because of the notion that "the truth of revelation could be pinned down in a dogmatic formula, binding on all

85. Dulles, *The Resilient Church*, p. 119.
86. Dulles, *The Resilient Church*, p. 120.
87. Dulles, *The Resilient Church*, p. 124.

future generations," and because these statements "enjoy such infallibility 'by themselves and not by the consent of the Church.'"[88] Dulles believes that the main culprit here is the cultural and philosophical transitions that have occurred since Vatican I. During the council, all the bishops agreed that the supreme teaching authority in the church must be infallible. The primary question, then, was where this infallibility resides, and the council answered that the pope, under certain conditions, enjoys the same infallibility Christ gave the church. But Dulles suggests that the council "leaves open the tremendous question: What kind and measure of infallibility did Christ choose to confer upon his Church?"[89]

Dulles believes that *Pastor Aeternus* "demands a sophisticated interpretation, according to the methods of modern hermeneutics." While doctrinal statements are subject to the same limitations present in all human communication, Dulles argues that doctrinal statements "contain an element of special obscurity" since they touch on the transcendent and divine. Therefore all the doctrines of the church, including papal infallibility, "are subject to ongoing reinterpretation in the Church."[90]

Regarding the *ex sese* clause, Dulles argues that Vatican I was rejecting Gallicanism, which according to Manning and others challenged the independence of the church through the influence of national governments. Vatican I, though, did not intend to separate the pope from the church, and Vatican II affirms this interpretation by stressing that the pope cannot teach anything in opposition to the faith of the church or the teaching of the bishops. In fact, Dulles argues, "If in a given instance the assent of the Church were evidently not forthcoming, this could be interpreted as a signal that the pope had perhaps exceeded his competence and that some necessary condition for an infallible act had not been fulfilled." Further, Dulles suggests that *Pastor Aeternus* does not necessarily exempt a pope from falling into heresy. He states,

> In order to teach infallibly the pope must align himself with the faith of the whole Church — a faith already objectified in Scripture

88. Dulles, *The Resilient Church*, p. 124.
89. Dulles, *The Resilient Church*, p. 124.
90. Dulles, *The Resilient Church*, p. 125.

and in the documents of tradition. If he were to separate himself from this faith, which lives on in the body of the faithful, the pope could well become a heretic or, to use the harsh term of some reformers, an Antichrist.[91]

Like Newman and other moderates, Dulles believes the inopportunists at Vatican I succeeded in adding many restrictions to the text of *Pastor Aeternus,* so that the "celebrated definition of papal infallibility really commits one to very little." Dulles concludes,

Minimalistically, or even strictly, interpreted, [papal infallibility] is hardly more than an emphatic assertion that the pope's primacy, as previously set forth in the first three chapters of *Pastor aeternus,* extends also to his teaching power. He is not only the first pastor but also the first teacher in the Church. In view of his special responsibility for the unity of the whole Church in the faith of the apostles, it is antecedently credible that in him the infallibility of the whole Church may come to expression.[92]

Therefore, the doctrine of papal infallibility simply emphasizes papal primacy in teaching. However, Dulles still views an infallible papacy as a necessary element of an infallible church, and without infallibility, the church cannot retain unity or remain in the truth of the gospel.

Dulles's view of papal infallibility is given further treatment in a second key article entitled "Moderate Infallibilism: An Ecumenical Approach."[93] Here Dulles explicitly identifies his position as "moderate infallibilism" and contrasts this position with "absolutistic infallibilism" and "fallibilism," which correspond to our categories "maximal infallibility" and "minimal infallibility" respectively.[94] According to Dulles, the moderate position is characterized by two traits:

91. Dulles, *The Resilient Church,* p. 125.
92. Dulles, *The Resilient Church,* p. 127.
93. In *A Church to Believe In,* pp. 133-48. This article is a revision of Avery Dulles, "Moderate Infallibilism," in *Teaching Authority and Infalliblity in the Church: Lutherans and Catholics in Dialogue VI,* pp. 81-100.
94. Dulles, *A Church to Believe In,* p. 133. Dulles borrows these terms from George Lindbeck, *Infallibility* (Milwaukee: Marquette University Press, 1972).

In the first place, it affirms that the pope is infallible or at least that he has on certain occasions a charism that may not too deceptively be called infallibility. Second, the position asserts that papal infallibility, being limited, is subject to inherent conditions which provide critical principles for assessing the force and meaning of allegedly infallible statements.[95]

While Dulles believes this position holds great promise for ecumenical dialogue, he is aware that many Christians outside the Catholic tradition will still find the doctrine problematic. Nonetheless, he believes the doctrine is a plausible faith claim for Christians who hold the following beliefs:

1. God provides for the Church effective means by which it may and will in fact remain in the truth of the gospel till the end of time.

2. Among these means are not only the canonical Scriptures but also . . . the pastoral office. Without such a pastoral office the Christian community would not be adequately protected against corruptions of the gospel.

3. The pastoral office is exercised for the universal Church by the bearer of the Petrine office (which means, for Catholics, by the pope). . . . It is therefore reasonable to suppose that the pope is equipped by God with a special charism . . . for correctly interpreting the gospel to the universal Church. . . .

4. In order that the papacy may adequately discharge its function of preserving unity in the faith and exposing dangerous errors, the papal charism must include the power to assert the truth of the gospel and to condemn contrary errors in a decisive manner. Authoritative pronouncements from the Petrine office that are seriously binding on all the faithful must have adequately certified truth, for there could be no obligation to believe what could probably be error.[96]

However, the moderate position insists that papal infallibility has substantial limits. In addition to the limitations inherent in all human

95. Dulles, *A Church to Believe In,* p. 134.
96. Dulles, *A Church to Believe In,* p. 135.

communication, Dulles discusses other limitations that were mentioned in debates on the council floor and in *Pastor Aeternus* itself. For instance, an infallible definition must be a free, rational act of the pope and not involve any form of coercion or mental illness. Further, an infallible definition must meet the conditions found in *Pastor Aeternus,* which Dulles lists as four. First, "The pope must be speaking not as a private person but as a public person and more specifically in his capacity as 'supreme pastor and teacher of all Christians.'" Second, the pope "must appeal to his supreme apostolic authority, i.e., that which pertains to him as successor of Peter." Third, the pope "must be teaching within the sphere of 'faith and morals.'" While the phrase "faith and morals" is not completely clear, Dulles believes it is probably a general term for matters of doctrine as opposed to matters of discipline and polity. At the same time, Dulles notes that infallibility likely extends beyond revealed doctrines, that is, the primary object of infallibility, to include "doctrines necessary to maintain, preach, or defend the content of revelation," that is, the secondary object of infallibility. And fourth, "The pope must be proposing the doctrine as something to be held by the whole Church, that is to say, as a doctrine having universal obligatory force."[97]

In addition to these conditions, Dulles lists four other properties of infallible statements that have widespread support. First, infallible definitions must agree with scripture and tradition. This condition is based on the nature of the charism of infallibility, as it does not properly reveal new doctrines to the pope but rather allows the pope to guard and interpret the divine revelation already given. Second, the infallible definition must agree with the present faith of the church. While the consent of the church is not the source of the irreformability of infallible doctrines, Dulles observes that Vatican I "did not deny that the consent of the church will be present or even that such consent is necessary as a condition for recognizing an authentic exercise of the infallible magisterium." Dulles's observation is supported by the interpretation of papal infallibility found in *Lumen Gentium* 25 from Vatican II, which states, "The assent of the church, however, can never fail to be given to these definitions on account of the activity of the same Holy Spirit, by which the whole flock of Christ is preserved in the unity of faith and

97. Dulles, *A Church to Believe In*, pp. 136-38.

makes progress."[98] Third, infallible definitions will agree with the teaching of the universal episcopate. Concerning this point, Dulles states,

> Because the assistance of the Holy Spirit is promised both to the pope and to the bishops as a corporate body, it seems clear that they would not fail to assent to any valid papal definition of the faith. If the bishops with moral unanimity held the contrary, one would be put on notice that the conditions for a genuinely infallible act on the part of the pope might not have been fulfilled.[99]

Fourth, the definition should follow only after sufficient theological investigation. The need for careful investigation is again related to the nature of the pope's charism: new doctrines are not revealed to the pope, but the pope is aided by the Holy Spirit in guarding and interpreting the revelation already given. But further complications can arise here. For example, Dulles asks, "What if it were evident that in a given case the pope did not have access to certain essential data or did not take the requisite measures to ascertain what was in Scripture or tradition?" While some Catholic theologians appeal to divine providence to guide the pope in such circumstances, Dulles finds this position unsatisfactory and maintains that sufficient theological investigation should be a condition of infallibility.[100]

Next, Dulles turns to *Mysterium Ecclesiae* to examine two limiting factors of infallible definitions that correspond well to his own theological emphases: "the transcendence of divine revelation and the historicity of human formulations." Concerning divine revelation, Dulles presents a position similar to the "dialectical presence" model found in *Models of Revelation*. He writes,

> It must be recognized that the categories used in ecclesiastical definitions are human and that the definitions therefore fall short of adequately expressing the content of revelation itself.

98. *Lumen Gentium,* in Jaroslav Pelikan and Valerie Hotchkiss, eds., *Creeds and Confessions of Faith in the Christian Tradition,* vol. 3 (New Haven: Yale University Press, 2003), p. 358.

99. Dulles, *A Church to Believe In,* p. 140.

100. Dulles, *A Church to Believe In,* pp. 138-42.

Dogmas must be seen as human formulations of the Word of God, formulations not undialectically identified with the revelation they transmit.[101]

Dulles gives significant attention to the historicity of the formulation of papal infallibility at Vatican I and asks a number of exploratory questions regarding *Pastor Aeternus*. He organizes these questions around four areas found in *Mysterium Ecclesiae:* how *Pastor Aeternus* may have been influenced by

the presuppositions (i.e., the "context of faith or human knowledge"), the concerns (i.e., "the intention of solving certain questions"), the thought categories (i.e., "the changeable conceptions of the given epoch"), and the available vocabulary (i.e., the "expressive power of the language used at a certain point of time").[102]

Regarding the presuppositions of Vatican I, Dulles asks the following questions. First, "Did Vatican I assume, in its statements on infallibility, that revelation could be directly and adequately embodied in human propositions?" Second, "Did Vatican I assume that every doctrine deemed requisite for an adequate profession of faith at one time must always remain requisite?" Third, "Did Vatican I assume that the Christian Church was fully and adequately present in Roman Catholicism?" Fourth, "Did Vatican I assume too easily that faith is a collection of divinely guaranteed propositions, so that a mistake about these would involve the destruction of faith itself?" And fifth, "Did Vatican I assume too rapidly that the faithful were abjectly dependent for the content of their faith on the authoritative teaching of the pope, so that if he erred they would all be led inevitably into the same errors?"[103]

Regarding the concerns of Vatican I, Dulles believes Gallicanism was the primary issue dealt with at the council. Therefore, the council was more concerned about the locus of supreme teaching authority than the question of infallibility itself. If this is the case, Dulles asks if one could still accept the teaching of Vatican I "if one accepted the su-

101. Dulles, *A Church to Believe In*, pp. 142-43.
102. Dulles, *A Church to Believe In*, p. 143.
103. Dulles, *A Church to Believe In*, pp. 143-44.

preme teaching authority of the pope, quite independently of any formal or juridical approval by the bishops, but denied that this teaching power could properly be called infallible." Dulles believes that this is the position of Hans Küng. Dulles, though, maintains,

> I would not myself go so far as to say that one could be faithful to Vatican I while denying that the pope has any kind of infallibility under any circumstances, but I do think that the vagueness of the Council gives very large scope for interpreting what is really involved when "infallibility" is referred to.[104]

Regarding the thought categories and vocabulary used at Vatican I, Dulles suggests that terms like *ex cathedra,* "irreformable," "definition," and "infallibility" reflect a strong authoritarian mentality that emphasizes juridical and metaphysical categories. Today these terms strike readers differently than they would have a century ago. To deal with the problem of evolving terminology and concepts, Dulles turns to the two options offered in *Mysterium Ecclesiae.* Dulles explains,

> In some cases theologians of a later generation continue to use the same terms but make "suitable expository and explanatory additions" to clarify what has become obsolete. In other cases the formulas themselves give way to new expressions which convey more clearly to a new generation what the older expressions really intended.

Thus a term like "infallibility" may "eventually be rejected as being excessively burdened with the conceptuality and polemics of a bygone era." However, Dulles follows the less radical option and believes the term should be retained, but carefully clarified. He states, "In the interests of the historical continuity and the identity of the Roman Catholic communion, I believe that the key terms of Vatican I should be salvaged if possible."[105]

Dulles concludes by examining the obligation of Catholics to hold papal infallibility and the two Marian dogmas that have been defined by

---

104. Dulles, *A Church to Believe In,* p. 145.
105. Dulles, *A Church to Believe In,* pp. 145-46.

the pope. He observes that many practicing Catholics, especially younger ones, have substantial misgivings about these three doctrines. While Dulles believes that these three doctrines are true and meaningful when properly interpreted, he holds that they are "too unclear in their meaning and too peripheral in importance to be of decisive moment for good standing in the Church." Appealing to the notion of a "hierarchy of truths," Dulles argues that papal infallibility in particular is distanced from the core of the gospel since it deals with the guarding of divine revelation rather that the substance of revelation. Further, Dulles is an advocate of lifting the anathemas that appear at the end of these definitions. His tolerance, though, should not be interpreted as a rejection of the doctrines, especially papal infallibility. He clearly states,

> I am convinced that the occupants of the papal office do enjoy special assistance from the Holy Spirit and the privileged means of access to the tradition of the whole Catholic communion of churches. Hence I acknowledge that the infallibility of the universal Church and of the worldwide body of pastors comes to expression in a singular way in the definitive teaching of the Roman pontiffs. I believe that, prudently and moderately interpreted, the definition of *Pastor aeternus,* chapter IV, should be accepted.[106]

Dulles strongly endorses papal infallibility, properly interpreted.

Analysis

In many ways, the concerns driving Dulles are the same concerns driving this work. As a young man, Dulles was rightly leery of Protestant churches that lacked strong doctrinal commitments, and as a mature theologian he continues to point out problems with a simple *sola scriptura* position. At the same time, he believes that acceptance of all Catholic doctrines, especially papal infallibility and the Marian dogmas, is not necessary for ecumenical union. For Dulles, ecumenical unity should be based on foundational Christian beliefs set forth "in

106. Dulles, *A Church to Believe In,* pp. 147-48.

the New Testament and in the historical creeds." So Dulles would likely affirm the proposal of this work that ecumenical unity should be centered on the theism found in the canonical heritage of the undivided church.

While Dulles takes epistemological reflection seriously, his primary concern is ontology and soteriology. Dulles is more interested in Christians understanding the core of the gospel and being transformed by the Spirit of God than reaching epistemic certainty on all matters of doctrine. When Dulles does take up epistemological issues, his weak foundationalism has many similarities to the position argued for here. Dulles has dedicated much of his life to ecumenical dialogue, and he desires to present a vision of Catholicism that is true to its own heritage, intellectually honest, and ecumenically fruitful.

However, Dulles is the consummate "moderate's moderate."[107] While his moderate disposition can be a great strength for theological reflection, it can also be a great weakness. Dulles has the tendency to appreciate and adopt conflicting theological and philosophical positions. The problem with this is it blurs substantial conceptual issues and never allows him to develop fresh proposals that aid in overcoming conflict. At the same time, he opens himself up to positions that can lead to conclusions he clearly wants to avoid. Dulles's use of symbolic realism for theological reflection brings more confusion than clarification.

Take for example Dulles's symbolic realist approach to divine revelation and doctrine. Dulles rejects an extreme, caricatured version of revelation and doctrine as propositional, and yet he still retains a propositional understanding of revelation and doctrine in his notion of "symbolic communication." With a strong emphasis on the mystery and transcendence of God, Dulles argues that revelation and doctrine are necessarily mediated through symbol, and such symbols give more profound truth, and bring about greater transformation, than mere propositions. Further, the symbolic nature of revelation and doctrine explains the need for multiple, conflicting models in theological reflection, and it justifies Dulles's adoption of different models to support his various concerns. When Dulles wants to counter liberals, he appeals to the propositional nature of revelation and doctrine. When he wants

---

107. I first heard this depiction of Dulles from Bruce Marshall. Whether he remembers it or not, I find the phrase to be quite descriptive.

to counter conservatives, he appeals to revelation and doctrine as symbolic or dialectical communication that can never be fully grasped in propositional statements.

However, in an evaluation of Dulles's theology of revelation, Ross Shecterle correctly, though disapprovingly, suggests, "Dulles occasionally slips into a 'cognitive-propositional' approach, one which perceives symbols as subordinate to propositional speech."[108] The reason this is the case is because revelation must include, though not necessarily be limited to, propositions if it is to communicate actual knowledge of God.[109] While Dulles argues that revelation is fundamentally expressed in symbols, not propositions, the opposite is actually the case. Revelation includes propositional statements that can make use of symbols. Imagine, for instance, that the symbol of the cross was revealed to us apart from any propositional communication. It would be impossible to know exactly what this symbol meant if we were not given a propositional account of the cross. Other symbols that Dulles employs, such as the church as a vine or sacrament, cannot even be communicated without the use of propositions. A more adequate approach to revelation, then, would view symbolic language as a type of propositional speech. Propositional speech can make use of symbols, and through these symbols can communicate information that is provocative and transformative.

Viewing symbolic language as a form of propositional speech is important for at least two reasons. First, it points us to a much richer view of propositions than the dry and nearly unrecognizable picture that is often painted by critics of propositions. Propositions can be used to make plain, factual statements, but they can also be used to paint pictures through symbols, similes, metaphors, and analogies. Further, propositions can be used to tell stories that capture the imagination. It is no wonder that those who defend the propositional nature of revelation and doctrinal statements have a difficult time recognizing the straw man that is often erected by critics of propositions.

108. Ross A. Shecterle, *The Theology of Revelation of Avery Dulles, 1980-1994: Symbolic Mediation* (Lewiston, NY: Edwin Mellen Press, 1996), p. 203.

109. For instance, revelation does include events in human history, the presence of God, and, in a qualified sense, the work of God in the experience of all human beings. But we can never adequately interpret these events, theophanies, and experiences in a way that would actually give us revelation without the assistance of propositional speech.

Second, propositions make available cognitive truth claims that can be confessed or rejected, and that are open to argumentation and falsification. For example, Christians believe that Jesus, the Son of God, is fully divine as the Father is fully divine. Further, this same Jesus experienced a bodily resurrection in human history. These statements can be confessed or rejected, and at least the latter claim is open to falsification. Dulles, on the other hand, stresses the symbolic, nebulous nature of revelation and doctrine that is open to "hermeneutical treatment" even in core areas of Christian belief. It is one thing to submit papal infallibility and the Marian dogmas to hermeneutical treatment, but one wonders to what extent the doctrines of the Trinity and the resurrection of Christ — not to mention the overarching Christian vision of sin, salvation, and new life — are open to similar hermeneutical treatment. Dulles suggests that such core beliefs are candidates for hermeneutical examination. So, would a book entitled *Models of the Trinity* include Arianism and Modalism as legitimate expressions of the Christian faith? Dulles would surely answer No, but his symbolic realism opens the Christian faith to this possibility and confuses the issues at stake in theological discussion.

Dulles's symbolic realist treatment of tradition faces a similar fate, in part because tradition includes past doctrinal statements. In addition, his adoption of Newman's idea of doctrinal development leads him to similar problems we observed with Newman. It is interesting to recall the reasons Dulles rejects the traditional Roman Catholic understanding of tradition in favor of his symbolic view that takes account of doctrinal development. Among other reasons, Dulles argued that the traditional view involves a *deus ex machina* and is difficult to utilize as an actual doctrinal source. However, the same can be said about contemporary Catholic views of doctrinal development, where doctrinal development can be, and is, appealed to as a *deus ex machina* to justify all present developments. Here it is difficult to see how tradition in the objective sense, that is, the actual content of the teaching of the church after the writing of the New Testament, can serve as a doctrinal source. In theories of doctrinal development, any present belief or action can be seen as a legitimate development of the tradition, and as such the present belief or action is beyond critique, even from tradition itself. Catholic theories of doctrinal development, and Dulles's conception of tradition as symbolic communication open to creative hermeneutical treatment, undermine tradition and historical study as important epistemic resources for the contemporary church.

The weakness of Dulles's symbolic realism is clearly seen in his discussion of papal infallibility. On the one hand, it is plain that for Dulles papal infallibility does not provide epistemic certainty. The doctrine of papal infallibility and the Marian dogmas are open to hermeneutical treatment that often results in creative interpretive possibilities. And the collegial nature of the church leads to a complex system of checks and balances that, ultimately, can be understood only in light of the working of the Holy Spirit. For all practical purposes, Dulles has reinterpreted infallibility as the traditional notion of indefectibility, where the church will not stray so far as to lose the truth of the gospel. While Dulles's interpretation of indefectibility might be called something like "indestructibility," it is clear that his use of the term is meaningless apart from his use of infallibility. The church is no longer the church once it has completely abandoned the core beliefs of the gospel. Dulles keeps the term "infallibility" to maintain continuity with his Catholic heritage, reinterprets the term so that the pope is no longer viewed as an infallible belief-producing mechanism, and adopts particularism in epistemology. At this point, Dulles is quite close to the position argued here, though we drop the term "infallibility" because of its usual connection with epistemic certainty.

On the other hand, Dulles's attraction to symbol and models leads him to maintain conflicting views on papal infallibility as a proposal in religious epistemology. While Dulles rejects an epistemic conception of the canons of the church, he also treats ecclesial canons as epistemic criteria. While he adopts particularism in epistemology, he is also a methodist. For instance, Dulles argues that the church must be infallible, and this infallibility must come to expression in the papacy, if the church is to remain united in the truth of the gospel. Dulles's inconsistency allows him to affirm traditional Roman Catholic beliefs while simultaneously addressing substantial problems with these traditional beliefs. However, it confuses the epistemic and doctrinal issues that are at stake, and it does not help Dulles transcend the impasse that has divided Catholics and Protestants since the time of the Reformation. Dulles is headed in the right direction, but his symbolic realism confuses important conceptual issues.

The problem with this conceptual confusion is clearly illustrated in

George Lindbeck's analysis of moderate infallibility. Lindbeck believes proponents of moderate infallibility have the best chance of uniting Catholics and Protestants because they maintain continuity with past Catholic doctrines while interpreting these doctrines in ways that are agreeable to Protestants. He concludes with a puzzling comment: "Common sense may accuse them of dubious compromises, but theologically they are remarkable for comprehensiveness and balance."[110] The problem, of course, is that papal infallibility was originally an epistemic proposal that was supposed to secure epistemic certainty. Now, because of insoluble problems with the doctrine, it leads to dubious compromises that confound common sense. Our final theologian, Hans Küng, refuses to ignore the inadequacy of doctrines of infallibility. Unfortunately, these epistemic doctrines are not the only beliefs he rejects.

110. George Lindbeck, *Infallibility*, p. 59.

CHAPTER 6

Minimal Infallibility:
Hans Küng

The final theologian we will consider is quite different from the others. Unlike Manning, Newman, and Dulles, Küng's native tongue is German, not English. Küng is not a convert to Catholicism, but was born and raised Catholic, a self-described "dyed-in-the-wool Catholic."[1] Küng was never elevated to Cardinal, but instead had his canonical mission to teach revoked by Pope John Paul II. And Küng does not defend papal infallibility, but has openly challenged the doctrine. However, no work on the contemporary reflection of papal infallibility could ignore Hans Küng. As Werner Jeanrond notes,

> Hans Küng is a unique phenomenon in twentieth-century theology: No other theologian has been published, translated, and read so widely in this century; no other theologian has been the focus of such a major controversy; no other contemporary theologian has covered such a broad spectrum of theological themes.[2]

While Küng has written widely, his works on infallibility have been particularly influential, primarily because of the reaction they received from the Catholic authorities as well as the public at large.

1. Hans Küng, *Erkämpfte Freiheit: Erinnerungen* (Munich: Piper, 2002). ET: *My Struggle for Freedom: Memoirs,* trans. John Bowden (Grand Rapids: Eerdmans, 2003), p. 42. This is the first of a two-volume autobiography. The second volume has yet to appear.

2. Werner G. Jeanrond, "Hans Küng," in *The Modern Theologians,* 2nd ed., ed. David F. Ford (Malden, MA: Blackwell, 1997), p. 162.

163

A few words need to be said about the category Küng represents. Since Küng rejects papal infallibility and other attempts to locate the infallibility of the church, it seems strange to call him an infallibilist of any kind, even if "minimal." This categorization, though, is a standard way of describing Küng and others like him who reject the teaching on infallibility yet still remain Catholic.[3] Küng has made it quite clear that he has no desire to leave the Catholic Church, and even in his opposition he remains loyal to the Catholic Church and the pope.[4] Further, Küng does insist that the universal church will be "maintained in truth" through the work of the Holy Spirit, even in spite of some errors. So while Küng rejects the notion of infallibility as "incapable of erring," he does hold that the universal church is "incapable of failing," and in this sense his position can be called minimal infallibility. The standard terminology will be adopted, but minimal infallibility, at least as used here, should not be confused with attempts to rescue papal infallibility as a form of religious epistemology.

The Life of Küng

Hans Küng, the oldest of seven children, was born on March 19, 1928, in the Swiss town of Sursee near Lucerne.[5] Küng's father, Hans Küng-Gut, owned a shoe business during a time of great political and economic instability. The early years of Küng's life were deeply impacted by Hitler and the threat Germany posed to the freedom of Switzerland. According to Küng, the strong tradition of freedom that characterized his homeland became embedded in him as well. In his autobiography, *My Struggle for Freedom,* he writes,

3. See, for instance, J. Robert Dionne, *The Papacy and the Church: A Study of Praxis and Reception in Ecumenical Perspective* (New York: Philosophical Library, 1987), pp. 30-31.

4. See, for instance, *My Struggle for Freedom,* pp. 106-7.

5. A number of Küng biographies have appeared at different stages in his career and from different theological perspectives. In addition to his autobiography, this section is indebted to the following: Hermann Häring, *Hans Küng: Breaking Through,* trans. John Bowden (New York: Continuum, 1998); Robert Nowell, *A Passion for Truth: Hans Küng and His Theology* (New York: Crossroad, 1981); and John Kiwiet, *Hans Küng* (Waco, TX: Word, 1985).

Yes, I come from a tradition with a sense of civic freedom and will never deny it. Our national "project" and my Swiss nature have an almost instinctive antipathy to all dictatorship in state, church and society, to all state totalitarianism and ecclesiastical integralism; they are also resistant to the worship of church leaders and the idolization of institutions, whether party or church. And there is commitment . . . to democracy, federalism, tolerance and the freedom and dignity of the individual and smaller communities.[6]

This national heritage would later compel and sustain Küng in his conflicts with the Catholic hierarchy.

Küng was raised in a Catholic family in the Catholic part of Switzerland. He described the church of his childhood as "fundamentally mediaeval and baroque." Yet, "It isn't gloomy; rather, it delights the senses."[7] The Catholic Church of Küng's youth was strongly institutional and hierarchical, and Küng insists he would never have joined the clergy under this model. Instead, it was the influence of his youth chaplain Franz-Xaver Kaufmann, who wore plain clothes and was deeply involved in the life of his parishioners, that gave him an alternative vision of the ecclesiastical life.[8] After deciding to pursue ordination, Küng made the unusual move of attending the coeducational grammar school in Lucerne, which had the reputation of being "liberal" and "free-thinking." Küng describes his grammar school education as "a farewell to intellectual, terminological, religious ghetto Catholicism and a move to an openly humanistic culture."[9]

After graduating from grammar school in 1948, Küng made another surprising move and decided to pursue his theological education under the Jesuits at the Pontifical Gregorian University in Rome, a school known for its strict discipline and adherence to traditional Catholic theology. Küng spent seven years at the Gregorian University completing his licentiates in philosophy and theology. During this time he witnessed several important events, including the definition of the assumption of Blessed Virgin Mary by Pope Pius XII in 1950. However, his

6. Küng, *My Struggle for Freedom*, p. 16.
7. Küng, *My Struggle for Freedom*, p. 27.
8. Küng, *My Struggle for Freedom*, pp. 29ff.
9. Küng, *My Struggle for Freedom*, p. 36.

reaction to this definition as a student was much different than his later position. He states,

> The definition of the Assumption . . . struck me as a suitable expression of the Catholic understanding of the faith on the basis of the organic theory of the development of dogma being served up to us at that time. And in talking to students from German universities I used to criticize the "arrogance" and the "mania for criticism" shown by the German professors of theology who had their doubts on this question and who were described as rationalistic.[10]

The development of Küng's more critical position was a long process, but it had its beginnings in Rome. For Küng, "being able every day to look behind the scenes of this pontificate brought about a demythologization of this Pope whom formerly we had all idealized." Further, Küng came to believe that the neoscholastic theology he was being taught in Rome "didn't deliver what it promised."[11]

Küng's thesis for his philosophy licentiate was on the existential philosopher Jean-Paul Sartre. Early on Küng was interested in atheistic philosophers, and this interest would resurface in his apologetic works. For his theology licentiate, he followed the guidance of his spiritual supervisor, Father Wilhelm Klein, and focused his attention on G. W. F. Hegel and Karl Barth. Küng was ordained to the priesthood in 1954, and in the following year he defended a thesis on Barth's doctrine of justification. This thesis was the basis of his doctoral dissertation that he defended in 1957 at the Catholic Institute in Paris. Küng's dissertation, which sought to show the essential agreement between the Protestant Barth and the Tridentine doctrine of justification, was lauded by the likes of Catholic theologian Karl Rahner and Barth himself. In fact, the dissertation was the beginning of a close friendship between Küng and Barth. That same year the German edition of the dissertation, *Justification: The Doctrine of Karl Barth and a Catholic Reflection,* was published and immediately brought attention to Küng.[12] In Rome, however, the

10. Hermann Häring and Karl-Josef Kuschel, eds., *Hans Küng: His Work and His Way,* trans. Robert Nowell (Garden City, NY: Image Books, 1980), p. 132.

11. Häring and Kuschel, eds., *Hans Küng: His Work and His Way,* p. 133.

12. Hans Küng, *Rechtfertigung: Die Lehre Karl Barths und eine Katholische Besinnung*

book was looked upon with suspicion. Although the book was never placed on the Index, a dossier was begun on Küng in what is now called the Congregation for the Doctrine of the Faith.

Upon receiving his doctorate in 1957, Küng returned to Lucerne to serve as an assistant priest. Although this is what Küng had prepared himself for, and although he performed his duties well, Küng's tenure at Lucerne did not last long due to a rapid series of events. In 1958 Pope Pius XII died and a new pope, John XXIII was elected. On January 19 of the next year, Küng was invited to the University of Basel by Barth to address the topic *"Ecclesia semper reformanda,"* the Protestant slogan that the church is in need of continual reform. Six days after Küng's lecture, Pope John XXIII announced his plans for an ecumenical council to complete the work begun at Vatican I and to reconsider the relationship of the Catholic Church to non-Catholic Christians and the world at large. Küng quickly began to expand the notes from his lecture at Basel, and later that year published the German edition of *The Council, Reform and Reunion*.[13] The book was a bold attempt by the young priest to propose an agenda for the upcoming council. During his work on this book, Küng accepted an invitation from the University of Münster to join the Catholic faculty as an assistant professor of dogmatics. Less than a year later, Küng accepted an appointment as full professor of systematic theology in the Catholic faculty at the prestigious and progressive University of Tübingen.[14] Küng remained at Tübingen until his retirement in 1996.

In *The Council, Reform and Reunion* Küng presents a number of "reforming ideals which the Church has been working to achieve, if not completely, yet effectually, during the last seventy years,"[15] which in later years he summarized as seven points:

- The Catholic Church must take seriously the religious motives in the Protestant Reformation.

(Einsiedeln: Johannes, 1957). ET: *Justification: The Doctrine of Karl Barth and a Catholic Reflection,* trans. Thomas Collins, Edmund E. Tolk, and David Granskou (New York: Thomas Nelson, 1964).

13. Hans Küng, *Konzil und Wiedervereinigung* (Freiburg: Herder, 1959). ET: *The Council, Reform and Reunion,* trans. Cecily Hastings (New York: Sheed & Ward, 1961).

14. Kiwiet, *Hans Küng,* p. 25.

15. Küng, *The Council, Reform and Reunion,* p. 103.

- There must be a growing regard for scripture in the Catholic Church.
- The Catholic liturgy needs to be a liturgy for the people.
- There must be a new understanding of the universal priesthood that stresses the importance of the laity in the life of the Catholic Church.
- The Catholic Church must adapt to various cultures and be in dialogue with them.
- There must be a reform of excessive popular piety.
- There must be a reform of the Roman Curia.[16]

As Küng himself notes, he was not the first to state these reforming ideals, but his summary and presentation of these ideals had a substantial impact. According to Peter Hebblethwaite, "It was reasonable to conclude that whatever the Preparatory Commission might be doing, Küng had provided the real agenda for the Council, and drawn up the battle lines for its first session." Fergus Kerr agrees, "Like it or not, in historical perspective this book has done more than any other to get the Council going."[17]

The Council, Reform and Reunion was a commercial success that led Küng on speaking engagements and media appearances around the world. He also began work on an ecclesiology, *Structures of the Church*, which presented a theology of ecumenical councils within a conciliar and collegial understanding of the Catholic Church.[18] As the quintessential "man of the hour" had done before and would do again, this book appeared with remarkable timing just four weeks prior to the opening of Vatican II. In the meantime, Küng was asked by Bishop Leiprecht of Rottenburg to be his personal *peritus* at the council. When Küng arrived in Rome, he was asked to be an official *peritus* of the council.

At the council Küng worked with other progressive theologians like Yves Congar, Karl Rahner, and Edward Schillebeeckx to press for reform. In addition, he joined Rahner, Schillebeeckx, and publisher Paul Brand in the founding of *Concilium,* a progressive Catholic scholarly

---

16. Küng, *The Council, Reform and Reunion,* pp. 101-11, and summarized in *My Struggle for Freedom,* p. 443.

17. Quoted in Küng, *The Council, Reform and Reunion* and *My Struggle for Freedom,* pp. 320, 450.

18. Hans Küng, *Struckturen der Kirche* (Freiburg: Herder, 1962). ET: *Structures of the Church,* trans. Salvator Attanasio (New York: Crossroad, 1964, 1982).

journal. After the first session of the council, though, Pope John XXIII died, and with him the dreams of many of the progressives. The pope's successor, Paul VI, was elected in 1963, and although he brought the council to completion, Küng and his fellow progressives saw him as overly hesitant and the ultimate reason for numerous compromises in the conciliar documents. The council had brought about considerable changes in the Catholic Church, but not as many as Küng desired.

After the council Küng published his most substantial work in ecclesiology, *The Church,* as an attempt to provide direction to the Catholic Church after Vatican II.[19] While other works of Küng had received scrutiny before, his lengthy clash with the Congregation for the Doctrine of the Faith began here. In May 1971 Küng received a letter from the Congregation outlining two points of concern with the book. One, "It seems as if the author's mind is attracted to the notion that the Church of Christ, whose unity is torn asunder, consists of all the churches and ecclesial communities." And two, "the author conjectures that, in abnormal cases, the Eucharist may be consecrated by non-ordained baptized persons."[20]

In the summer of 1971, with the Congregation's proceedings against *The Church* still in progress, Küng published the most controversial work of his career, *Infallible? An Inquiry.*[21] This would be Küng's final installment to the ecclesiology he had developed over the past decade, and in it he openly questioned all doctrines of infallibility, including papal infallibility. Once again, the timing of publication was impeccable, as the book appeared just before the centennial celebration of the definition of papal infallibility at Vatican I. Küng begins *Infallible?* with a "candid preface" that insists, "The renewal of the Catholic Church sought by the second Vatican Council, with its prospect of ecumenical understanding with other Christian Churches and a new open-

19. Hans Küng, *Die Kirche* (Freiburg: Herder, 1967). ET: *The Church,* trans. Ray and Rosaleen Ockenden (New York: Sheed & Ward, 1967).

20. United States Catholic Conference, *The Küng Dialogue: A Documentation of the efforts of the Congregation for the Doctrine of the Faith and of the Conference of German Bishops to achieve an appropriate clarification of the controversial views of Dr. Hans Küng* (Washington, DC: United States Catholic Conference, 1980), p. 45.

21. Hans Küng, *Unfehlbar? Eine Anfrage* (Zurich: Benziger, 1970). ET: *Infallible? An Inquiry,* with a new introduction by the author, trans. Edward Quinn (Garden City, NY: Doubleday & Co., 1983).

ing out toward the modern world, has come to a standstill."[22] Another clear concern behind the work is the encyclical *Humanae Vitae,* issued in 1968, which condemns all forms of artificial birth control. Küng contends that the encyclical

> makes the weakness and backwardness of Roman theology clearly evident to the astonished general public throughout the world and within the Catholic Church has aroused opposition such as had not hitherto existed, from simple Church members, theologians, bishops, and bishops' conferences.[23]

As a final act of defiance against the Roman hierarchy, Küng refused to seek an Imprimatur for the work, which he never would have found anyway.

The contents of *Infallible?* will be examined in more detail below. For now it should be noted that several expected results came from the book. The book was a commercial success and caused quite a stir in the popular and academic religious world. Also, the book did not help Küng's case with the Congregation for the Doctrine of the Faith. However, one unexpected result was the opposition Küng received from some of his progressive colleagues, especially Karl Rahner. Rahner wrote a stinging critique of Küng's book that led to a heated written exchange between the authors.[24] Rahner argued that, since

---

22. Küng, *Infallible? An Inquiry,* p. 17.

23. Küng, *Infallible? An Inquiry,* p. 31.

24. The exchange included the following: Karl Rahner, "Kritik an Hans Küng: Zur Frage der Unfehlbarkeit theologischer Sätze," *Stimmen der Zeit* (December 1970): 361-77. ET: "A Critique of Hans Küng: Concerning the Infallibility of Theological Propositions," *Homiletic and Pastoral Review* (May 1971): 10-26. Hans Küng, "Im Interesse der Sache: Antwort an Karl Rahner," *Stimmen der Zeit* (January 1971): 43-64. ET: "To Get to the Heart of the Matter: Answer to Karl Rahner," *Homiletic and Pastoral Review* (June 1971): 9-29. Hans Küng, "Im Interesse der Sache: Antwort an Karl Rahner," *Stimmen der Zeit* (February 1971): 105-22. ET: "To Get to the Heart of the Matter: Answer to Karl Rahner — Part II," *Homiletic and Pastoral Review* (July 1971): 17-32. Karl Rahner, "Replik Bemerkungen zu Hans Küng: Im Interesse der Sache," *Stimmen der Zeit* (March 1971): 145-60. ET: "Reply to Hans Küng: In the Form of an Apologia Pro Theologia Sua," *Homiletic and Pastoral Review* (August/September 1971): 11-27. Küng's final word did not appear in *Stimmen der Zeit* but was published in English. Hans Küng, "Postscript," *Homiletic and Pastoral Review* (August/September 1971): 28-31.

Küng rejected the Catholic methodological principle, his discussion with him could not proceed as an inner-Catholic dialogue but rather as a discussion with a Liberal Protestant or even a skeptical philosopher.[25] In his reply Küng especially resented being called a Liberal Protestant, but this label would follow him the rest of his career.[26] Rahner's final installment of the debate retracted some of his harsh words toward Küng, but he insisted that an obvious methodological divide remained.

More importantly, in 1973 the Congregation for the Doctrine of the Faith issued *Mysterium Ecclesiae,* which, while not mentioning Küng by name, was clearly directed at him. The declaration confirmed the two points raised earlier against *The Church,* and emphasized the significance of the doctrine of infallibility taught at Vatican I and Vatican II. The Congregation offered to drop its investigations into *The Church* and *Infallible?* if Küng would ascribe to the declaration. Küng declined, opting instead to launch a public campaign and accuse the Congregation of unfair procedures. While the Congregation was seeking clarification on doctrinal issues, Küng wanted answers to the objections he had raised in his works. The Congregation issued another, similar declaration in 1975. After *Infallible?* Küng's research turned away from ecclesiology to other issues in theology. But once again he encountered controversy.

In two substantial apologetic works, *On Being a Christian*[27] and *Does God Exist?,*[28] Küng presented a christology that many, including some of his progressive Catholic colleagues as well as Protestants, saw as denying basic christological affirmations found in the Nicene Creed and the Chalcedonian Definition. While Küng maintained he did not deny these basic statements of faith, he refused to speak of the divinity of Jesus Christ in ontological categories and instead employed functional categories, where God acts in Jesus in a dynamic way.[29] Küng's christology will be considered more carefully in the next section, but obviously

25. Rahner, "A Critique of Hans Küng," pp. 13, 20.
26. Küng, "To Get to the Heart of the Matter: Answer to Karl Rahner," p. 11.
27. Hans Küng, *Christ Sein* (Munich: Piper, 1974). ET: *On Being a Christian,* trans. Edward Quinn (London: Collins, 1978).
28. Hans Küng, *Existiert Gott?* (Munich: Piper, 1978). ET: *Does God Exist?* trans. Edward Quinn (Garden City, NY: Doubleday & Co., 1980).
29. Häring, *Hans Küng: Breaking Through,* p. 142.

his new works did not help his situation with the Congregation nor the German bishops.

The conflict reached a high point in 1979 when Küng wrote a preface entitled "The New Situation in the Infallibility Debate" for the German edition of August Hasler's controversial book *How the Pope Became Infallible*.[30] The preface was viewed negatively by the Congregation as an attempt on Küng's part to further the infallibility debate, which the Congregation had warned him against. Later that year on December 18, 1979, the Congregation for the Doctrine of the Faith, under the leadership of Pope John Paul II, withdrew Küng's canonical mission to teach Catholic ministerial students. A few weeks later on January 7, 1980, the German bishops met to sign a joint declaration in support of the decision of Rome. The Declaration of the Congregation emphasized "the matter of the opinion which at least puts in doubt the dogma of infallibility in the church or reduces it to a certain fundamental indefectibility of the church in truth." Further, the Congregation expressed concern over "some essential points of the Catholic faith (e.g., those teachings which pertain to the consubstantiality of Christ with his Father, and to the Blessed Virgin Mary)" which it saw as "consequences of this opinion [on infallibility]."[31]

This move by the Congregation brought widespread attention to the popular Küng and his plight. Opinions varied as some viewed the Congregation's action as an appropriate and even overdue response to the wayward theologian, while others saw it as an unjust inquisitional attempt to suppress academic freedom and freedom of conscience. Küng clearly thought the latter. The University of Tübingen, however, faced the legal responsibility of removing Küng from his position on the Catholic faculty. The university decided against placing Küng in a non-theological department and instead appointed him professor of ecumenical theology and director of the now independent Institute for Ecumenical Research. From this position Küng continued his voluminous publishing career and focused his attention on ecumenical concerns and the world religions. After retiring from Tübingen in 1996,

30. August Hasler, *Wie der Papst unfehlbar wurde* (Munich: Piper, 1979). ET: *How the Pope Became Infallible,* trans. Peter Heinegg (Garden City, NY: Doubleday & Co., 1981).

31. United States Catholic Conference, *The Küng Dialogue*, p. 201.

Küng became president of the Global Ethic Foundation, where he presently serves.

Significant Theological Themes

Since Küng ultimately rejects papal infallibility, it is important to see how he proceeds in the theological task. In this section we will examine his theological method and how this methodology influences two key doctrines, ecclesiology and christology. We will also briefly consider the weak foundationalism that he presents in his apologetic works, which will help us compare Küng to the other Catholic theologians and the position argued for in this work.

The basic contours of Küng's theological method are present early in his career. In *The Council, Reform and Reunion* Küng argues that renewal in the church can be measured by one norm alone, "Jesus Christ, the Lord of the Church, who speaks to the Church of every century in his Gospel, making his demands upon her."[32] This emphasis on an existential encounter with Jesus Christ and scripture as an epistemic norm is clearly a result of Küng's contact with Karl Barth. In *Structures of the Church* Küng expands this methodological principle with the embrace of historical-critical exegesis of scripture, along with the anti-supernatural presuppositions that sometimes accompany this approach. The influence here was his colleague at Tübingen, the Protestant biblical scholar Ernst Käsemann.[33]

In a later programmatic work, *Theology for the Third Millennium,* Küng affirms the methodological orientation of his earlier books. He states that, in his mind, it is

> beyond dispute that in the quest for solid ground there is no other way but the one which the New Testament Scriptures themselves point to, on which their authority reveals itself, in which alone they find their inner unity, and which opens up in a new manner with the historico-critical method: the way to the Jesus of history, who was experienced and attested to by the community of his dis-

32. Küng, *The Council, Reform and Reunion,* p. 56.
33. Kiwiet, *Hans Küng,* p. 27.

ciples as God's Messiah and the Lord. On this subject it has been shown in addition that this way back "before" the testimonies collected in the New Testament, in other words back to Jesus himself, is possible, despite all we know about our roots in our own historical situation.[34]

For Küng, the authentic tradition of Jesus Christ is the *norma normans* of the church while all later tradition is *norma normata*. Since this authentic tradition exists before the writing of the New Testament, and since the New Testament itself includes some later tradition, the historical-critical exegesis of scripture is required. It should be noted, then, that while Küng adamantly rejects Rahner's description of him as a liberal Protestant and while Küng does remain Catholic, he does adopt a methodology characteristic of Liberal Protestantism.[35]

Although the gospel of Jesus Christ is Küng's theological criterion, he recognizes the importance of other theological resources. This is evident in *The Church — Maintained in Truth,* where Küng stresses the importance of the Christian community and tradition for discerning the gospel. He states, "The community and the tradition of the Church . . . form an essential part of the process of discovering Christian truth. This is precisely what is meant by catholicity in space and time."[36] Further, Küng stresses the importance of right living as well as right belief. He insists that

> the Church is maintained quite concretely in the truth of Jesus Christ not only where the right words are produced but wherever *discipleship is fully realized in practice:* wherever, that is, Jesus is not only proclaimed and believed but imitated and given living expression in a spirit of faith.[37]

---

34. Hans Küng, *Theologie im Aufbruch* (Munich: Piper, 1987). ET: *Theology for the Third Millennium,* trans. Peter Heinegg (New York: Doubleday, 1988), p. 85.

35. Schubert Ogden gives a standard presentation of Liberal Protestant methodology, which has many similarities to Küng's. See "The Authority of Scripture for Theology," in *On Theology* (San Francisco: Harper & Row, 1986), pp. 45-68.

36. Hans Küng, *Kirche — gehalten in der Wahrheit?* (Zurich: Benziger, 1979). ET: *The Church — Maintained in Truth,* trans. Edward Quinn (New York: Seabury Press, 1980), p. 41.

37. Küng, *The Church — Maintained in Truth,* p. 20, italics Küng.

Included here is an emphasis on the character of the believer. "The totality of faith consists in the integrity of commitment, not in completely correct propositions."[38] So Küng rounds out his emphasis on the historical-critical exegesis of the New Testament with a recognition of the importance of tradition, the Christian community, and character.

Küng's methodology is crucial for his work in ecclesiology because, like the Reformers of the sixteenth century, he sought a norm that would allow him to question the absolute authority of ecumenical councils and popes in favor of a more collegial understanding of the church. In *Structures of the Church* Küng argues that ecumenical councils, while beneficial for the life of the church, are not necessary *per se* since they are not directly authorized by Jesus or the apostles. Further, they appear in a variety of forms throughout history. For these reasons, Küng suggests that ecumenical councils are a matter of ecclesiastical law rather than theology or dogma, although a theology of ecumenical councils can be constructed if one begins with ecclesiology.[39]

For Küng, the universal church, the mysterious assembly of all who believe in Christ, is an "ecumenical council by divine convocation." This "ecumenical council by divine convocation" can call an "ecumenical council by human convocation," and the latter "is *only,* but at the same time *really,* the representation of the ecumenical council by divine convocation."[40] But this ecumenical council by human convocation is under the same gospel as the ecumenical council by divine convocation, and any decisions of an ecumenical council by human convocation can be critiqued on the basis of the gospel of Jesus Christ. Küng argues that this recognition is standard in Catholic literature, where councils are said to be "assisted" rather than "inspired" by the Holy Spirit. He concludes that "it is obvious . . . that Holy Scripture is the norma *normans,* whereas the definitions of the councils indeed were also norma but only norma *normanta,* that is, they can only be norms regulated by Holy Scripture."[41]

Although Küng seeks a principle of critique, he never rejects the need for ecclesiastical offices. He maintains that ecclesiastical offices

---

38. Küng, *The Church — Maintained in Truth,* p. 36.
39. Küng, *Structures of the Church,* pp. 6-7.
40. Küng, *Structures of the Church,* p. 15.
41. Küng, *Structures of the Church,* p. 54.

are more than a result of utilitarian needs, as some Protestants hold, but rather have a divine origin and are a divine institution. However, due to the collegial nature of the church and the fact that the church is under the gospel of Jesus Christ, all offices have concrete limits. More importantly, ecclesiastical offices must be held and exercised in the spirit of the gospel. At this time Küng presents a moderate interpretation of papal infallibility much like that of Dulles, which is also characterized by a collegial understanding of the church and limitations on papal authority.[42]

Küng develops his ecclesiology further in *The Church*. Here he distinguishes the essence of the church from the various forms that the church has assumed throughout history. While the essence and historical form of the church are not separable, neither are they identical. To discern the essence of the church, one must return to the gospel of Jesus Christ as found in the New Testament, the *norma normans*.[43] Even here a number of different forms of the church appear. So, the theologian must take "the New Testament as a *whole* with *all* its writings as the positive witness of the Gospel of Jesus Christ" to avoid the temptation of too hastily dissociating or harmonizing conflicting statements in scripture.[44] The historical-critical method is utilized because it gives the theologian "an overall view of the changes in the Church and in theology since New Testament times" as well as "insight into the extremely important changes which were taking place while the New Testament was being written (approximately between A.D. 50 and 150) and to some extent into the changes of the preceding years (from A.D. 30 to 50)."[45] The earliest tradition of the gospel serves as a standard for the church as it tries to fulfill its mandate in the present.

Again, Küng takes up the issue of ecclesiastical offices. His discussion begins with a strong emphasis on Jesus as the only mediator of the church, and on the corresponding notion of the priesthood of all believers. These emphases do not exclude the need for ecclesiastical offices, as apostles and other church leaders can be found in the New Testament. However, Küng stresses that in the New Testament, the titles

---

42. Küng, *Structures of the Church*, chaps. VI–VIII.
43. Küng, *The Church — Maintained in Truth*, pp. 5, 16.
44. Küng, *The Church — Maintained in Truth*, p. 19, italics Küng.
45. Küng, *The Church — Maintained in Truth*, p. 20.

used for leaders in the church emphasize service rather than power or honor. Further, the early church included charismatic figures who exercised authority and taught apart from an official position. Notable here are teachers and prophets, whom Küng views as precursors to present-day theologians.[46]

At the end of *The Church* Küng once more offers a moderate interpretation of papal infallibility. He also suggests that the pope embrace a "primacy of service" that differs from the Orthodox and Protestant preference for a primacy of honor and the Catholic concern for a primacy of jurisdiction. He states,

> This primacy of service is more than a primacy of honour *(primates honoris)*, which belongs to no one in a Church of service and in its passivity could help no one. This primacy of service is also more than a primacy of jurisdiction *(primates iurisdictionis)*, which, interpreted solely in terms of power and dominion, would be a fundamental misunderstanding and which, interpreted solely in terms of the words themselves, would leave out of account, if not contradict, the essential element, that of service.[47]

In all of this it is evident that Küng seeks a collegial understanding of the church and a magisterium that is more interested in pastoral ministry than privileges and rights. Küng maintains that ecclesiastical offices, including the papacy, play a crucial role in the life of the church, especially when exercised in the right spirit. However, these offices must be viewed in light of the gospel and within the context of the whole church. In particular, he is interested in the role of theologians as charismatic figures who help balance the teaching authority of the magisterium.

In *Infallible? An Inquiry,* Küng rejects the idea of an infallible magisterium as an epistemic criterion for Christian doctrine. For all practical purposes, Küng had already established another criterion in his earlier works, the gospel of Jesus Christ as found in the historical-critical exegesis of the New Testament. However, since Küng's earlier works focused on ecclesiology, he had not yet fleshed out the specific

46. Küng, *The Church — Maintained in Truth,* part E.
47. Küng, *The Church — Maintained in Truth,* p. 477.

content of the Christian message. He takes up this task in his next major work, *On Being a Christian,* and continues it, with similar results, in *Does God Exist?* In both works Küng investigates christology with the tools of historical-critical exegesis. The following paragraph from *On Being a Christian,* quoted in full, summarizes Küng's approach well.

> The Christian message aims at making intelligible what Jesus Christ means and is for man today. But does this Christ become really intelligible for man today if we simply start out dogmatically from established teaching on the Trinity? Can he be understood if we simply take for granted the divinity of Jesus, the pre-existence of the Son, and then merely ask how this Son of God could unite to himself, could assume, a human nature, frequently leaving the cross and resurrection to appear as something which happened purely as a result of his "becoming man"? Can modern man understand if we emphasize the title of Son of God and suppress as much as possible the humanity of Jesus, denying him existence as a human person? Will he understand if Jesus is more adored as divinity than imitated as earthly and human? Would it not perhaps correspond more to the New Testament evidence and to modern man's historical way of thinking if we started out like the first disciples from the real human being Jesus, his historical message and manifestation, his life and fate, his historical reality and historical activity, and then ask about the relationship of this human being Jesus to God, about his unity with the Father. In a word, therefore: can we have less of a Christology in the classical manner, speculatively or dogmatically "from above," but — without disputing the legitimacy of the older Christology — more of a historical Christology "from below," in light of the concrete Jesus, more suited to modern man?[48]

Küng wants to present a christology for the modern person that sets aside the classical christological statements of the Nicene Creed and the Chalcedonian Definition and begins with the historical, human existence of Jesus. However, while he wants to do so "without disputing the legitimacy of the older Christology," he does in fact reinterpret key

48. Küng, *On Being a Christian,* pp. 132-33.

elements of these traditional statements, thus essentially rejecting them. For example, Küng revisions the pre-existence of Jesus, or better the Word or Son, that is confessed in these classical statements as well as the New Testament. Although the pre-existence of Jesus is found in John's prologue and throughout John's Gospel, as well as the pre-Pauline hymn in Philippians and Paul's own writings, Küng argues that these texts simply reflect the metaphysical outlook that permeated the Hellenistic world. Properly interpreted, they do not mean that Jesus pre-existed in some way before his birth, but rather point to his unique claim to be a real revelation of the eternal God.[49]

A related issue is the identity of Jesus as divine or God. While Küng is right to argue that Jesus should not be identified with the Father, he never affirms the Chalcedonian confession that Jesus is ontologically fully human and fully divine. Instead, he presents an exegetical and hermeneutical critique of the Definition, stating,

> The two-natures doctrine [of the Chalcedonian Definition], in the opinion of many exegetes, is by no means identical with the *original* New Testament message about Christ. Some regard it as displacing or — up to a point — even corrupting the original message, others as at least not the sole possible and certainly not the best interpretation.[50]

Once again Küng finds the divinity of Jesus in the New Testament, but he argues that such texts represent a corruption of the original message of Jesus. Even if these texts do represent the authentic preaching about Jesus, they can be given a better interpretation than that found in the Chalcedonian Definition. In *Does God Exist?* Küng makes a similar argument regarding the designation "God" that is given to Jesus in the New Testament. He suggests, "Apart from John's Gospel, written fifty years later . . . Jesus is designated as 'God' in only a few, all likewise late, Hellenistically influenced, exceptional cases."[51] For Küng, New Testament language of the divinity of Jesus is a corruption of the original gospel and should not be interpreted to mean that Jesus was ontologically

---

49. Küng, *On Being a Christian*, pp. 445-46.
50. Küng, *On Being a Christian*, pp. 131-32, italics Küng.
51. Küng, *Does God Exist?* p. 685.

divine. Rather, such language points to Jesus' unique identity as the human through whom God worked in a decisive way. Jesus is an exceptional human, but he is only human.

Küng's interpretation of Jesus' pre-existence and divinity is hard to reconcile with the orthodox Christian belief in the incarnation. His response is that such criticism does not do justice to his desire to conceive christology in functional and "from below" categories instead of ontological and "from above" categories.[52] However, his own position has important similarities to the Nestorian position that was rejected at Chalcedon and continues to be rejected today in Catholic, Orthodox, and Protestant confessional statements. Like the Nestorian position, Küng posits a two-subject christology that distinguishes the man Jesus and the God who is at work in this man. Küng's Jesus would have lived whether or not God decided to work in him in a decisive way. Moreover, while Küng attempts to avoid ontological categories, he does in fact present a picture of Jesus with ontological implications. Regardless of one's opinion on Küng's christology, it is clear that his understanding of the identity of Jesus differs significantly from the traditional one.

Another issue we need to consider briefly is the epistemology Küng presents in *On Being a Christian* and *Does God Exist?* In both works Küng seeks a "middle way between a purely authoritative assertion of God in the sense of 'dialectical theology' and a purely rational proof in the sense of 'natural theology.'"[53] Or, in the categories we used in the introduction, he seeks an alternative to the fideism of Barth and the strong foundationalism of his Catholic heritage. Küng rejects the former because he believes we can offer reasons for accepting the Christian faith, but he rejects the latter because he believes these reasons are never enough to prove the existence of God and the truth of the Christian faith. For this reason Küng, like Newman and Dulles, is best described as a weak foundationalist in the realm of epistemology. He does make a unique contribution to religious epistemology by uniting this reasonable belief with existential trust. Küng's question to the unbeliever is, "Why do we as humans maintain a basic trust in reality instead of a basic mistrust?"[54] From this existential confidence in reality Küng goes

---

52. See Häring, *Hans Küng: Breaking Through*, pp. 227-28.
53. Küng, *On Being a Christian*, p. 67. See also *Does God Exist?* pp. 509-28.
54. See *On Being a Christian*, pp. 70, 71.

on to argue for the God who makes this trust possible, and then more specifically for the Christian faith.[55]

Papal Infallibility

Küng's mature position on papal infallibility is found in *Infallible? An Inquiry*. However, before this time he espoused a moderate position, as seen especially in the last chapter of *Structures of the Church*. Since his early position has many similarities to that of Newman and Dulles, and since we have already presented their moderate positions on papal infallibility, we will not concentrate on Küng's early view. It will be beneficial, though, to briefly present his early, moderate position and consider why he ultimately abandoned this view.

In *Structures of the Church* Küng presents the infallibility of the pope and the councils as a preservation of "office as a whole in the Church from apostasy: from falling away from faith, from a substantial error which would destroy Christ's message."[56] Like Dulles, he essentially defines infallibility as what has traditionally been called indefectibility. However, he goes on to say that "this office [of the pope and of the councils] with and in the Church is an infallible norm for the faith of the individual Christian."[57] While he calls the teaching office a "norm for the faith," he is careful to emphasize that the teaching office of the church does not exalt itself above scripture. Rather, as a charism promised to the church by the Holy Spirit, the infallibility of the teaching office does not offer new revelation, but properly interprets revelation for each new generation. As noted earlier with Newman and Dulles, there are several areas of tension in Küng's early position, and this tension is compounded in Küng's case due to his strong epistemic view of scripture.

In *Structures* Küng holds that only one doctrine has been defined *ex cathedra* since 1870, the assumption of the Blessed Virgin Mary in 1950. While the pope does not require the consent of the Catholic Church when making an infallible definition *(ex sese non autem ex consensu ecclesiae)*, he insists that under no circumstances can the pope define a

55. Küng, *Does God Exist?* chaps. E-G.
56. Küng, *Structures of the Church*, p. 314.
57. Küng, *Structures of the Church*, p. 314.

doctrine without the consensus of the church.[58] Küng affirms the development of doctrine, stating that "as human — and as historical formulations — the definitions of the Church are inherently capable and in need of improvement." However, doctrinal development is not simply "logical" development or "a question of organic growth and elaboration." Further, many doctrines have a "polemical orientation," that is, they are defined in opposition to a specific heresy. Such polemical doctrines are susceptible to denying the truth that is usually present with the error of the heresy. While Küng does not present a clear picture of the nature of doctrinal development, he does emphasize the need for all Christians to consider "the truth in the error of the others and the possible error in their own truth."[59]

It was Küng's quest for truth that ultimately led him to deny papal infallibility and certain forms of doctrinal development. This is especially apparent in his work *Truthfulness: The Future of the Church*,[60] which anticipates many of the themes found in *Infallible? An Inquiry*. Here Küng argues,

> Today — very differently from former times — we do not take it badly if anyone says that he has changed his opinion, that he has revised, corrected his view, that today he would see it differently, better, or in the opposite way. We respect a person for saying this. We take it badly only if someone changes his mind but does not admit it; when a person says the opposite of what he said before, but now asserts that he had always said it. For modern man it is not the revision of a position but the negations of a revision which offend against truthfulness.[61]

Because of this new cultural outlook, and because of difficulties with past doctrinal statements, Küng suggests that infallibility be under-

58. Küng, *Structures of the Church*, pp. 326-36.

59. Küng, *Structures of the Church*, pp. 346-51. An earlier discussion of the development of dogma and the "polemic of dogma" can also be found in *The Council, Reform and Reunion*, p. 113. In *The Council, Reform and Reunion* he describes doctrinal development as "an unfolding of what is implicit so as to make it explicit, under the influence of the Holy Spirit."

60. Hans Küng, *Truthfulness: The Future of the Church* (New York: Sheed & Ward, 1968).

61. Küng, *Truthfulness*, p. 130.

stood as *"a basic persistence of the Church in truth, which is not destroyed by errors in detail."* The church can claim this type of infallibility because of the Holy Spirit who has promised to "maintain the Church in the truth of the gospel, in *spite* of all errors and *through* all errors."[62] For Küng, the existence of errors does not negate the infallibility of the church as long as the church owns up to these errors and the Holy Spirit keeps the church from fatal heresy.

Küng also disassociates himself from theological methods that seek to ingeniously reinterpret problematic doctrinal statements through "speculative interpretation." He states,

> [T]his kind of speculative dissociation from the original meaning, while the old formula was still adhered to, was indeed the sole method that was accepted — or, more accurately, at least tolerated — in the Catholic theology of the pre-conciliar age. But the fact still cannot be ignored that the reinterpretation together with the retention of the same formula is just what renders innocuous the formula itself, empties it of its original meaning and turns it into its opposite. Thus the procedure leads to an *unwanted* theological untruthfulness, which says "Yes" and "No" simultaneously, frequently leaves the person without theological prejudices perplexed, and in fact leads to ever greater difficulties.[63]

Instead of this kind of speculative exegesis, which does not lead to truthfulness, Küng opts for a historical interpretation of doctrinal statements that takes seriously the old formulation and the new doctrinal concern. *Truthfulness,* then, foreshadows the position Küng would present in *Infallible?* as well as the debate that would follow between Rahner and him on theological method.

In *Infallible?* Küng addresses all forms of infallibility claimed by the Catholic magisterium, including but not limited to papal infallibility. In this work he picks up the "neoscholastic textbook" definition of infallibility as "the impossibility of falling into error."[64] He begins with a listing of several "classical errors of the ecclesiastical teaching office":

62. Küng, *Truthfulness,* p. 136, italics Küng.
63. Küng, *Truthfulness,* pp. 146-47.
64. Küng, *Infallible? An Inquiry,* p. 74.

the excommunication of Photius, the Ecumenical Patriarch of Constantinople and of the Greek Church, which made formal the schism with the Eastern Church, a schism which is now almost a thousand years old; the prohibition of interest at the beginning of modern times, on which the ecclesiastical teaching office after a variety of compromises changed its mind, much too late; the condemnation of Galileo and the measures adopted as a consequence of this action, which are essentially responsible for the estrangement between the Church and the natural sciences (not yet overcome today); the condemnation of new forms of worship in the Rites controversy, which is one of the main reasons for the large-scale breakdown of the Catholic missions of modern times in India, China, and Japan; the maintenance up to the First Vatican Council of the medieval secular power of the Pope, with the aid of all secular and spiritual means of excommunication, which in large measure rendered the papacy incredible as a spiritual ministry; finally, at the beginning of our century, the numerous condemnations of the approach of modern critical-historical exegesis to the authorship of the books of the Bible, to source-criticism in the Old and New Testaments, to historicity and literary forms, to the Comma Johanneum, to the Vulgate; and also the condemnations in the dogmatic field, particularly in connection with "modernism" (theory of evolution, conception of development of dogma) and most recently of all in connection with Pius XII's encyclical *Humani Generis,* and the consequent ecclesiastical disciplinary measures, etc.[65]

Catholic theologians, Küng continues, defend infallibility in spite of these errors with "a basically simple recipe: either it was not an error or — when at last and finally an error could no longer be denied, reinterpreted, rendered innocuous or belittled — it was not an infallible decision."[66] A clear example of the latter was the response of the bishops at Vatican I to the condemnation of Pope Honorius I. Although Honorius clearly promoted a monothelite christology, the bishops at Vatican I argued that he never presented his teaching as an *ex cathedra* definition

65. Küng, *Infallible? An Inquiry,* pp. 37-38.
66. Küng, *Infallible? An Inquiry,* pp. 38-39.

— a theological category that appears in *Pastor Aeternus* but did not exist in the seventh century when Honorius was pope.[67] For Küng, such defense strategies are an evasion of the obvious and lead the Catholic Church further away from truthfulness.

The primary example Küng highlights, though, is Pope Paul VI's encyclical *Humanae Vitae,* which prohibits Catholics from using artificial contraception. Küng chooses this example since it occurs after Vatican I and is a pressing contemporary issue. His argument is that the encyclical is not based on scripture but faulty natural-law reasoning, and the encyclical has not been accepted by the majority of the scientific community, non-Catholic Christians, and even Catholics.[68] So Küng feels he has a good, contemporary example where the teaching office of the Catholic Church has made a wrong decision. He suggests that the reason Pope Paul VI and the Catholic Church continue to maintain the immorality of artificial birth control is not the material aspect of the doctrine, the immorality of artificial birth control *per se,* but the formal aspect of the doctrine, the infallibility of the Catholic Church.[69]

The question remains, is the immorality of artificial contraception an infallible teaching of the Catholic Church? Küng insists that, even though *Humanae Vitae* was not defined *ex cathedra,* the restriction against artificial contraception still functions infallibly. This prohibition has been taught by the bishops of the Catholic Church scattered throughout the world, a condition which, according to Vatican II, makes a doctrine infallible even if not infallibly defined.[70] While the restriction against artificial contraception is not an example of extraordinary papal magisterium, it is an example of ordinary papal magisterium and ordinary universal magisterium, the latter of which makes a teaching infallible. For Küng, though, all forms of infallibility claimed by the Catholic Church suffer similar difficulties.

Historically, Catholic claims to infallibility do not rest on firm foundations. Regarding the infallible exercise of universal magisterium, Küng argues, "The whole substantiation of episcopal infallibility depends on the presupposition that the bishops in a definite, direct, and

---

67. Küng, *Infallible? An Inquiry,* p. 39.
68. Küng, *Infallible? An Inquiry,* p. 41.
69. Küng, *Infallible? An Inquiry,* pp. 53-69.
70. Küng, *Infallible? An Inquiry,* pp. 71-85.

exclusive way are the successors of the apostles and that the apostles claimed infallibility for themselves."[71] However, there is no evidence from the New Testament and other early Christian sources that the apostles, as a whole or individually, ever claimed infallibility. Nor is it possible to prove that bishops are, in a strict sense, the direct and exclusive successors of the apostles. Further, other pastoral leaders and teachers, like presbyters, priests, and charismatic prophets, played an important role in the early church and continue to do so today.[72]

Concerning papal infallibility, other historical difficulties arise. For instance, although *Pastor Aeternus* describes papal infallibility as a divinely revealed dogma, the doctrine is based on highly speculative and controversial exegesis of scripture. Early attempts of the Roman church to claim juridical primacy were always opposed by other bishops, and even here juridical primacy did not include infallibility. This is clear in the excommunication of Pope Vigilius at the Fifth Ecumenical Council at Constantinople, upon which Vigilius recanted; and even more so by the condemnation of Pope Honorius I at the Sixth Ecumenical Council at Constantinople, a condemnation confirmed by subsequent popes and councils. Küng suggests that the primary theological foundation for Vatican I was the writings of Thomas Aquinas, but Thomas based his teaching on a number of documents now proven to be forgeries, including the Pseudo-Isidorian Decretals.[73] Küng's contention is that the doctrines of infallibility at Vatican I and II are based less on biblical and historical considerations and more on other factors such as the rejection of Gallicanism, the increasing loss of papal temporal power, and the concern over modernism.

While the historical foundations of doctrines of infallibility are far from secure, Küng proposes to have discovered the central problem of Catholic doctrines of infallibility. He begins with a rejection of other attempts to deal with infallibility, including: appealing to a lack of freedom for the minority at Vatican I; focusing on the issue of papal primacy, as papal infallibility remains the chief obstacle in the ecumenical arena; emphasizing the rights of conscience over papal definitions; exploring the opportuneness, conditions, and limits of the infallibility

71. Küng, *Infallible? An Inquiry,* pp. 86-87.
72. Küng, *Infallible? An Inquiry,* pp. 87-91.
73. Küng, *Infallible? An Inquiry,* pp. 114-25.

definition; redefining the term "infallibility"; and stressing the truth, mandate, and authority of the church as such, a point on which both the Orthodox and Protestants agree. These attempts cloud the central issue rather than bring clarification. For Küng, the primary question is, "is the Church's infallibility dependent on infallible *propositions?*"[74]

Küng agrees that the church is dependent on propositions, especially summary professions of Christian belief and polemical demarcations that distinguish Christian from non-Christian beliefs. However, he does question whether the church is dependent on infallible propositions. He defines infallible propositions as "statements which must be considered as guaranteed a priori to be free from error; sentences, propositions, definitions, formularies, and formulas, which are not only *de facto* not erroneous but in principle simply cannot be erroneous."[75] Küng argues that, while the church depends on propositions, even binding ones, this does not mean that such propositions must be or even can be infallible. With regard to the infallibility definition, he believes the two Vatican councils wrongly presupposed that "the 'infallibility' of the Church simply could not be realized without infallible propositions" and were unaware of the problematic nature of infallible propositions.[76]

What exactly is problematic about the notion of infallible propositions? Küng argues that articles of faith, while they point us to God, are never directly God's word but rather are God's word mediated to us by human words. As human words, articles of faith suffer from the same limitations inherent in all human propositions. For instance, propositions as such always fall short of the reality they intend to convey. It is impossible for propositions to adequately capture the complexity of reality, and this is especially the case when we seek to speak of faith and God. Furthermore, propositions are inevitably open to misunderstanding. Others, even with the best intentions, may misunderstand what I intend to communicate. Matters are complicated even more when propositions are read in a different time period or translated into different languages. Words and expressions in a given language change meaning over time, and when a proposition is translated into another

---

74. Küng, *Infallible? An Inquiry,* pp. 131-49, italics Küng.
75. Küng, *Infallible? An Inquiry,* p. 156.
76. Küng, *Infallible? An Inquiry,* p. 158.

language, meaning always varies however slightly. Also, propositions can be taken out of their original context and abused for ideological purposes.[77] Küng believes that Catholic doctrines of infallibility simply reflect the modern project of pursuing propositional clarity that began during the Enlightenment. However, this project inevitably failed because of the limitations of propositions. While the limitations of propositions are being increasingly recognized in the academic world, the Catholic Church has yet to integrate this realization in its own understanding of doctrine.

Because of the limitations of propositions, Küng states that "propositions can be true *or* false — and add to it: propositions can be true *and* false."[78] This is especially the case when propositions are offered in a polemical context, as people are often more aware of the truth of their own position than the truth of their opponent's position. One example he gives is the debate over justification during the Reformation. Protestants argued for the doctrinal proposition "The just man lives by faith (and does no good works)" while Catholics defended the doctrinal proposition "the just man does works of charity." As is increasingly recognized by Protestants and Catholics, both of these propositions affirm part of the truth of the gospel. Justification is based solely on the graciousness of God, and justification manifests itself in works of love. But both propositions can also be understood in a heretical manner. Justification cannot exist apart from human acts of love, nor is justification "works righteousness."[79]

The Catholic Church, then, appears to face a dilemma. "With the disappearance of infallible propositions, the promises given to the Church also seem to have disappeared, and the infallibility of the Church itself seems to have gone. But does the infallibility of the Church really stand or fall with infallible propositions?"[80] This is the main presupposition Küng challenges, and he answers with an emphatic No. Just because we

77. Küng, *Infallible? An Inquiry*, pp. 164-68.

78. Küng, *Infallible? An Inquiry*, p. 176.

79. Küng, *Infallible? An Inquiry*, pp. 176-77. Küng's observation was officially recognized by Lutheran and Roman Catholic officials in 1999. See the Lutheran–Roman Catholic Dialogue, *Joint Declaration on the Doctrine of Justification*, in Jaroslav Pelikan and Valerie Hotchkiss, eds., *Creeds and Confessions of Faith in the Christian Tradition*, vol. 3 (New Haven: Yale University Press, 2003), pp. 878-88.

80. Küng, *Infallible? An Inquiry*, p. 181.

cannot have infallible propositions does not mean that Jesus' promise to preserve the church in truth has failed. Rather, Küng offers an alternative: *"The Church will persist in the truth IN SPITE OF all ever possible errors!"*[81] Even with some errors in particular beliefs, God can preserve the church in the fundamental truth of the gospel. For this reason we can still speak of the "infallibility" of the church in the sense of a *"fundamental remaining of the Church in truth, which is not annulled by individual errors."*[82] However, because the term "infallibility" is so easily misunderstood, Küng prefers the terms *"'indefectibility' or 'perpetuity' in truth."*[83] The Holy Spirit preserves the church in the truth of the gospel in spite of errors, which are inevitable since the church is made up of finite and sinful human beings.

Küng believes his position has positive ecumenical implications. While Orthodox and Protestant Christians disagree with Catholics on the infallibility of the church, they do agree on the indefectibility of the church. Further, Küng's critique of papal infallibility also applies to Orthodox and Protestant Christians to the extent that they affirm either the infallibility of ecumenical councils or biblical inerrancy. The ecumenicity of councils is not *a priori* certain, and councils have corrected one another.[84] Scripture, which witnesses to divine revelation, is still the product of human authors and contains errors in details.[85] Since conciliar documents and scripture are composed of propositions, they suffer the same limitations inherent in all human propositions. Nonetheless, God can and does work through scripture and ecumenical councils to lead the church into the truth of Jesus Christ and to preserve the church in this truth.

Küng concludes *Infallible?* with suggestions found in his other works in ecclesiology. He argues for a collegial understanding of the church that takes seriously not only the teaching role of the magisterium but also the charismatic gift of teaching that is possessed by others in the church, particularly theologians.[86] He suggests an understanding of the papacy that is based not on a primacy of jurisdiction or a

81. Küng, *Infallible? An Inquiry*, p. 181, italics Küng.
82. Küng, *Infallible? An Inquiry*, p. 187, italics Küng.
83. Küng, *Infallible? An Inquiry*, p. 188, italics Küng.
84. Küng, *Infallible? An Inquiry*, pp. 206-14.
85. Küng, *Infallible? An Inquiry*, pp. 215-27.
86. Küng, *Infallible? An Inquiry*, pp. 227-46.

primacy of honor, but rather a primacy of service.[87] Such a view of the church, Küng believes, rightly emphasizes the pastoral nature of ecclesial leadership, takes seriously the giftedness of all the members of the church, and leads toward ecumenical understanding and unity.

As noted earlier, Küng's *Infallible?* aroused considerable discussion and brought numerous responses, several of which need to be considered. J. Robert Dionne represents one response, noting that "none of the examples given by Küng and his followers have to do with what since the latter part of the nineteenth century came to be called with increasing frequency the extraordinary papal magisterium."[88] Richard McBrien makes a similar observation, stating,

> I agree with Avery Dulles and others that Küng is mistaken when he argues that the teaching of *Humanae Vitae* and the doctrine of papal infallibility stand or fall together. . . . Küng certainly knows that this encyclical does not fulfill all the conditions for an infallible pronouncement as set down by Vatican I.[89]

The charge against Küng is that *Humanae Vitae* should not be identified as an infallible *ex cathedra* definition, and therefore his book does not adequately critique the doctrine of papal infallibility. In defense of Küng, it should be observed that there is nothing in *Pastor Aeternus* that prevents *Humanae Vitae* from being an infallible pronouncement if one maintains a maximal interpretation of *Pastor Aeternus*. Cardinal Manning would have viewed *Humanae Vitae* as an infallible papal pronouncement. Of course, Dionne and McBrien are right that *Humanae Vitae* is not an infallible pronouncement when *Pastor Aeternus* is given a moderate interpretation.

However, this critique misses Küng's point. His contention is not that *Humanae Vitae* is an exercise of extraordinary papal magisterium, but rather ordinary universal magisterium. *Humanae Vitae* is an infallible teaching because it has been taught worldwide by the bishops of the Catholic Church. Based on this example of an infallible teaching that

---

87. Küng, *Infallible? An Inquiry,* p. 253.

88. J. Robert Dionne, *The Papacy and the Church* (New York: Philosophical Library, 1987), p. 31.

89. Richard McBrien, in *The Infallibility Debate,* ed. John J. Kirvan (New York: Paulist Press, 1971), p. 39.

Küng believes is clearly wrong, he argues for the inadequacy of all doctrines of infallibility. Francis Sullivan offers a more precise critique when he observes, "Karl Rahner and most other Catholic theologians ... do not agree that according to the official Catholic doctrine on the infallibility of the ordinary universal magisterium, the sinfulness of artificial contraception has been infallibly taught."[90] Sullivan, however, is overstating his case, for a number of conservative Catholic theologians believe that the sinfulness of artificial contraception has been infallibly taught. Küng's supporters agree. For example, Herbert Haag argues that Pope John Paul II held the immorality of artificial contraception as an infallible teaching.[91] We will return to this debate at the end of the chapter.

A second response is that Küng's historical critiques of doctrines of infallibility do not take sufficient account of the Catholic idea of doctrinal development. For example, Peter Chirico states,

> Now many who have undertaken to investigate the history of infallibility (like Küng and [Brian] Tierney) assume that for a doctrine to be of divine faith it must be articulated in the sacred books, or it must be reducible to articulation from two or more scriptural articulations, or it must be implicit in the actions performed by the scriptural Church. Further, one must be able to trace the doctrine through history from the scriptural beginnings. These assumptions, it seems to me, are too facile.[92]

Chirico argues that doctrines of infallibility do not have to be explicit in the New Testament or early Christian sources since these doctrines are implicit in these sources and have developed through history. However, Chirico's response, while a popular one, does not deal adequately with Küng's rejection of the notion of doctrinal development. Küng is well aware of the idea of doctrinal development — he employed it in his own early writings on infallibility. But in his latter work he explicitly rejects

90. Francis A. Sullivan, *Magisterium: Teaching Authority in the Catholic Church* (New York: Paulist Press, 1983), p. 120.

91. Herbert Haag, "Preface: An Unresolved Enquiry," in *Infallible? An Unresolved Enquiry*, by Hans Küng (New York: Continuum, 1994), pp. xvii-xviii.

92. Peter Chirico, *Infallibility: The Crossroads of Doctrine* (Wilmington, DE: Michael Glazier, 1983), p. 226.

the appeal to doctrinal development because, in his view, such appeals conceal important conceptual problems and lead the church away from truthfulness.

A third response concerns Küng's analysis of language and knowledge, which, Robert Murray observes, "even his admirers find rather embarrassing."[93] Representative here is the critique of Lutheran theologian George Lindbeck. While Lindbeck affirms Küng's suggestion of supplanting "magisterial infallibility" with "ecclesial indefectibility," he asks,

> Is it really the case that all true propositions can become infected with error, with falsehood? Above all, does this hold for all religious statements, for all affirmations of Christian faith, for all — not just some — dogmas? Is it true, for example, of "Jesus is Lord"?[94]

Lindbeck believes that Küng's linguistic analysis overlooks the basic distinction between the judgments one makes, or "propositions"; and the words one uses to articulate these judgments, or "sentences." He explains,

> It is difficult to imagine that [Küng] has not often been exposed to the suggestion that the same basic affirmation, such as "Jesus is Lord," may be expressed in different languages or conceptualities (e.g., "Jesus is Messiah," "God-man," etc.), some more and some less adequate, but that *qua* affirmation, it always remains either true or false. Conversely, the same sentence — let us once again cite "Jesus is Lord" — may be used to express different propositions, not only true ones, but false ones such as "Jesus is the one for whose sake it is mandatory to kill heretics." But that doesn't make the same proposition true *and* false. It simply means that the same sentence can be used to enunciate different propositions. In this approach, every true proposition, including those about the impermanent, are eternally true, incapable of being erroneous, and in this improper sense, "infallible."[95]

93. Quoted in Nowell, *A Passion for Truth*, pp. 214-15.
94. George Lindbeck, in *The Infallibility Debate*, p. 111.
95. Lindbeck, in *The Infallibility Debate*, p. 112.

Propositions, then, are affirmations that are either true or false. The same proposition may be expressed in varying ways using different sentences. If the proposition is true, the sentence, when properly interpreted, is also true. In this sense we can and should affirm that there are true propositions, or in Küng's terms, infallible propositions. However, the same sentence can be interpreted to mean different propositions. A sentence can be true and false, based on which proposition is intended by the sentence. While Küng argues that there are no infallible propositions, his discussion proceeds with an analysis of what Lindbeck calls sentences. Lindbeck rightly proposes that Küng needs to distinguish propositions, which are either true or false, and sentences, which can be true and false.

Lindbeck continues with an insightful critique. He observes,

> Religious thinkers, perhaps especially Catholics rebelling against too much of the wrong kind of Scholastic logic, seem more inclined at the moment than their secular colleagues to propose complicated and puzzling theories of truth which are far removed from traditional ones. Thus they get into the odd position of attacking the presumed irrationality of dogmatic infallibility by means of theories of propositional truth which are positively antirational to most secular specialists in these problems.[96]

In Küng's case, he argues that doctrines of infallibility and the immorality of artificial contraception are false, but with a theory of language that suggests all propositions can be both true and false. This argument leaves him in a strange bind, to say the least. Further, it is easy to see how Küng's opponents could use his analysis to argue for the necessity of continual reinterpretation and even reformulation of past doctrinal statements in order to retain their proper meaning. The intended meaning would remain "infallible" even as doctrinal statements are reinterpreted or reformulated.[97] But this is the theological exercise that Küng adamantly opposes as leading to untruthfulness.

The most celebrated response to Küng and *Infallible?*, and one that

---

96. Lindbeck, in *The Infallibility Debate*, p. 113. Lindbeck's own proposal is discussed in more detail in the introduction.

97. See Nowell, *A Passion for Truth*, p. 215.

incorporates and expands upon the critiques already mentioned, is that of Karl Rahner. Rahner proposes that Küng, as well as many of his opponents, holds a "basically rationalistic" conception of history. While Küng's opponents look to history for evidence of the immutability of the Catholic Church, Küng questions the teaching and structure of the Catholic Church whenever historical support appears to be lacking. In Rahner's opinion, neither Küng nor his opponents can account for the abiding identity of the Catholic Church in the midst of historical change.[98] Using the classifications laid out in this work, Rahner represents the moderate position on infallibility while those he labels "Küng's opponents" represent maximal infallibility. However, Rahner's primary target is the minimal infallibility of Küng.

In terms of theological methodology, Rahner believes that Küng's proposal "contradicts all Catholic theology at least since the Reformation and it contradicts the explicit teaching of Vatican I and II."[99] By rejecting papal infallibility and the infallibility of the Catholic Church in favor of the historical-critical exegesis of scripture, Küng explicitly denies defined teachings of the Catholic Church as well as basic Catholic methodology. Rahner states, "One can carry on such a discussion with Küng under the given presuppositions certainly only as one would with a liberal Protestant for whom a council and also Scripture are not matters that make an absolute claim on him."[100] Therefore, in Rahner's view, "We can no longer consider the controversy over Küng's thesis, from the nature of the case, as an inner-Catholic theological controversy."[101]

Next, Rahner challenges Küng's use of *Humanae Vitae*. Rahner believes Küng nowhere proves that *Humanae Vitae* is in fact false, or that *Humanae Vitae* is an infallible teaching of the ordinary universal magisterium.[102] To defend Küng, it should be noted that he does offer arguments for both points in *Infallible?*, although obviously these arguments are not convincing to Rahner. And Rahner never lays out what such proof would include. Nonetheless, Rahner maintains that *Humanae Vitae* does not meet the requirements of an infallible teaching as laid out in *Lumen Gentium* at Vatican II. As we have already seen, there is

98. Rahner, "A Critique of Hans Küng," p. 11.
99. Rahner, "A Critique of Hans Küng," p. 13.
100. Rahner, "A Critique of Hans Küng," p. 13.
101. Rahner, "A Critique of Hans Küng," p. 14.
102. Rahner, "A Critique of Hans Küng," pp. 12, 15.

considerable debate on this point among Catholic theologians from across the theological spectrum.

Rahner agrees that Küng's rejection of true, infallible propositions is highly problematic. For one, as we have already noted, it makes Küng's own proposal self-defeating, and to the extent that Küng maintains his position then "one could speak with him as one would with a skeptical philosopher."[103] However, Rahner's main concern is that, "If there is an indefectible remaining-in-the-truth for the Church, then there are also propositions which are 'in themselves' indefectible and are realized *as such.*"[104] For the Catholic Church to remain in the truth, there must be some indefectible propositions which the Catholic Church must continue to uphold. If this is the case, there must be some way of identifying these infallible propositions. For Rahner, it is the magisterium that identifies these infallible propositions; and in situations of conflict, it is the magisterium that pronounces a ruling, not theologians.[105]

Rahner invites Küng to adopt his own methodology, which is characteristic of moderate infallibility. Rahner states,

> Küng would have done us a great service if he had worked out a more precise theory of the historicity of propositions as such — a theory pointing out that every human proposition, because of the unity and the still remaining history of human consciousness, fundamentally and necessarily remains open to the future for a further interpretation. Thus, the history of the interpretation of even the most "infallible" proposition always perdures and a new interpretation cannot simply be suspected as a clever re-interpretation (as Küng is inclined to do for the sake of his thesis) because an ultimate identity of the old propositions and their necessarily ever new interpretation, given every concern for the grasp of historical and ideal continuity between the old and the new propositions themselves, can only be understood in a trusting faith in the permanency of the Church in the truth.[106]

103. Rahner, "A Critique of Hans Küng," p. 20.
104. Rahner, "A Critique of Hans Küng," p. 21, italics Rahner.
105. Rahner, "A Critique of Hans Küng," p. 24.
106. Rahner, "A Critique of Hans Küng," p. 22.

Stated briefly, Rahner argues that the theologian should accept the defined dogmas of the church, but because of the historicity of propositions as such, the theologian must ever attempt to properly interpret the defined dogmas. In Küng's reply, however, this is exactly the approach he refuses to adopt. He maintains that "in Rahner's approach we do not have interpretation but re-interpretation, that formulas are retained while the content is quietly changed. In brief: His method is not a positivistic but rather a speculative interpretation of dogma which is opposed to a truly historical one."[107]

As the debate continued, Rahner and Küng agreed that the primary difference between them was one of methodology, and they both defended the superiority of their own approach. However, Küng believes his disagreement with Rahner shows that,

> we are not dealing here simply with a "question of faith," but with a "complex problem of theological scholarship." Accordingly, Church leadership would overstep its competence if it wanted to direct this discussion with any kind of administrative measure or even to suppress it.[108]

As we have already seen, the Catholic authorities did not agree with Küng's assessment of their place in this debate. The Congregation for the Doctrine of the Faith warned Küng to no longer teach on the issue of infallibility. After *Infallible?* Küng focused his scholarly attention on the issues of christology and apologetics.

Küng followed the demands of the Congregation until 1979, when he wrote the preface for August Hasler's controversial work, *How the Pope Became Infallible.* Here Küng restates his position in *Infallible?* and highlights recent studies that support his position, but he does not offer new arguments. Against the methodology of the supporters of moderate infallibility, he maintains,

> Opportunistic reinterpretation, ultimately leading to outright denial of the text, is a common feature of all authoritarian systems,

107. Küng, "To Get to the Heart of the Matter: Answer to Karl Rahner — Part I," p. 28.

108. Küng, "To Get to the Heart of the Matter: Answer to Karl Rahner — Part II," p. 32.

but it only obscures the problems, violates intellectual integrity, and delays a comprehensive solution. Of course, read in their original sense, knowing what we know today, the texts on infallibility pose a still greater challenge to every Catholic than they did one hundred years ago.[109]

He continues to hold that the decisive question is whether there are "judgments, statements, definitions, and *creedal propositions* which are not only de facto true (which no one denies) but *infallibly true?*"[110] His answer is still a resounding No. And he suggests, "Thus far the recent debate over infallibility has not been marked by excommunications, suspensions, or professors losing their jobs, and such things are not likely to occur in the future."[111] On this last point Küng was mistaken. Before the year was over his canonical mission to teach Catholic theology would be revoked.

Analysis

Our analysis of Hans Küng must first recognize the many positive contributions he makes. Küng raises a number of concerns that are shared by many who reject doctrines of infallibility, especially papal infallibility. His emphasis on truthfulness and his refusal to conceal real difficulties has no doubt led to his widespread appeal. In his mature position, Küng refuses to retain the word "infallibility" when he is, in fact, speaking of indefectibility. Küng presents historical problems that raise substantial questions about doctrines of infallibility, even if one does not subscribe to all of his historical critiques. And Küng refuses to call a doctrinal change a "development" if such terminology is used to cover past errors in order to preserve doctrines of infallibility. Surely Küng is to be commended for facing these issues in an effort to overcome important conceptual difficulties.

109. Hans Küng, "Introduction: The Infallibility Debate: Where Are We Now?" in August Bernhard Hasler, *How the Pope Became Infallible* (Garden City, NY: Doubleday & Co., 1981), pp. 4-5.
110. Küng, "Introduction: The Infallibility Debate," in Hasler, *How the Pope Became Infallible,* p. 7, italics Küng.
111. Küng, "Introduction: The Infallibility Debate," in Hasler, *How the Pope Became Infallible,* p. 21.

Küng proceeds in the right direction when he stresses that the indefectibility of the church, and not doctrines of infallibility, is the primary belief to be affirmed. As Küng points out, this is the position of Orthodox and Protestant Christians, and a shift in Catholic theology from infallibility to indefectibility would have positive ecumenical implications. Although many Catholic theologians argue that infallibility is implied by indefectibility, Küng is right to question this implication.

Further, Küng's ecclesiology has much that should be commended. In his treatment of ecclesial authorities, Küng recognizes the necessity and divine origin of these authorities. His proposal that the pope should embrace a primacy of service instead of a primacy of jurisdiction or honor extends well the concern of this work, that ecclesial authorities be primarily conceived in soteriological rather than epistemic categories. He stresses the giftedness and responsibility of all members of the church in the quest for truth. Perhaps the main concern with Küng's ecclesiology is not his theory but his own practice. In his ongoing conflict with Catholic authorities, it is difficult to see where Küng accepts the role of ecclesial authorities to make doctrinal decisions on behalf of the church. One gets the sense that, in his treatment of the giftedness of the whole church and especially theologians, Küng is pushing his own agenda and seeking to circumvent the legitimate role of Catholic authorities.

Unfortunately, Küng's solution to the issues he raises is mired in the same conceptual mistakes that afflict doctrines of infallibility. Rejecting Catholic doctrines of infallibility, Küng adopts another theological method based on an epistemic understanding of the canons of the church. He simply shifts from the traditional Catholic position, which views the magisterium as an epistemic norm, to a Liberal Protestant emphasis, which adopts scripture subjected to historical-critical exegesis as an epistemic norm. In both cases, the canons of the church are viewed first and foremost as epistemic criteria. With his new criterion, Küng, like the defenders of papal infallibility, proceeds along methodist rather than particularist lines. In Küng's case his epistemic method is historical criticism.

On the basis of this new method, Küng not only questions doctrines of infallibility, but core beliefs affirmed in the canonical heritage of the church. He questions whether the pre-existence of the Son and the ontological divinity of Jesus are actually found in the original apostolic preaching, although both are found in the New Testament, the Nicene Creed, and the Chalcedonian Definition. He adopts a functional christology, where God acts in a dynamic way in the man Jesus, and he refuses to profess the ontological divinity of Jesus. Küng's christology, which he believes results from his new theological method, alienates him from many Orthodox and Protestant Christians who might otherwise agree with his rejection of papal infallibility. In addition, his revisionist version of the faith gives ammunition to the defenders of papal infallibility. Küng becomes a textbook example of what happens when one denies the epistemic doctrines of infallibility — one eventually denies material doctrines of the faith such as the ontological divinity of Jesus.

It is evident the Catholic authorities also proceed along methodist lines in epistemology. While they are concerned with Küng's rejection of orthodox christology, they are especially troubled by his rejection of infallibility. In their opinion, it is Küng's rejection of the latter that ultimately leads to his rejection of the former. Again, though, the presuppositions underlying methodism need to be questioned, especially in light of the many Orthodox and Protestant Christians who reject papal infallibility but still affirm orthodox christology.

Küng's discussion of "infallible propositions" only adds to the confusion of the debate. First of all, if we adopt the standard use of propositions as George Lindbeck does, it is better to speak of propositions as true or false, not infallible or fallible. Once this is done, we can then ask if there are propositions, whether true or false, that are essential to the identity of orthodox Christianity. Here the truth of the proposition is one issue, and whether or not the proposition is essential to the identity of orthodox Christianity is another. A proposition may be essential for a certain religion without being true.

Küng agrees that the Christian faith relies on propositions. When he addresses the truth of propositions or sentences (unfortunately he never distinguishes these terms as Lindbeck suggests), he repeatedly states that propositions or sentences may be *de facto* true but never infallibly true. Using Lindbeck's distinctions, Küng apparently means that a proposition may be true, but the sentence that expresses the proposition can always be interpreted in a false way. However, Küng's point about the nature of sentences is simply stretched too far. Unless Küng adopts an extreme hermeneutical skepticism, which he does not appear to do, his point can be granted and he can still be asked about the truth of the proposition under consideration. This work suggests that *ad hoc* arguments be offered for the truth or falsehood of particular propositions, an approach that fits well with the weak foundationalism Küng employs in his apologetic writings.

Rahner is right to press Küng for clarification on whether or not certain propositions are essential to orthodox Christian identity. The indefectibility of the church, which Küng affirms, requires that certain propositions of faith endure through time. Küng's own apparent denial of orthodox christology, which many would consider essential for the Christian faith, only makes more pressing the issue of whether or not certain propositions are essential to orthodox Christian identity. This work argues that the Christian faith includes essential, enduring propositions that are ultimately given by divine revelation and affirmed in the canonical heritage of the church. To be a Christian includes, but is not limited to, assent to these essential propositions.

This work maintains that emphasis should be given to particular propositions of belief instead of the epistemic methods used to arrive at these beliefs. The truth or falsehood of particular propositions can be argued for with various arguments, but no single epistemic method is sought and stringently followed in an effort to secure epistemic certainty. Thus the concern with Küng is not so much his use of the historical-critical exegesis of scripture, a method that can be and has been beneficial in the church's quest for truth, especially when anti-supernatural presuppositions are rejected. Instead, the concern is Küng's rejection of particular propositions of belief, such as his rejection of orthodox christology. Any proposed epistemic method must be combined with a profession of essential beliefs, particularly the theism found in the canonical heritage of the church. Other helpful proposals in epistemology and hermeneutics, such as the importance of community, tradition, and virtue — all of which Küng rightly affirms — must also be combined with a profession of essential beliefs. As suggested in the introduction, epistemic truisms alone are not enough.

Finally, the debate over *Humanae Vitae* clearly demonstrates the inability of doctrines of infallibility to provide epistemic certainty. In *Infallible?* Küng, a renowned Catholic theologian trained at the Gregorian University, argues that the immorality of artificial contraception has the status of an infallible teaching of the Catholic Church. Other renowned and well-trained theologians disagree, arguing that *Humanae Vitae* is not an *ex cathedra* definition. However, while Küng himself does not make this argument, we noted that *Humanae Vitae* would be an *ex cathedra* definition under a maximal interpretation of *Pastor Aeternus*. Küng, though, states that the immorality of artificial contraception is an infallible teaching of the ordinary universal magisterium. Once again there is disagreement, but this time it is much more widespread. Many conservative Catholic theologians agree with Küng and his supporters that the immorality of artificial contraception is an infallible teaching of the Catholic Church. Regardless of the merits or demerits of Küng work, the debate he sparked plainly illustrates the problem of identifying and interpreting infallible pronouncements. Such problems make it difficult to see how Catholic doctrines of infallibility bring the epistemic certainty that the Ultramontanes at Vatican I desired.

CHAPTER 7

Conclusion:
Orthodoxy Without Infallibility

Our survey of Catholic theologians has clearly demonstrated that there are problems with the doctrine of papal infallibility as a proposal in religious epistemology. The strongest desire for epistemic certainty is found in Manning, who was a leading advocate of papal infallibility at Vatican I. Manning's maximal infallibility, which stressed the problems of private judgment in theological reflection, looked to the pope to decisively settle theological disputes and secure doctrinal unity. Maximal infallibility envisions an infallible pope who speaks often and on a wide array of pressing topics. While many proponents of moderate infallibility argue that the limitations in *Pastor Aeternus* prevent a maximal position, we saw that this is not the case. Manning promoted maximal infallibility both before and after Vatican I, using the terminology found in *Pastor Aeternus,* and in no instance was he censured for doing so. In fact, he was elevated to Cardinal by Pope Pius IX after the Vatican council.

However, Manning's maximal infallibility is fraught with problems. His position is dependent on a strong foundationalism with unfeasibly high standards for knowledge that has been largely abandoned in contemporary epistemology. Rather than rescuing Manning from the problem of private judgment, maximal infallibility only continues his pursuit of epistemic certainty on an endless cycle. Infallible papal pronouncements must be properly identified, and then they too, like scripture and tradition, are subject to private interpretation. In this regard, papal pronouncements bring no more certainty than scripture and tradition do. If, as Manning suggests, religious certainty is needed to preserve Christian doctrine and maintain unity in the church, then Christians need to abandon theological and ecumenical endeavors. The certainty and unity Manning seeks is found nowhere, not even in the Catholic Church.

Not only does Manning's position fail to bring religious certainty, it leads to a host of epistemic problems. His maximal infallibility makes it difficult to deal with past papal errors, as illustrated in his treatment of Pope Honorius. In this instance either Honorius was a heretic, or subsequent popes and ecumenical councils were in error to condemn him. Either way, Manning's conception of the papacy as an infallible belief-producing mechanism does not fare well. Manning also maintains the traditional Catholic idea of doctrinal immutability. However, the events of Manning's lifetime, especially the definition of the doctrines of the immaculate conception and papal infallibility, made doctrinal immutability difficult to sustain. Leaving the legitimacy of these definitions aside, they are not clearly found in the New Testament or patristic church. Manning's standard response to these problems was to disparage historical research, but in doing so he gives up important epistemic resources for the sake of an epistemic method that does not deliver on its promises.

In a last-ditch effort to salvage maximal infallibility, Manning deals with the problems of identifying and interpreting papal pronouncements by turning to the pope. The pope alone can judge which pronouncements are infallible and how they are to be interpreted. This move still does not solve the problem of epistemic certainty, as now one must interpret infallible papal interpretations of infallible papal pronouncements. But this move does lead to a form of absolutism that is extremely problematic. The Catholic Church rightly rejected papal absolutism for a more collegial understanding of the church at Vatican II.

Newman's moderate infallibility and his theory of doctrinal development were proposed to address many of the problems that result from maximal infallibility. The moderate position substantially limits the number of infallible papal pronouncements, and the theory of doctrinal development explains the lack of historical support for recent Catholic doctrines. Newman, though, shares many of Manning's assumptions in epistemology. Like Manning, Newman is seeking epistemic certainty, and this certainty is required for religious claims to qualify as knowledge. In his case, religious certainty is found in an infallible church and an infallible pope that properly distinguish legitimate and illegitimate doctrinal developments. Without an infallible judge of doctrinal development, the church cannot be maintained in doctrine or unity.

However, the complexity of Newman's proposal subtly undermines the epistemic certainty he seeks. To avoid papal absolutism, Newman highlights the problem of identifying and interpreting infallible papal pronouncements. For Newman, the church as a whole has a part in adopting infallible papal pronouncements, and theologians in particular play a crucial role in interpreting infallible doctrines. While Newman recognizes the problem of past papal errors, he offers explanations for these errors, some of which are quite inventive, in an attempt to preserve papal infallibility. When he considers the possibility of future papal errors, he employs a number of epistemic resources, primarily conscience, to counter these potential errors. Thus, while Newman desires epistemic certainty, his moderate infallibility highlights the complexity of religious epistemology. Far more is at work in Newman's proposal than infallible popes and infallible councils that secure epistemic certainty for the church.

Further, Newman's theory of doctrinal development, like Manning's view of doctrinal immutability, undermines important epistemic resources. Like Manning, Newman emphasizes the tentative and uncertain nature of historical research, in his case to support his theory of doctrinal development. Since recent doctrines may be legitimate developments adopted by an infallible pope, historical support is not strictly required for Catholic doctrines. While the theory of doctrinal development worked in Newman's favor for the doctrines he supported, it was also used against him by proponents of doctrines he opposed. Suddenly, Newman could no longer appeal to historical problems in contemporary doctrinal proposals since such doctrines could be legitimate doctrinal developments. Further, proponents of theological liberalism could appeal to doctrinal development to bypass historical beliefs like the Trinity and Chalcedonian christology. In an attempt to shore up religious epistemology, Newman proposes a theory of doctrinal development that is based on questionable assumptions and rejects important epistemic resources.

With Dulles the declining fortunes of moderate infallibility as a form of religious epistemology come to view. Dulles adopts a symbolic realism that stresses the symbolic and incomprehensible nature of re- ality, especially the divine. Because of the mysterious nature of reality, it is impossible to adequately express reality in propositional statements. Thus all propositional statements, especially theological statements, are open to hermeneutical treatment and reinterpretation. With this symbolic realism in hand, Dulles affirms traditional doctrines of infal- libility, and he maintains that an infallible pope is needed for the church to remain united in the truth of the gospel. But Dulles's sym- bolic realism also allows him to argue that all doctrinal statements, in- cluding the doctrine of papal infallibility, are open to continual reinter- pretation by the church if such doctrines appear implausible. For example, Dulles interprets infallibility much like the traditional notion of indefectibility, although he retains the term "infallibility" to empha- size doctrinal continuity. Further, Dulles emphasizes the collegial na- ture of the church, since the church as a whole is needed to discern the mysterious nature of the divine. But as we have seen with Newman, an emphasis on the collective discernment of the church raises the ques- tion of how to locate and properly interpret infallible pronouncements. For Dulles, such epistemic problems only serve to demonstrate his no- tion of the symbolic view of reality.

However, several problems flow from Dulles's moderate infallibility. First, since all doctrinal statements are open to reinterpretation, one wonders to what extent the theism found in the canonical heritage of the church can be reinterpreted. Dulles suggests that such doctrines are open to reinterpretation, and surely we should want to present these doctrines in a way that clearly communicates the gospel to contempo- rary society. But would it suffice to interpret the doctrine of the Trinity as Arianism, even if we retained the term Trinity? Are there any limits to the mysterious nature of the divine and the process of reinterpretation?

Second, the theological method of Dulles and other proponents of moderate infallibility raise questions about the integrity of Christian theology. Dulles affirms the need for infallibility, yet doubts the reality of epistemic certainty. He stresses the doctrinal continuity of the Cath- olic Church, yet reinterprets past doctrines that are no longer plausible. The result is a dubious methodology that quickly creates suspicions in the believer and unbeliever alike. Third, Dulles knows from his exten- sive work in ecumenical dialogue that papal infallibility is a substantial ecumenical problem. Dulles's moderate infallibility, though, retains papal infallibility without clearly identifying and overcoming the problems of papal infallibility as a proposal in religious epistemology.

Küng's minimal infallibility, which is actually a rejection of papal infallibility, refuses to engage in the epistemic practices of moderate infallibility. Küng does not call doctrinal change a doctrinal development, and he does not retain the term "infallibility" when he is in fact speaking of indefectibility. Küng admits historical problems in the doctrinal history of the Catholic Church without attempting to explain these problems away. And he is not interested in retaining the notion of religious certainty. His entire project is characterized by a concern for truthfulness and epistemic integrity.

However, while Küng rejects papal infallibility, he adopts another theological method based on an epistemic conception of ecclesial canons, the historical-critical exegesis of scripture. Thus, his new position preserves two of the assumptions concerning religious epistemology that are questioned in this work: he continues to view ecclesial canons primarily in the arena of epistemology and he maintains methodist commitments in epistemology. On the basis of his new epistemic method, Küng calls for the rejection of fundamental Christian beliefs such as Chalcedonian christology. So Küng's rejection of orthodox christology appears to support the claim of the proponents of papal infallibility. It seems that the only real options are papal infallibility on one hand, and skepticism and heresy on the other. This work has argued that these are not the only two options. One can reject papal infallibility and still confess the theism found in the canonical heritage of the church.

The debate over Küng's *Infallible? An Inquiry* demonstrates once again the inadequacy of doctrines of infallibility. In *Infallible?* Küng gives the example of *Humanae Vitae,* which bans the use of artificial contraception, as an example of an erroneous teaching of the Catholic magisterium that has the status of an infallible doctrine. Küng's example, though, sparked a substantial debate over whether *Humanae Vitae* is indeed an infallible exercise of either the extraordinary papal magisterium or the ordinary universal magisterium. The debate clearly shows the problem of identifying infallible doctrines by the foremost officials and theologians of the Catholic Church. Obviously, doctrines of infallibility have not brought the epistemic certainty first envisioned by Manning and even Newman.

Now that specific articulations of papal infallibility have been examined, we can further consider the four conceptual errors of papal infallibility and the constructive proposal for religious epistemology presented in chapter 1. First, the doctrine of papal infallibility conceives ecclesial canons as epistemic criteria. Obviously Manning and Newman view scripture and ecumenical councils as epistemic criteria, and the pope as an infallible belief-producing mechanism who properly interprets, and in Newman's case properly develops, these criteria. While Dulles's proposal is more complex, he still defends the necessity of an infallible pope. Küng, of course, rejects the idea of the pope as an infallible belief-producing mechanism. Nevertheless, he still views scripture as an epistemic norm to be subjected to historical-critical exegesis.

This work argues that the ecclesial canons of the church are better viewed in the arena of soteriology than epistemology. In other words, ecclesial canons are primarily means of grace that lead one to salvation, not criteria for knowledge claims. This point needs to be carefully stated, because ecclesial canons can and should play a role in religious epistemology. For example, it is certainly appropriate to appeal to scripture in arguments for Christian beliefs since scripture provides access to divine revelation. The decrees of ecumenical councils give us access to the beliefs of Christians who lived before us. In some instances, creedal statements like the Apostles' Creed and Nicene Creed continue to be confessed, whether formally or informally, by a large majority of ecclesial traditions today. However, in all of these instances, an appeal to scripture, council, or creed is not necessarily an appeal to an epistemic criterion.

Conceiving ecclesial canons as epistemic criteria is highly problematic. For instance, when an error is found in scripture and scripture is viewed as an epistemic criterion, it appears that scripture should be abandoned altogether as an epistemic resource. At the very least, scripture is retained as a norm for Christian belief that is subjected to critical historical evaluation based on anti-supernatural presuppositions. Further, an epistemic conception of the papacy continues to be a primary component in the separation of Christian traditions. This work argues that ecclesial canons simply do not function as epistemic criteria. Even the staunchest defenders of papal infallibility and biblical inerrancy appeal to a wide variety of epistemic resources when defending alleged errors in these canons, or when properly interpreting these canons. Since ecclesial canons do not in fact function as epistemic criteria, it is far more fruitful to view them in the arena of soteriology. Here the role of scripture and the episcopacy is to communicate what God has done on our behalf and to be used by the Holy Spirit to transform us into the likeness of Christ.

Second, papal infallibility is committed to methodism in epistemology, usually in an attempt to secure epistemic certainty. This is especially clear in the case of Manning and Newman. For Manning, there is either a divine certainty of faith grounded in papal infallibility, or Christianity has not been preserved. Newman, based on his theory of doctrinal development in an infallible church, states that the only options are Trent and skepticism. Here we see stark contrasts, where one either follows the proper epistemic method or is lost in uncertainty and doubt. Dulles and Küng also maintain methodist commitments. Dulles ultimately argues that an infallible pope is necessary to secure doctrine and maintain unity in the church. And while Küng rejects papal infallibility, he adopts another epistemic method, the historical-critical exegesis of scripture. Küng follows this new method, along with its anti-supernatural assumptions about history, to the bitter end.

This work argues that particularism is more appropriate than methodism in epistemology. That is, the truth of particular knowledge claims, arrived at through a variety of *ad hoc* arguments, is more secure than any comprehensive method that is proposed to secure particular knowledge claims. For example, the doctrine of the Trinity, argued from scripture, tradition, and the historic consensus of the church, is more secure than proposals like papal infallibility and biblical inerrancy that are intended to secure this doctrine and others. Although papal infallibility cannot bring epistemic certainty, we do not necessarily give up particular Christian beliefs that the pope has affirmed.

The move from methodism to particularism in religious epistemology raises several questions that require attention. First, what specific beliefs are proposed as being fundamental for the Christian faith? This work suggests that the theism found in the canonical heritage of the church, or canonical theism, is a substantial candidate. Canonical theism is actually a complex web of beliefs that presents a specific vision of God, the human condition, and salvation. This theism is not the proposal of an individual theologian or ecumenical committee, but is articulated in the public, ecumenical decisions of the undivided church. Further, canonical theism can be defended by appealing to a variety of arguments.

Second, what about the many other issues that continue to divide Christian traditions? Ecumenical unity should be grounded first and foremost on the doctrinal commitments found in canonical theism, and even here careful discernment must be applied. However, other divisive issues can and should still be debated by appealing to arguments of various kinds. For example, Catholics and Protestants would still likely disagree over the Marian dogmas for many of the same reasons that they currently do. But discernment and time are needed to recognize which specific beliefs are central to Christian identity, and which beliefs are not central or are no longer tenable.

One of the problems here is that the Christian faith is too often viewed as an all-or-nothing affair where one either has the truth, or one is outside the truth. If we compare this notion, though, with how we view other cases of knowledge, it is apparent how misguided this view is. No one would claim that all of their general beliefs are true and that they hold no false beliefs. In fact, we regularly change our opinion and grow in our knowledge of the world. Such changes do not suggest that beforehand we were completely devoid of knowledge. Rather, growth in knowledge is viewed as a lifelong journey, and there is a confidence that much of what we believe is true. The same is true of the Christian faith. The church can be confident that the Holy Spirit has guided it, and that much of what we believe about the gospel is true. However, this does not mean that there will no differences of opinion, or changes in our own beliefs. The Christian life too is a journey. God can and does work in spite of some false beliefs on our part to bring about God's primary goal, our spiritual transformation.

Third, is it not inevitable that some epistemic method will be adopted, no matter how tentatively? The answer is Yes, and the superiority of various epistemic methods can be argued for as well. However, the move to particularism makes us aware of the liabilities inherent in all epistemic methods, and the need to focus on particular doctrinal commitments. Epistemology is a complex field of investigation, and it is not even the primary concern of the Christian community. William Abraham offers the following advice:

> We may have to be content with epistemic proposals which illuminate crucial tracts of Christian theology, rather than provide a single theory which will cover the whole terrain. It may even be the

case that the best way ahead in the epistemology of theology is to be epistemically agnostic, cautious about the success of any general epistemological theory as applicable to theology. As in many other areas of life, it may be that in theology we know much more than we can either explain or show that we know.[1]

Returning to the four conceptual errors, the third problem with papal infallibility is that it canonizes an epistemology. Papal infallibility was canonized in the Catholic tradition at Vatican I, and since then it has been problematic for Catholic theology and disastrous for Christian ecumenical dialogue. For this reason, we will offer suggestions for dealing with papal infallibility in Catholic theology below. It should be emphasized, though, that the task of the church is to preach the gospel, and not an epistemology, to the world. While epistemic arguments will need to be employed at times, these are secondary to the fundamental mission of the church.

And fourth, papal infallibility wrongly assumes that epistemic certainty is required for maintaining ecclesial unity. Proponents of papal infallibility argue that epistemic certainty is not only required to secure doctrine, but also to maintain unity in the church. However, epistemic certainty is not logically required for the effective exercise of teaching and organizational authority. Further, we have seen that papal infallibility simply does not bring the epistemic certainty it promises. If ecclesial unity depends on epistemic certainty, ecumenical proceedings should be discontinued.

The proposal offered here challenges much of Western theology, whether Catholic or Protestant. Western theology for the most part views ecclesial canons as epistemic criteria and is deeply wedded to methodism in epistemology. Further, Western Christians have been tempted to canonize epistemologies, either informally or formally. Given that papal infallibility is clearly canonized in the Catholic tradition, how might Catholic theologians proceed given the argument of this work? Here we can only provide suggestive hints, since this must be the task of Catholic theologians rather than a Protestant observer.

Before considering the following suggestions, it is necessary to re-

---

1. William J. Abraham, *Canon and Criterion in Christian Theology* (Oxford: Clarendon Press, 1998), pp. 479-80.

call the two related but separate proposals that are implicit in William Abraham's *Canon and Criterion in Christian Theology* and that are argued for in this work: the ecumenical proposal and the epistemological proposal. Both proposals include two major points. According to the ecumenical proposal, (1) ecumenical unity should be based on specific doctrinal beliefs, namely the theism found in the canonical heritage of the undivided church. Since canonical theism can be argued for with a variety of epistemologies, (2) no single epistemology should be canonized in the ecumenical arena. According to the epistemological proposal, (1) ecclesial canons should be viewed primarily in the arena of soteriology, not epistemology, and (2) particularist commitments in epistemology should be adopted in favor of methodist commitments. With these two proposals before us, it should be noted that one can adopt the ecumenical proposal without adopting the epistemological proposal. In fact, the ecumenical proposal stresses that no single epistemological vision should be made the basis for ecumenical unity. Therefore, at least two options are available to Catholic theologians based on whether they accept or reject our proposal in religious epistemology.

First, if the ecumenical proposal is accepted while the epistemological proposal is rejected, papal infallibility could be viewed as a local epistemology of the Catholic Church that is not binding on other Christians within a larger ecumenical union. The Catholic theologian may disagree that particularism is preferable to methodism in epistemology, and may affirm that papal infallibility offers the best available method for securing religious knowledge. Still, the Catholic theologian could affirm papal infallibility and the ecumenical proposal offered here by confessing the theism found in the canonical heritage of the undivided church, and refusing to canonize an epistemology in the ecumenical arena. Other Christians who confess canonical theism could also be a part of this ecumenical union, though they would not have to affirm papal infallibility.

Second, and by far more preferable, the epistemological proposal could be accepted along with the ecumenical proposal, and ecclesial canons would be conceived outside the realm of epistemology. One way this could be done that would be conversant with contemporary Catholic theology is to further interpret or develop the doctrine of papal infallibility in Catholic theology in light of the epistemic concerns presented

211

in this work. As has already been illustrated, Dulles's work in hermeneutics and Catholic theories of doctrinal development give Catholic theologians significant leeway in affirming past doctrinal statements while recognizing the philosophical limitations of those statements. While earlier it was suggested that such moves make claims to infallibility and epistemic certainty look unconvincing, these same moves could be used to relocate *Pastor Aeternus* outside the field of epistemology. *Pastor Aeternus* could be interpreted or developed in light of philosophical developments that question the possibility of epistemic certainty and the viability of methodist commitments in epistemology.

For instance, recall Dulles's suggestion that *Pastor Aeternus* is primarily concerned with establishing the primacy of the pope in his teaching ministry in the Catholic Church. This teaching primacy can be affirmed without viewing the papacy as an infallible belief-producing mechanism. Future interpretations and developments of *Pastor Aeternus* could recognize that the desire for an infallible epistemic method and religious certainty found in *Pastor Aeternus* was culturally conditioned and unnecessary for the primary concern of the council, which was to affirm the teaching authority of the pope. The pope could still serve as the final judge of doctrinal disputes in the Catholic Church without viewing teaching and organizational authority along epistemic lines.

This second option is attractive for several reasons. First, in chapter 2 we saw that the Ultramontanes at Vatican I were concerned with a number of issues, including Gallicanism, the increasing loss of papal authority, and modernism. While an epistemology was defined to address these issues, this is not the only possible response. Gallicanism can be rejected as an option in the Catholic Church, papal authority can be affirmed, and the excesses of modernism can be opposed without conceiving the papacy as an infallible belief-producing mechanism. Second, the epistemic proposal offered here is highly compatible with the weak foundationalism employed by many Catholic theologians, including Newman, Dulles, and Küng. Particularism can readily employ various arguments for specific beliefs, though it does question the need for and availability of a comprehensive epistemic method.

These suggestions will need further elaboration by Catholic theologians. It should also be noted that these suggestions do not solve all of the ecumenical issues posed by the papacy. For one, they do not deal with the issue of primacy.[2] Nevertheless, if the episcopacy is reconceived along the lines suggested here, the issue of primacy will be easier to address. The pope could still exercise primacy in the Catholic Church while exercising a different role of leadership in any potential ecumenical union, as the bishop of Rome did in the first millennium of the church's existence. Even if ecumenical union is not a possibility, the proposal given here offers viable resources for Catholic theologians in their conception of ecclesial authority.

2. See J. Michael Miller, *What Are They Saying About Papal Primacy?* (New York: Paulist Press, 1983).

Bibliography

Abraham, William J. *Canon and Criterion in Christian Theology.* Oxford: Clarendon Press, 1998.

———. *Crossing the Threshold of Divine Revelation.* Grand Rapids: Eerdmans, 2006.

———. *An Introduction to the Philosophy of Religion.* Englewood Cliffs, New Jersey: Prentice-Hall, 1985.

Abraham, William J., Jason E. Vickers, and Natalie E. Van Kirk, eds. *Canonical Theism: A Proposal for Theology and the Church.* Grand Rapids: Eerdmans, 2008.

Barraclough, Geoffrey. *The Medieval Papacy.* New York: Harcourt, Brace & World, 1968.

Barth, Karl. *Church Dogmatics: A Selection with Introduction by Helmut Gollwitzer.* Translated and edited by G. W. Bromiley. Louisville: Westminster John Knox Press, 1994.

Boff, Leonardo. *Trinity and Society.* Maryknoll, NY: Orbis Books, 1988.

Braaten, Carl E., and Robert W. Jenson, eds. *Church Unity and the Papal Office.* Grand Rapids: Eerdmans, 2001.

Butler, B. C. *The Church and Infallibility: A Reply to the Abridged "Salmon."* New York: Sheed & Ward, 1954.

Butler, Edward Cuthbert. *The Vatican Council: 1869-1870: Based on Bishop Ullathorne's Letters.* Edited by Christopher Butler. Westminster, MD: Newman Press, 1962.

Calvin, John. *Institutes of the Christian Religion.* Vol. 1. Edited by John T. McNeill. Translated by Ford Lewis Battles. Philadelphia: Westminster Press, 1960.

Chadwick, Owen. *From Bossuet to Newman.* Cambridge: Cambridge University Press, 1957.

———. *A History of the Popes: 1830-1914.* Oxford: Clarendon Press, 1998.

———. *The Secularization of the European Mind in the Nineteenth Century.* Cambridge: Cambridge University Press, 1975.

Bibliography

"Chicago Statement on Biblical Inerrancy." *Journal of the Evangelical Theological Society* 21, no. 4 (December 1978): 289-96.

Chirico, Peter. *Infallibility: The Crossroads of Doctrine.* Wilmington, DE: Michael Glazier, 1983.

Chisholm, Roderick M. *The Problem of the Criterion.* Milwaukee: Marquette University Press, 1973.

Cobb, John B., and David Ray Griffin, *Process Theology: An Introductory Exposition.* Philadelphia: Westminster Press, 1976.

Cone, James H. *A Black Theology of Liberation.* Twentieth Anniversary ed. Maryknoll, NY: Orbis Books, 1990.

De George, Richard T. *The Nature and Limits of Authority.* Lawrence, KS: University Press of Kansas, 1985.

Derrida, Jacques. *A Derrida Reader: Between the Blinds.* Edited by Peggy Kamuf. New York: Columbia University Press, 1991.

Dionne, J. Robert. *The Papacy and the Church: A Study of Praxis and Reception in Ecumenical Perspective.* New York: Philosophical Library, 1987.

Duffy, Eamon. *Saints and Sinners: A History of the Popes.* 2nd ed. New Haven: Yale University Press, 2001.

Dulles, Avery. *Apologetics and the Biblical Christ.* Paramus, NJ: Newman Press, 1963.

———. *A Church to Believe In.* New York: Crossroad, 1982.

———. *The Craft of Theology: From Symbol to System.* New expanded ed. New York: Crossroad, 1995.

———. *Models of the Church.* Expanded ed. New York: Image Books, 1987.

———. *Models of Revelation.* Maryknoll, NY: Orbis Books, 1999.

———. *Newman.* New York: Continuum, 2002.

———. *The Reshaping of Catholicism.* San Francisco: Harper & Row, 1988.

———. *The Resilient Church.* Garden City, NY: Doubleday & Co., 1977.

———. *Revelation and the Quest for Unity.* Washington, DC: Corpus Books, 1968.

———. *The Survival of Dogma.* New York: Crossroad, 1982.

———. *A Testimonial to Grace and Reflections on a Theological Journey.* Kansas City: Sheed & Ward, 1996.

Empie, Paul C., T. Austin Murphy, and Joseph A. Burgess, eds. *Teaching Authority and Infallibility in the Church: Lutherans and Catholics in Dialogue VI.* Minneapolis: Augsburg, 1978.

Femiano, Samuel D. *Infallibility of the Laity: The Legacy of Newman.* New York: Herder & Herder, 1967.

Fessler, Joseph. *The True and False Infallibility of the Popes.* New York: Catholic Publication Society, 1875.

Ford, David F., ed. *The Modern Theologians.* 2nd ed. Malden, MA: Blackwell, 1997.

Foucault, Michel. *A Foucault Reader.* Edited by Paul Rabinow. New York: Pantheon, 1984.

Gilley, Sheridan. "Manning: The Catholic Writings." In *By Whose Authority? Newman, Manning, and the Magisterium,* edited by V. Alan McClelland, pp. 244-58. Bath: Downside Abbey, 1996.

————. *Newman and His Age.* London: Darton, Longman & Todd, 1990.

Gladstone, W. E. *The Vatican Decrees in Their Bearing on Civil Allegiance.* London: John Murray, 1874.

————. *Vaticanism: An Answer to Replies and Reproofs.* London: John Murray, 1875.

Gratry, Auguste Joseph Alphonse. *Papal Infallibility Untenable: Three Letters.* 1st American ed. Hartford: Church Press, 1870.

Gray, Robert. *Cardinal Manning: A Biography.* London: Weidenfeld & Nicolson, 1985.

Haag, Herbert. "Preface: An Unresolved Enquiry." In *Infallible? An Unresolved Enquiry,* by Hans Küng, pp. xvii-xviii. New York: Continuum, 1994.

Hales, Edward E. Y. *Pio Nono: A Study in European Politics and Religion in the Nineteenth Century.* Garden City, NY: Doubleday, 1954.

Häring, Hermann. *Hans Küng: Breaking Through.* Translated by John Bowden. New York: Continuum, 1998.

Häring, Hermann, and Karl-Josef Kuschel, eds. *Hans Küng: His Work and His Way.* Translated by Robert Nowell. Garden City, NY: Image Books, 1980.

Hasler, August Bernhard. *Wie der Papst unfehlbar wurde.* Munich: Piper, 1979. ET: *How the Pope Became Infallible.* Translated by Peter Heinegg. Garden City, NY: Doubleday & Co., 1981.

————. *Pius IX. (1846-1878), papstliche Unfehlbarkeit und 1. Vatikanisches Konzil. Dogmatisierung und Durchsetzung einer Ideologie.* 2 vols. Papste und Papsttum, no. 12. Stuttgart: Verlag Anton Hiersemann, 1977.

Hodge, Charles. *Systematic Theology.* Vol. 1. New York: Scribner, Armstrong & Co., 1874.

Holmes, J. Derek, ed. *The Theological Papers of John Henry Newman on Biblical Inspiration and on Infallibility.* Oxford: Clarendon Press, 1979.

————. *The Triumph of the Holy See: A Short History of the Papacy in the Nineteenth Century.* London: Burns & Oates; Shepherdstown, WV: Patmos Press, 1978.

Jelly, Fredrick M. *Madonna: Mary in the Catholic Tradition.* Huntington, IN: Our Sunday Visitor Publishing, 1986.

Johnson, Luke Timothy. *Scripture and Discernment: Decision Making in the Church.* Nashville: Abingdon Press, 1996.

Ker, Ian. *John Henry Newman: A Biography.* Oxford: Clarendon Press, 1988.

Kirvan, John J., ed. *The Infallibility Debate.* New York: Paulist Press, 1971.

Kiwiet, John. *Hans Küng.* Waco, TX: Word, 1985.

Kuhn, Thomas S. *The Structure of Scientific Revolutions.* Chicago: University of Chicago Press, 1962.

Küng, Hans. *Christ Sein.* Munich: Piper, 1974. ET: *On Being a Christian.* Translated by Edward Quinn. London: Collins, 1978.

————. *Erkämpfte Freiheit: Erinnerungen.* Munich: Piper, 2002. ET: *My Struggle for Freedom: Memoirs.* Translated by John Bowden. Grand Rapids: Eerdmans, 2003.

————. *Existiert Gott?* Munich: Piper, 1978. ET: *Does God Exist?* Translated by Edward Quinn. Garden City, NY: Doubleday & Co., 1980.

————. "Im Interesse der Sache: Antwort an Karl Rahner." *Stimmen der Zeit* (January 1971): 43-64. ET: "To Get to the Heart of the Matter: Answer to Karl Rahner." *Homiletic and Pastoral Review* (June 1971): 9-29.

————. "Im Interesse der Sache: Antwort an Karl Rahner." *Stimmen der Zeit* (February 1971): 105-22. ET: "To Get to the Heart of the Matter: Answer to Karl Rahner — Part II." *Homiletic and Pastoral Review* (July 1971): 17-32.

————. *Die Kirche.* Freiburg: Herder, 1967. ET: *The Church.* Translated by Ray and Rosaleen Ockenden. New York: Sheed & Ward, 1967.

————. *Kirche — gehalten in der Wahrheit?* Zurich: Benziger, 1979. ET: *The Church — Maintained in Truth.* Translated by Edward Quinn. New York: Seabury Press, 1980.

————. *Konzil und Wiedervereinigung.* Freiburg: Herder, 1959. ET: *The Council, Reform and Reunion.* Translated by Cecily Hastings. New York: Sheed & Ward, 1961.

————. "Postscript." *Homiletic and Pastoral Review* (August/September 1971): 28-31.

————. *Rechtfertigung: Die Lehre Karl Barths und eine Katholische Besinnung.* Einsiedeln: Johannes, 1957. ET: *Justification: The Doctrine of Karl Barth and a Catholic Reflection.* Translated by Thomas Collins, Edmund E. Tolk, and David Granskou. New York: Thomas Nelson, 1964.

————. *Struckturen der Kirche.* Freiburg: Herder, 1962. ET: *Structures of the Church.* Translated by Salvator Attanasio. New York: Crossroad, 1964, 1982.

————. *Theologie im Aufbruch.* Munich: Piper, 1987. ET: *Theology for the Third Millennium.* Translated by Peter Heinegg. New York: Doubleday, 1988.

————. *Truthfulness: The Future of the Church.* New York: Sheed & Ward, 1968.

————. *Unfehlbar? Eine Anfrage.* Zurich: Benziger, 1970. ET: *Infallible? An Inquiry.* With a new introduction by the author. Translated by Edward Quinn. Garden City, NY: Doubleday & Co., 1983.

LaCugna, Catherine Mowry. *God for Us: The Trinity and Christian Life.* San Francisco: HarperCollins, 1991.

Lash, Nicholas. *Newman on Development.* Shepherdstown, WV: Patmos Press, 1975.

Leslie, Shane. *Henry Edward Manning: His Life and Labours.* London: Burns, Oates & Washbourne, Ltd., 1921.

Lindbeck, George A. *Infallibility.* Milwaukee: Marquette University Press, 1972.

————. *The Nature of Doctrine: Religion and Theology in a Postliberal Age.* Philadelphia: Westminster Press, 1984.

McClelland, V. A. *Cardinal Manning: His Public Life and Influence, 1865-1892.* London: Oxford University Press, 1962.

McCord, Peter J., ed. *A Pope for All Christians: An Inquiry into the Role of Peter in the Modern Church.* New York: Paulist Press, 1976.

McGrath, Alister. *The Genesis of Doctrine: A Study in the Foundation of Doctrinal Criticism.* Grand Rapids: Eerdmans, 1990.

Manning, Henry Edward. *The Centenary of St. Peter and the General Council: A Pastoral Letter to the Clergy.* London: Longmans, 1867.

———. *The Oecumenical Council and the Infallibility of the Roman Pontiff: A Pastoral Letter to the Clergy.* 2nd ed. London: Longmans, 1869.

———. *The Temporal Mission of the Holy Ghost; or, Reason and Revelation.* New York: D. Appleton, 1866.

———. *The True Story of the Vatican Council.* London: Henry S. King, 1877.

———. *The Vatican Council and Its Definitions: A Pastoral Letter to the Clergy.* New York: D. & J. Sadlier, 1871.

———. *The Vatican Decrees in Their Bearing on Civil Allegiance.* New York: Catholic Publication Society, 1875.

Manning, Henry Edward, and Robert G. Ingersoll. *Rome or Reason? A Series of Articles Contributed to the North American Review.* New York: C. P. Farrell, 1914.

Merrigan, Terrence. "Models in the Theology of Avery Dulles: A Critical Analysis." *Bijdragen* 54 (1993): 141-61.

Milbank, John, Catherine Pickstock, and Graham Ward, eds. *Radical Orthodoxy: A New Theology.* New York: Routledge, 1999.

Miller, J. Michael. *What Are They Saying About Papal Primacy?* New York: Paulist Press, 1983.

Misner, Paul. *Papacy and Development: Newman and the Primacy of the Pope.* Leiden: E. J. Brill, 1976.

Moltmann, Jürgen. *The Trinity and the Kingdom.* Minneapolis: Fortress Press, 1993.

Mozley, J. B. *The Theory of Development: A Criticism of Dr. Newman's Essay on the Development of Christian Doctrine.* London: Rivingtons, 1878.

Musser, Donald W., and Joseph L. Price, eds. *A New Handbook of Christian Theologians.* Nashville: Abingdon Press, 1996.

Newman, John Henry. *Apologia Pro Vita Sua.* London: Oxford University Press, 1964.

———. *An Essay on the Development of Christian Doctrine.* Notre Dame: University of Notre Dame Press, 1990.

———. *Fifteen Sermons Preached Before the University of Oxford.* London: Longmans, Green & Co., 1898.

———. *A Grammar of Assent.* New York: Longmans, Green & Co., 1947.

———. *Letter to the Duke of Norfolk.* In *Newman and Gladstone: The Vatican Decrees.* Edited by Alvan Ryan. Notre Dame: University of Notre Dame Press, 1962.

———. *On Consulting the Faithful in Matters of Doctrine.* London: Collins, 1986.

———. *The Via Media of the Anglican Church.* Edited by H. D. Weidner. Oxford: Clarendon Press, 1990.

Newsome, David. *The Convert Cardinals: John Henry Newman and Henry Edward Manning.* London: John Murray, 1993.

Nichols, Terence L. *That All May Be One: Hierarchy and Participation in the Church.* Collegeville, MN: Liturgical Press, 1997.

Niebuhr, H. Richard. *Christ and Culture.* New York: Harper & Row, 1951.

Nowell, Robert. *A Passion for Truth: Hans Küng and His Theology.* New York: Crossroad, 1981.

Ogden, Schubert. *On Theology.* San Francisco: Harper & Row, 1986.

Page, John R. *What Will Dr. Newman Do? John Henry Newman and Papal Infallibility, 1865-1875.* Collegeville, MN: Liturgical Press, 1994.

Pannenberg, Wolfhart, Avery Dulles, and Carl E. Braaten. *Spirit, Faith, and Church.* Philadelphia: Westminster Press, 1970.

Pelikan, Jaroslav, and Valerie Hotchkiss, eds. *Creeds and Confessions of Faith in the Christian Tradition.* Vol. 3. New Haven: Yale University Press, 2003.

Pereiro, James. *Cardinal Manning: An Intellectual Biography.* Oxford: Clarendon Press, 1998.

Popkin, Richard H. *The History of Scepticism from Erasmus to Descartes.* Assen: Van Gorcum, 1960.

Purcell, E. S. *Life of Cardinal Manning.* 2 vols. London: Macmillan & Co., 1896.

Rahner, Karl. "Kritik an Hans Küng: Zur Frage der Unfehlbarkeit theologischer Sätze," *Stimmen der Zeit* (December 1970): 361-77. ET: "A Critique of Hans Küng: Concerning the Infallibility of Theological Propositions." *Homiletic and Pastoral Review* (May 1971): 10-26.

————. "Replik Bemerkungen zu Hans Küng: Im Interesse der Sache." *Stimmen der Zeit* (March 1971): 145-60. ET: "Reply to Hans Küng: In the Form of an Apologia Pro Theologia Sua." *Homiletic and Pastoral Review* (August/September 1971): 11-27.

Rees, Thomas, ed. *The Racovian Catechism.* London: Longman, Hurst, Rees, Orme & Brown, 1818; Lexington, KY: American Theological Library Association, 1962.

Reno, R. R. "The Radical Orthodoxy Project." *First Things* 100 (February 2000): 37-44.

Salmon, George. *The Infallibility of the Church.* 4th ed. Searcy, AR: James D. Bales, 1914.

Shecterle, Ross A. *The Theology of Revelation of Avery Dulles, 1980-1994: Symbolic Mediation.* Lewiston, NY: Edwin Mellen Press, 1996.

Stickler, Alfons M. "Papal Infallibility — A Thirteenth-Century Invention? Reflections on a Recent Book." *Catholic Historical Review* 60, no. 3 (October 1974): 427-41.

Strachey, Lytton. *Eminent Victorians.* Garden City, NY: Garden City Publishing Co., 1918.

Sullivan, Francis A. *Magisterium: Teaching Authority in the Catholic Church.* New York: Paulist Press, 1983.

Taylor, Mark C. *Erring: A Postmodern A/theology.* Chicago: University of Chicago Press, 1987.

Tierney, Brian. *Origins of Papal Infallibility, 1150-1350.* Leiden: E. J. Brill, 1972.

Tillich, Paul. *Systematic Theology.* Vol. 1. Chicago: University of Chicago Press, 1951.

Troeltsch, Ernst. *Religion in History.* Minneapolis: Fortress Press, 1991.

Turner, Frank M. *John Henry Newman: The Challenge to Evangelical Religion.* New Haven: Yale University Press, 2002.

United States Catholic Conference. *The Küng Dialogue: A Documentation of the efforts of the Congregation for the Doctrine of the Faith and of the Conference of German Bishops to achieve an appropriate clarification of the controversial views of Dr. Hans Küng.* Washington, DC: United States Catholic Conference, 1980.

Vidler, Alec R. *The Church in an Age of Revolution: 1789 to the Present Day.* London: Hodder & Stoughton, 1962.

Volf, Miroslav. *After Our Likeness: The Church as the Image of the Trinity.* Grand Rapids: Eerdmans, 1998.

Ward, Wilfred. *The Life of John Henry, Cardinal Newman, Based on His Private Journals and Correspondence.* London: Longmans, Green & Co., 1912.

Warfield, Benjamin B. *The Inspiration and Authority of the Bible.* Edited by Samuel G. Craig. Philadelphia: Presbyterian and Reformed Publishing Co., 1948.

Watt, E. D. *Authority.* New York: St. Martin's Press, 1982.

Webster, William. *The Church of Rome at the Bar of History.* Edinburgh: Banner of Truth Trust, 1995.

Wiles, Maurice. *The Making of Christian Doctrine.* London: Cambridge University Press, 1967.

———. *The Remaking of Christian Doctrine.* London: SCM Press, 1974.

Williams, D. H. *Evangelicals and Tradition: The Formative Influence of the Early Church.* Grand Rapids: Baker Academic, 2005.

Wood, W. Jay. *Epistemology: Becoming Intellectually Virtuous.* Downers Grove, IL: InterVarsity Press, 1998.

Zagzebski, Linda. *Virtues of the Mind.* Cambridge: Cambridge University Press, 1996.

Index

Abraham, William, 8-10, 12-14, 105n.67, 209-11

Anathema, 26, 35, 44, 47, 111; in doctrinal statements, 143; lifting of, 157

Antecedent probability, 98-100, 121, 145, 151

Apostolic succession, 32, 37, 52, 56, 60, 71, 86, 128, 148, 186

Aquinas, Thomas, 43, 186

Arianism, 3n.6, 8, 89, 160, 119, 205

Aristotle, 101, 125

Artificial contraception, 40, 185, 191, 193, 200-201, 206

Assumption of Mary, 20, 27, 42, 46-47, 84, 165-66, 181

Atheism, 18, 58, 69, 80, 91, 105, 124, 166

Augustine, 43, 89, 126

Authority, 5-6; divine, 58, 61, 62, 64; ecclesial, 3, 15, 51, 75, 82, 118, 213; epistemic, 118; hierarchical conception of, 140; infallible, 68, 71, 98; organizational, 16-17, 210, 212; papal, 2, 6, 27, 30, 48, 79, 110, 128, 147, 176, 212; spiritual, 25, 48; teaching, 36, 39, 40, 42, 62, 64, 71, 131, 146, 150, 155, 156, 177, 212

Barth, Karl, 12, 166-67, 173, 180

Belief-producing mechanism, 14, 17, 48, 76, 83, 118, 120, 122, 142, 161, 203, 207, 212

Bonaventure, 34, 43

Canon, 13, 41, 72, 76, 99, 118, 122, 136; as epistemic criteria, 9, 14, 18, 161, 198, 207, 210

Canonical: heritage, 9-10, 13, 15, 82, 158, 198, 200, 205-6, 208, 211; mission, 18, 163, 172, 197; scriptures, 136, 152; theism, 8-12, 208-11

Catholic Church, 19-20; doctrinal continuity of, 205; hierarchical structure of, 5; immutability of, 58, 63-64, 72, 74, 79, 83, 92, 194, 203-4; infallible, 100, 104-5, 109, 128, 146, 185, 194, 200-201; unity in, 75

Chadwick, Owen, 21n.4, 25-26, 27n.15, 29, 30n.23, 31n.25, 43n.51, 96, 98n.47, 100, 122n.109

Chalcedonian: definition, 171, 178-

79, 199, 204, 206; Christology, 204, 206; confession, 179

Christology, 47n.64, 171, 173, 178, 180, 196, 199; monothelite, 4, 74, 184; orthodox, 199-200, 206

Church, 8, 37, 63, 87, 128, 145, 171, 203; canonical heritage of, 9-10, 13, 15, 82, 158, 198, 200, 205-6, 208, 211; doctrine of the, 72, 74, 113, 141; immutable tradition of, 64; immutability of, 58, 63, 194; indefectibility of, 38, 144-45, 161, 172, 181, 189, 192, 197-200, 205-6; infallibility of, 41, 57, 64-65, 74, 92, 98, 104-9, 114, 164, 183, 187, 188-89; pilgrim status of, 132; primitive, 52, 60, 72-73; as sacrament, 133, 139-41; undivided, 10, 12, 82, 158, 208, 211; unity of the, 56, 74, 148; universal, 74, 89, 149, 152, 157, 164, 175

Congar, Yves, 123, 129, 168

Congregation for the Doctrine of the Faith, 41, 167, 169-72, 196

Conscience, 14n.35, 90, 101-2, 111-12, 118, 120, 122, 172, 186, 204

Consensus fidelium, 92, 107, 120

Constantinople, 4, 25, 33, 184, 186

Council of Constance, 4, 73-74

Council of Trent, 52, 99, 119, 208

Cult of the Holy Father, 28-29

Cyprian, 33

Damasus I, 33

De Lubac, Henri, 123, 129

De George, Richard, 6, 16n.36

Deputation on the faith, 30, 31, 38

Descartes, René, 11-12, 125

Dionne, J. Robert, 17n.38, 18n.40, 36n.35, 40n.42, 40n.43, 41, 68n.63, 84n.1, 164n.3, 190

Divine providence, 59, 113, 115, 125, 144, 154

Divine revelation, 13-14, 34-35, 40-41, 59-61, 67, 86, 90, 98-99, 111, 114-16, 118-19, 129-60, 189, 200, 207

Doctrinal development, 4, 34-35, 53, 58, 73, 79, 90, 92, 95,-96, 98, 114, 117-18, 121, 137, 160, 182, 191-92, 203-4, 206, 208, 212

Duffy, Eamon, 32n.28, 81-82

Dulles, Avery, 17, 122, 123-62

Early church, 6, 12, 14, 52, 72, 87, 95, 100, 177, 186; fathers, 43, 45, 52, 86, 88, 136; historical practice of, 6

Ecclesiology, 38, 56-57, 110, 122, 130-32, 139, 141, 168-69, 171, 173, 175, 176-77, 189, 198; egalitarian, 5-7; institutional, 110n.83

Ecumenical council, 2, 10, 40, 74, 79, 93, 105, 116, 119, 148, 167, 168, 203, 207; authority of, 175; as epistemic criteria, 207; fifth, 186; infallibility of, 189; sixth, 4, 186; of Constance, 4, 73

Ecumenism, 48, 129, 130, 147

Egalitarianism, 5, 6

Emmanuel, Victor II, 26, 31, 59

Empiricism, 11, 12, 76

Enlightenment, the, 11, 21, 80, 188

Epistemic certainty, 3, 15-17, 20, 75-76, 78, 82, 103, 120-22, 158-62, 200-212

Epistemological proposal, 13, 19, 48, 76, 81, 120, 162, 209, 211

Epistemology, 5, 76-78, 82, 125, 132, 139, 199-212; foundationalism in, 56, 59, 95, 101; of theology, 10n.27, 15, 105n.67, 210; religious, 1, 3, 8, 10-11, 16, 18-20, 48, 78, 101-2, 118, 122, 161, 164, 180, 202, 204, 206-8, 211

Erastianism, 75, 83, 86; problem of, 54

Eutychians, 88

Ex Cathedra, 4, 27, 35-42, 65-80, 114, 115, 117, 156, 181, 184-85, 190, 201

Excommunication, 33, 79, 197; of Photius, 184; of Pope Vigilius, 186

Externalism, 118, 122

Faith and morals, 31, 35-41, 66-67, 69, 72, 77-78, 80, 110, 114, 126, 128, 153

Ferretti, Mastai. *See* Pius IX

Fessler, Joseph, 32, 84, 94

Fideism, 11-12, 180

Foundationalism: strong, 11, 16, 56, 59, 75, 76, 138, 180, 202; weak, 13, 95, 100-101, 118, 130, 139, 158, 173, 180, 200, 212

France: country, 22, 24, 26, 28, 31, 73, 129; revolutions, 21, 28

Franciscans, 33-34, 44

Galileo, 36, 115, 120, 184

Gallicanism, 21-22, 29, 31, 38, 67, 70, 73, 95, 146, 148, 150, 155, 186, 212

Gilley, Sheridan, 80, 84-85, 94n.35, 96, 101n.58, 108n.79, 108n.80, 120

Gladstone, W. E., 66-67, 69n.66, 77-78, 80, 84n.1, 94, 109-10, 113

Gratry, Auguste Joseph Alphonse, 78-79

Gray, Robert, 49n.2, 50n.6, 51n.8, 52n.9, 55, 60n.32, 80-81

Gregory VII, 33

Gregory XVI, 22

Gorham, G. E., 54, 58, 72

Hales, Edward E. Y., 23, 25, 27, 44n.52

Häring, Hermann, 164n.5, 166n.10, 166n.11, 171n.29, 180n.52

Hasler, August, 23, 31, 172, 196, 197n.109, 197n.110, 197n.111

Hegel, G. W. F., 21n.3, 166

Heresy, 3, 57, 66, 67, 74, 89, 90, 96, 105, 117, 146, 182, 206; church falling into, 146, 183; pope falling into, 150

Hermeneutics, 8, 147, 150, 160-61, 179, 199-200, 205, 212

Historical criticism, 2, 3n.6, 5, 62, 173-78, 184, 194, 198, 200, 206-8

Holy Spirit, 15, 42, 52, 60, 137, 153, 161, 164 181, 182n.59, 183, 189, 208, 209; aid of, 2, 35, 70-71, 154; guidance of, 2-4, 45, 92, 93, 209; indwelling of, 45, 57, 63; inner enlightenment of, 135; inspired by, 175; working of, 10, 13, 161

Honorius I, 4, 74, 78-79, 106, 114, 115n.96, 117, 184-86, 203

Humanae Vitae, 170, 185, 190, 194, 200-201, 206

Immaculate conception, 20, 26, 28-29, 42-47, 79, 84, 92, 105, 113-15, 118, 203

Inerrancy, biblical, 2-5, 11, 14, 189, 207-8

Infallibility, 8, 42, 207; doctrine of, 171; maximal, 17-18, 49-83, 84, 94, 109, 117-18, 122, 151, 194, 202-3; minimal, 17-18, 151, 163-201, 206; moderate, 17, 78, 84-122, 123-62, 195-96, 202-6

Ingersoll, Robert G., 58, 80

Inopportunists, 29, 31, 64, 68, 83, 108, 151

Italian, 25, 29-30, 59; nationalists, 21n.5, 29; risorgimento, 24, 28

Jelly, Frederick M., 43-46

Jesuit, 123, 129, 165

John XXII, 33

John XXIII, 38, 129, 167, 169

John Paul II, 1n.1, 131, 163, 172, 191

Ker, Ian, 85, 86n.9, 88n.13, 89n.20, 91,

93n.34, 101n.58, 101n.59, 103, 104, 107, 147, 168, 193

Küng, Hans, 4-5, 17-18, 41n.46, 144, 156, 162, 163-201, 206-7, 212

Laity, 26, 43, 107, 168, 215

Lash, Nicholas, 85, 95n.37, 98n.47, 122n.109

Leo I, 33

Leo XIII, 59, 68, 80-81, 94

Lindbeck, George, 6, 7, 10, 138, 139, 151n.94, 162, 192, 193, 199

Locke, John, 11-12, 96, 102

Lord Acton, 31, 62

Lumen Gentium, 17n.37, 20, 38, 39, 40, 42, 48, 85, 153, 154n.98, 194

Magisterium, 34n.31, 36, 40-41, 46, 57, 74, 80n.94, 114, 122n.109, 140, 142, 153, 177, 183, 185, 189, 190-91, 194-95, 201, 206; as epistemic criteria, 198; hierarchical, 137, 141

Manning, Henry Edward, 17, 18n.41, 28, 30, 31, 49-83, 85, 88, 92, 94, 101, 117, 118, 119, 121, 124, 128, 150, 163, 190, 202-8

Marian dogmas, 20, 38, 42-43, 46, 48, 84, 118, 142, 146-47, 156-57, 160-61, 209

Mary, virgin, 20, 37, 43-48, 91, 116, 118, 120, 136, 140, 165, 172, 181; as new Eve, 43-45; as type of the church, 47

Merrigan, Terrance, 133, 135

Methodism in epistemology, 10-12, 15, 18, 76, 119, 122, 161, 198-99, 206, 208, 210-12

Monophysites, 88-89, 90, 119

Monothelite, 4, 74, 114, 117, 184

Mysterium Ecclesiae, 41, 154-56, 171

Narrative theology. *See* Postliberal Theology

Nestorians, 90, 180

Newman, John Henry, 17, 18n.41, 49, 51-54, 58-59, 62, 80n.94, 84-122, 124, 128, 135, 137, 151, 160, 163, 180-81, 203-8, 212

Newsome, David, 49, 54n.13, 54n.14, 59, 68-69, 85n.3, 85n.7, 87, 92n.31

Nicene Creed, 33, 57, 90, 171, 178, 199, 207

Nicholas III, 33

Nowell, Robert, 164n.5, 166n.10, 192n.93, 193n.97

Old Catholic Church, 32

Olivi, Peter, 33-35

Ontology, 10, 11, 13, 132, 158

Particularism, 10-13, 15, 103n.63, 161, 198, 208-9, 211-12

Pastor Aeternus, 20, 31, 35, 37, 38, 40, 42, 48, 65-71, 73, 77, 79, 106, 114, 115, 117, 118, 120, 146, 150, 151, 153, 155, 157, 185, 186, 190, 201, 202, 212; moderate interpretation of, 7, 122

Paul VI, 1, 169, 185

Peter, apostle, 31, 110, 112, 128-29, 148, 153; office of, 32-33, 35-39, 70-73

Pius IX, 20, 21-31, 44-45, 55, 59, 68, 69, 79, 95, 202

Pius XII, 27, 47, 165, 167, 184

Plato, 96, 118, 125

Pope, 1, 25, 71, 112, 150, 185, 205; as antichrist, 87, 151; authority of, 27, 29, 156, 212; infallibility of, 29, 30, 32, 35, 36, 38, 57, 70, 71, 72, 114, 120, 146, 181; as judge of Christian faith, 34; as pastor of all Christians, 59, 65, 153; as successor of Peter, 37-39, 70, 128-29, 153; as teacher of revelation, 30; spiritual power of, 25-26; supporters of, 27; teaching of, 39, 155; temporal power of, 25, 58, 92; as

universal teacher, 65, 70; as witness, 30
Postliberal theology, 6, 12
Purcell, E. S., 49-50

Quanta Cura, 27, 68, 112

Rahner, Karl, 123, 132, 139, 166, 168, 170-71, 174, 183, 191, 194-96, 200
Rationalism, 11-12, 27, 61-62, 65, 73
Religious certainty, 2-3, 14, 76, 103, 203-4, 206, 212
Resurrection, 48, 143, 160, 178
Rome, 4, 80, 96, 149, 165, 172; bishop of, 23, 32-33, 37-38, 72, 110, 149, 213; church of, 52, 87, 90; invasion of, 69

Sacraments, 51, 56, 72, 79-80, 87, 128, 133, 136, 139-41, 159
Saints, 41, 62, 90-91, 120; canon of, 9
Schola Theologorum, 101, 107, 117, 120, 141, 143, 166, 196
Scotus, John Duns, 44-45
Scripture, 10, 45, 88, 115, 138, 189; canon of, 9, 13; as epistemic criteria, 2, 13, 207; as inerrant, 1-2, 8, 9, 13, 76; historical-critical exegesis of, 5, 173-78, 194, 198, 200, 206-7; private interpretation of, 52-53, 113, 202
Sensus Fidelium, 45, 47, 92, 107, 120
Separation of church and state, 21, 27
Sin: actual, 44; doctrine of, 6; mortal, 10, 44; original, 43-44; problem of, 143
Skepticism, 11-12, 15, 59, 75, 91, 119, 125-26, 199, 206, 208
Socinians, 2, 8
Sola scriptura, 2, 10, 77, 88, 157
Spinoza, Benedict, 2n.2, 125

Spiritual transformation, 10, 13, 15, 158, 209
Stoicism, 96, 118
Strachey, Lytton, 50, 78
Stephen, bishop of Rome, 33
Sullivan, Francis, 34, 41-42, 191
Syllabus of Errors, 69, 108, 112; historical setting, 28; summary, 26-28
Symbolic: communication, 135-40, 158, 160; realism, 132-41, 158-61, 205

Tierney, Brian, 4n.8, 33-34, 63n.42, 191
Tillich, Paul, 11, 129
Tractarian, 51-53, 77, 86-88
Tradition, 2, 14, 31, 46, 73, 89, 136, 162, 176; as epistemic criteria, 14; immutable, 64; living, 46; scripture and, 2, 3, 10, 14, 53, 76, 89, 106, 115, 122, 138, 153-54, 202
Transubstantiation, 105, 120, 142-43
Trinity, 3n.6, 40, 48, 86, 95, 143, 160, 178, 204-5, 208; as foundational Christian belief, 2; egalitarian understanding of, 5
Truth, 2, 11-12, 15, 30, 111-16; intrasystemic, 7; ontological, 7-9; revealed, 41, 132, 143, 146, 149

Ullathorne, bishop, 23n.8, 93-94, 113
Ultramontanism, 22, 26, 28-31, 55, 64, 68, 84, 92, 94, 108-9, 112, 117, 121, 201, 212
Unity, 16, 57, 62, 75-75, 122, 148-53, 178, 202; catholic, 56, 62, 82; of the church, 16, 56-58, 62, 71, 74-75, 82, 84, 148, 203, 208, 210; of the faith, 42; organic, 56-57; moral, 56-57

Vatican I, 3-4, 14n.35, 16-34, 48, 50, 68-71, 83, 85, 92-93, 104, 109, 140-

56, 169, 171, 184-86, 190, 194, 201,
202, 210, 212
Vatican II, 14, 20, 39, 48, 57, 72, 83,
85, 109, 123, 130, 136, 139, 141,
147-50, 153, 168-71, 185, 194, 203
Veuillot, Louis, 28
Via media, 88-90, 119
Victor I, 32

Victor Emmanuel II, 26, 31, 59
Vidler, Alec R., 21, 22n.6, 27-28
Vigilius, 106, 186
Von Döllinger, Johann Joseph Ignaz,
3n.6, 18n.40, 32

Ward, Wilfred G., 12n.32, 85, 107
Weigel, Gustave, 129-31